Published with the assistance of the

V. RAY CARDOZIER FUND

*an endowment created to support
publication of scholarly books.*

CONTESTED
TERRITORY

Murray R. Wickett

CONTESTED TERRITORY

Whites, Native Americans, and
African Americans in Oklahoma
1865–1907

LOUISIANA STATE UNIVERSITY PRESS
BATON ROUGE MM

Copyright © 2000 by Louisiana State University Press
All rights reserved
Manufactured in the United States of America
First printing
09 08 07 06 05 04 03 02 01 00
5 4 3 2 1

Designer: Bob Nance
Typeface: ITC Galliard
Typesetter: Coghill Composition
Printer and binder: Thomson-Shore, Inc.

Library of Congress Cataloging-in-Publication Data

Wickett, Murray R., 1965–
    Contested territory : whites, Native Americans, and African Americans in Oklahoma,
    1865–1907 / Murray R. Wickett.
        p.   cm.
    Includes bibliographical references and index.
    ISBN 0-8071-2584-9 (cloth : alk. paper)
    1. Oklahoma—Race relations.   2. Oklahoma—History.   3. Indians of North
America—Oklahoma—History.   4. Afro-Americans—Oklahoma—History.   5. Ex-slaves
of Indian tribes—Oklahoma.   6. Afro-Americans—Oklahoma—Relations with
Indians.   I. Title.
F705.A1 W53   2000
976.6004'96073—dc21   00-032122

Portions of Chapter 7 appeared in a somewhat different form as "The Fear of Negro
Domination: The Rise of Segregation and Disfranchisement in Oklahoma, 1865–1910," in
the May 2000 issue of *Chronicles of Oklahoma*, published by the Oklahoma Historical
Society. The author is grateful to the Oklahoma Historical Society for permission to use
material from that article in this book.

The paper in this book meets the guidelines for permanence and durability of the Committee
on Production Guidelines for Book Longevity of the Council on Library Resources. ⊗

CONTENTS

ILLUSTRATIONS AND TABLES

PREFACE

THE LATE NINETEENTH CENTURY was a period of tremendous upheaval in American race relations. Studies abound documenting the changes in relations between whites and African Americans in the northern and southern states during this era. Few historians, however, have studied this topic in the lands of the frontier West. In addition, few historical studies exist which seek to understand the inter-relationships of not only whites and African Americans, but also Native Americans. Hence this study is an attempt to fill a gap in our historical knowledge by analyzing the inter-relations of whites, Native Americans, and African Americans in Indian and Oklahoma Territories from the end of the Civil War to Oklahoma statehood in 1907. It describes the relations of these groups within the economic, political, and social spheres.

By the late nineteenth century, Indian and Oklahoma Territories represented the only place where the three "founding" cultures of American society co-existed in significant numbers. In addition, because the territories fell under the control of the federal government, they provided a unique chance for governmental officials and concerned reformers to implement their racial policies. Therefore, Indian and Oklahoma Territories afford the historian a case study for certain crucial questions about the nature of American race relations the answers to which far transcend the territorial boundaries of Oklahoma. The unique circumstances of the territories allow the historian to distinguish the differences in racial policies aimed at Native Americans and African Americans and demonstrate clearly that white policy-makers in Washington had very different views of the appropriate roles of Native Americans and African Americans in shaping the destiny of the Nation. This study contends that, ironically, whites discouraged in African Americans the very ideals and values they so ardently attempted to instill in Native Americans. While in the late nineteenth century white governmental officials and humanitarian reformers sought ways to ensure the assimilation of Native peoples into Anglo-American society, they sought, at the same time, to secure the strict segregation of African Americans.

Throughout my research in Washington, D.C., I benefited greatly from the assistance of several librarians and archivists. I would like to thank the staff of the National Archives for their guidance. I would also like to thank the staff of the Library of Congress for their help.

Throughout my research in Oklahoma, I was indebted to many for their courteous treatment and patient guidance. I would like to give special recognition to the staff of the Afro-American Cultural Center at Langston University, Langston, Oklahoma, and to the staff of the Archives and Manuscript Division of Oklahoma State University, Stillwater, Oklahoma. I would particularly like to call attention to the efforts of the employees of the Western History Collection at the University of Oklahoma, Norman, Oklahoma. Special recognition is due Donald L. DeWitt, Curator, John R. Lovett Jr., Librarian, and Kristina Southwell, Kim Brewer, Kelli Cupp, Shari McLaughlin, Library Assistants.

My heartfelt thanks are due to the wonderful men and women of the Archives and Manuscripts Division of the Oklahoma Historical Society, Oklahoma City, Oklahoma. I would like to express my sincere appreciation for the help and support I received during my eight-month research stay with my "Oklahoma family." This project would not have been possible without the expertise and support of William D. Welge, Director, Patsy Cooley, Office Administrator, Chester R. Cower, Photographic Archivist, Rodger G. Harris, Oral Historian, Ross Jury, Microfilmist, Judith L. Michener, Assistant Oral Historian, and Joe L. Todd, Manuscript Archivist. Thanks also to Delbert Amen and Scott Dowell, Newspaper Archivists.

I must admit a special intellectual debt to Dr. Daniel F. Littlefield Jr., Director of Native Press, University of Arkansas at Little Rock. His work about the Freedmen of the Five Civilized Tribes was a constant source of inspiration as I began my research. His subsequent thoughtful criticism of the manuscript has made the work much stronger.

I owe tremendous gratitude to my supervisors at the University of Toronto. Professor W. Bruce White provided invaluable service in establishing the parameters of the subject area of my dissertation. Professor John N. Ingham has been a constant source of encouragement and support throughout my graduate career. My greatest intellectual debt, however, is owed to my principal supervisor, Professor Michael Wayne. He has instilled upon me in our fifteen-year association a tremendous love for the study of history. Any success I may have, I owe to his constant inspiration and faith in my abilities. I shall forever be proud to have had him as my mentor.

In the process of changing a dissertation into a publishable book, I came across a variety of computer problems beyond my limited abilities to solve. Therefore, I must offer my sincere thanks to Ruth Watson for her invaluable help in the designing of macros and other computer aids that made the revisions of this manuscript much easier.

I would like to extend my heartfelt thanks to the staff of Louisiana State

University Press for their assistance and support in the publication of this book. Special recognition is due Maureen G. Hewitt, Associate Director and Editor-in-Chief; Sylvia Frank, Acquisitions Editor; John Easterly, Executive Editor; and Patricia Hoefling, Marketing Manager. The book was carefully copyedited by Eivind A. Boe, whose attention to detail and thoughtful insight have improved the presentation. I wish to also acknowledge the painstaking work of Kay Banning on the index. I know that readers will appreciate her hard work as much as I do. Everyone involved in the publication has been a joy to work with, and I look forward to future collaborations with all of you.

Finally, my greatest debt is to my family. I would like to express my love and devotion to my wife and daughter, whose support and encouragement are a constant source of inspiration to me. You make my life complete. I would also like to acknowledge the profound faith my parents and sister have had in me through the often difficult times experienced in writing this book. For all their patience, kindness, and love, this book is dedicated to them.

ABBREVIATIONS
Used in the Notes

CCRP   Carl Coke Rister Papers, Western History Collection, University of Oklahoma, Norman, Okla.

CIA   Commissioner of Indian Affairs

DDOHI   Doris Duke Oral History Interviews, Western History Collection, University of Oklahoma, Norman, Okla.

FBP   Fred Barde Papers, Oklahoma Historical Society, Oklahoma City, Okla.

FCSA   Franklin Campbell Smith Autobiography, Western History Collection, University of Oklahoma, Norman, Okla.

FOP   Florence Ogden Papers, Western History Collection, University of Oklahoma, Norman, Okla.

GFPHC   Grant Foreman Pioneer History Collection, Oklahoma Historical Society, Oklahoma City, Okla.

GMP   Green McCurtain Papers, Western History Collection, University of Oklahoma, Norman, Okla.

HIP   Hiram Impson Papers, Western History Collection, University of Oklahoma, Norman, Okla.

ILGP   I. L. Garvin Papers, Western History Collection, University of Oklahoma, Norman, Okla.

JFPP   James Franklin Parman Papers, Western History Collection, University of Oklahoma, Norman, Okla.

JRWP   John Robert Williams Papers, Western History Collection, University of Oklahoma, Norman, Okla.

JWP   John Womack Papers, Oklahoma Historical Society, Oklahoma City, Okla.

LR-RBIA   Microfilm Publication 234, RG 75, Letters Received, Correspondence of the Office of Indian Affairs (Central Office) and Related

	Records, Records of the Bureau of Indian Affairs, National Archives, Washington, D.C.
M	Microfilm
NRCIS	National Records of the Chilocco Indian School, Oklahoma Historical Society, Oklahoma City, Okla.
NRCN	National Records of the Cherokee Nation, Oklahoma Historical Society, Oklahoma City, Okla.
NRSFA	National Records of the Sac and Fox Agency, Oklahoma Historical Society, Oklahoma City, Okla.
OHP	Oral History Project Collection, Pioneer Interviews, Oklahoma Historical Society, Oklahoma City, Okla.
OHS	Oklahoma Historical Society, Oklahoma City, Okla.
OSU	Oklahoma State University, Stillwater, Okla.
PPP	Peter Perkins Pitchlynn Papers, Western History Collection, University of Oklahoma, Norman, Okla.
R	Roll
RDI	Records of the Department of the Interior, National Archives, Washington, D.C.
RIIIA	Report of the Indian Inspectors of Indian Affairs, Microfilm Publication 1070, RG 48, Reports of the Inspection of the Field Jurisdictions of the Office of Indian Affairs, Indian Division, Records of the Secretary of the Interior, National Archives, Washington, D.C.
RSI	United States Department of the Interior, *Report of the Secretary of the Interior* (Washington, D.C.: Government Printing Office, 1865–1907). In the citations, *"RSI"* is followed by the year of issue. Reports in some years consist of two volumes; volume number is indicated for these years.
RSIA	Record of the Superintendent of Indian Affairs, Microfilm Publication 856, RG 75, Records of the Superintendencies and Agencies of Indian Affairs, Records of the Bureau of Indian Affairs, National Archives, Washington, D.C.
RSIAI	Report of Superintendents of Indian Affairs Inspectors, Microfilm Publication 1070, RG 48, Reports of the Inspection of the Field Jurisdictions of the Office of Indian Affairs, Indian Division, Records of the Secretary of the Interior, National Archives, Washington, D.C.
SCP	Samuel Checote Papers, Western History Collection, University of Oklahoma, Norman, Okla.
SFCTR	Superintendent of the Five Civilized Tribes Report
SHMP	Samuel Houston Mayes Papers, Western History Collection, University of Oklahoma, Norman, Okla.
SI	Secretary of the Interior
SIA	Superintendent of Indian Affairs

TAP	Thomas Athey Papers, Oklahoma Historical Society, Oklahoma City, Okla.
USDCR	United States District Court Records, Western History Collection, University of Oklahoma, Norman, Okla.
WCJP	W. C. Jarboe Papers, Western History Collection, University of Oklahoma, Norman, Okla.
WHC	Western History Collection, University of Oklahoma, Norman, Okla.
WNJP	Wilson N. Jones Papers, Western History Collection, University of Oklahoma, Norman, Okla.
WPA	Works Progress Administration
WSFP	Walter Scott Ferguson Papers, Western History Collection, University of Oklahoma, Norman, Okla.

CONTESTED
TERRITORY

ONE

After the Trail of Tears
The Indian Nations in the West

AMERICAN SOCIETY began a major reorientation in race relations during the administrations of President Andrew Jackson. In the early 1830s, William Lloyd Garrison's abolition movement began to gather attention and support in the northern states. At the same time, southern slaveholders began to articulate a defense of slavery based upon the supposed racial inferiority of African Americans. Although there was an obvious division of opinion in America over the practice of slavery, there was widespread agreement among whites on the inferiority of people with African ancestry. Across America there was a movement to restrict the rights of free blacks. In the North, the movement was centered upon a campaign to segregate blacks from whites in public facilities. In the South, free blacks suffered from numerous constraints: they were subjected to curfews; in some states they had to wear badges and carry special passes; and they were punished for crimes in the same manner as slaves. Free blacks were so discriminated against in southern society that one historian has come to argue they were "slaves without masters." Hence, most white Americans, North and South, at this time, clearly saw African Americans as a distinct, separate, and inferior people.[1]

While these changes were taking place in whites' attitude towards blacks, a profound transformation occurred in whites' attitude towards Native Americans. In the early decades of the nineteenth century many whites had adopted Thomas Jefferson's view of Native Americans as "noble savages," a people lacking civilized habits but possessing the inherent solemnity and honor to make civilization possible for them in the future. However, by the time of the election of Andrew Jackson to the presidency, many Americans saw Native Americans simply as "savages," not only uncultivated but without the potential ever to become civilized. Hence some Americans argued that the government

---

1. Leon Litwack, *North of Slavery: The Negro in the Free States, 1790–1860* (Chicago: University of Chicago Press, 1961); Ira Berlin, *Slaves without Masters: The Free Negro in the Antebellum South* (Oxford: Oxford University Press, 1974).

should remove Indians from their present dwellings in the East and relocate them elsewhere so that their "evil influence" would not degrade white society.[2]

By the 1830s, then, both African Americans and Native Americans were considered separate and inferior castes in American society. There was one essential difference between the two groups, however—Native Americans held vast tracts of richly coveted agricultural lands. This was particularly true in the Southern states of North Carolina, Tennessee, Georgia, Alabama, Mississippi, and Florida, where members of the Cherokee, Chickasaw, Choctaw, Creek, and Seminole tribes resided. These tribes had gone the furthest in adopting Anglo-American technology and culture, later gaining a reputation among whites as the "Five Civilized Tribes." These Indians had never been nomadic; they had lived in permanent farming villages since before initial contact with white settlers. They built log cabins and frame houses and dressed like whites. Their subsistence economy based on raising corn and livestock mirrored that of their white neighbors. Some wealthy chiefs grew cotton and other staple crops using black slaves to labor on their plantations. Many of them sent their children to schools operated under the guidance of white missionaries, where they were exposed to Christianity. One Cherokee, named Sequoyah, devised a syllabary for the Cherokee language, and the Cherokee government published its own newspaper, entitled *The Cherokee Phoenix,* in both the English and Cherokee languages. In Anglo-American eyes, these were extraordinary accomplishments, and the federal government welcomed them as signs of advancing "civilization" among the Indians. But many local whites and officials in Washington proved more concerned with the opening of millions of acres of land to white settlers.[3]

President Andrew Jackson contended that the Indians of the Southeast should be removed west of the Mississippi River, by force if necessary, to enable white settlement upon their former land. Jackson claimed to represent the interests of the yeomen farmers who were fast finding themselves shut out of available land. In 1830, he was able to convince a divided Congress to pass the Indian Removal Act, which appropriated new funds for negotiating treaties with the southern tribes to entice them to relocate to the West. Jackson had the support of the various southern state governments, which wished to rid themselves of the potentially violent repercussions of white settlers intent on encroaching upon Indian lands.[4]

2. Bernard Sheehan, *Seeds of Extinction: Jeffersonian Philosophy and the American Indian* (Chapel Hill: University of North Carolina Press, 1973); Ronald N. Satz, *American Indian Policy in the Jacksonian Era* (Lincoln: University of Nebraska Press, 1975).

3. Angie Debo, *And Still the Waters Run* (Princeton: Princeton University Press, 1940), 5; Harry L. Watson, *Liberty and Power: The Politics of Jacksonian America* (New York: Hill and Wang, 1990), 105–106; Arrell M. Gibson, *Oklahoma: A History of Five Centuries* (Norman: University of Oklahoma Press, 1981), 65.

4. Watson, *Liberty and Power,* 107, 109.

The Native American tribes resisted efforts to entice them to move west voluntarily. The Cherokees took the state of Georgia to the United States Supreme Court, and in the case of *Worcester* v. *Georgia,* Chief Justice John Marshall ruled that the Cherokees had "distinct political communities, having territorial boundaries within which their authority is exclusive." Undaunted, Jackson defied Marshall to enforce his ruling, and proceeded to enter negotiations with Indian leaders who were willing to sign treaties of removal in return for bribes and consolidation of their political position within the tribe. Jackson, for example, was able to negotiate a treaty with a minority faction of the Cherokee tribe, who agreed to relocate. The Treaty of New Echota (1835) ceded all the Cherokee lands to the United States in exchange for $5 million and free transportation west. Most Cherokees denounced the treaty, and a party of militants later took revenge by murdering three of its principal signers. But the Cherokees' fate had been sealed.[5]

The Indian Intercourse Act of 1834 created a huge Indian Territory west of the Mississippi River (carved out of lands acquired in the Louisiana Purchase of 1803) to which the Southern tribes were to be relocated. The territory, bordering the future state of Arkansas, was considered sufficiently removed from existing white settlements and consisted of land deemed undesirable by government officials. Bordered on the west by land that explorers had christened the "Great American Desert" because of its aridity, government officials felt it was unlikely that whites would ever settle along the western border of the Indian Territory, which meant that further encroachment by whites upon Indian lands would be avoided.[6]

Many members of the Five Civilized Tribes over the course of the early 1830s began the long trek across the Mississippi to their new homeland. Others refused to go voluntarily. The Seminoles, Creeks, and Cherokees violently resisted relocation. The Seminoles engaged in fierce warfare with local militia and government troops which lasted until 1842, when the government abandoned the effort to force the few remaining Seminoles who had not removed or been killed in the resistance to move west. The Creeks likewise violently resisted efforts to remove them, but to no avail. Resistance culminated in what came to be known as the "Creek War of 1836." Cherokee resistance was also unsuccessful. The army endeavored to round up every Cherokee man, woman, and child at bayonet point. They placed the Indians in stockades guarded by soldiers until plans were completed for their relocation.[7]

By the end of the 1830s most members of the Five Civilized Tribes had been

5. *Worcester* v. *Georgia,* 1832, in Francis P. Prucha, ed., *Documents of United States Indian Policy* (Lincoln: University of Nebraska Press, 1990), 60; Gibson, *Oklahoma,* 66.

6. Gibson, *Oklahoma,* 66.

7. Arrell M. Gibson, *The History of Oklahoma* (Norman: University of Oklahoma Press, 1984), 44–45.

removed from their homelands. The tribes had ceded over 100 million acres of eastern land to the federal government in return for $68 million and 20 million acres of far less hospitable land west of the Mississippi. The journey westward proved a tragic one for members of the Five Civilized Tribes. The winter was bitterly cold and few of the tribes had warm clothing. Rations were poor and often stolen, there were so few wagons that many of the people were forced to walk the long distance, and disease was rampant. As a result, nearly 4,000 of the 18,000 Cherokees perished. Other tribes had fatality rates almost as high. Possibly the highest mortality rates belonged to the African American slaves who were forced to remove along with their Indian masters. Black slaves performed much of the manual labor connected with removal—they loaded freight wagons and cleared new trails for the overland march. The survivors of the ordeal, Native American and African American, remembered the terrible journey as the "Trail of Tears."[8]

Andrew Jackson, and most of his white contemporaries, believed that Native Americans were doomed to extinction because they were unable to compete with white Americans. Hence, Jackson publicly extolled his removal policy as a benevolent effort to give Native Americans one last chance to assimilate and give up their Indian ways. In December of 1833, he told Congress that Indians "have neither the intelligence, the industry, the moral habits nor the desire for improvement." He concluded that if not removed elsewhere, the Indians "must necessarily yield to the force of circumstance and ere long disappear." Across the Mississippi, Jackson claimed, Native Americans might yet survive for a while.[9]

Survive they did. In fact, Native societies flourished in their new homeland. Historian Grant Foreman refers to this era "as an interlude of peace in the lives of these Indians, a short span reaching from their enforced migration to the devastation of the Civil War." Foreman concludes, "in spite of tremendous difficulties[,] their progress year after year and their achievements in the field of culture and government have no parallel in the history of our Indians."[10]

The new home of the Five Civilized Tribes was quite large and endowed with a diversity of natural resources. The Creek and Chickasaw Nations contained some of the finest agricultural lands on the frontier; the Choctaw Nation was covered in valuable timber; and coal fields (and later, oil fields) were opened in each of the Indian nations after the Civil War.[11]

Each of the Five Civilized Tribes was given complete sovereignty over its

8. Watson, *Liberty and Power,* 111; Gibson, *The History of Oklahoma,* 42.

9. Watson, *Liberty and Power,* 111; William G. McLoughlin, *After the Trail of Tears: The Cherokees' Struggle for Sovereignty, 1839–1880* (Chapel Hill: University of North Carolina Press, 1993), 3.

10. Grant Foreman, *The Five Civilized Tribes* (Norman: University of Oklahoma Press, 1934), preface.

11. Debo, *And Still the Waters Run,* 6.

own territory. For example, by the terms of the Treaty of New Echota, the United States promised that the lands ceded to the Cherokees "shall in no future time, without their consent, be included within the territorial limits or jurisdiction of any State or Territory." The treaty also specified that the Cherokee Council had the right "to make and carry into effect all such laws as they deem necessary."[12]

Control over local government, the judiciary, and the educational system was placed in the hands of the Indians. The Cherokee, Choctaw, and Chickasaw tribes each had a constitutional government modeled after the United States system, with a Principal Chief and other executive officers, a General Council, and a system of courts. All of the offices, including that of Principal Chief, were elective. Political interest was high, and the electorate was kept well informed of political issues by the local press.[13]

In the years after removal, an extensive educational system, funded by the tribal governments and white missionary societies, provided opportunities for young Native Americans. The Cherokees, Choctaws, and Chickasaws created a school system for their youth, and some had academies (the equivalent of high schools) for young adults. Many of the elite Indian families sent their children to private boarding schools in the East. After 1850, the community leaders of the tribes were often college graduates. William P. Ross, nephew of Chief John Ross, was a graduate of Princeton. He returned to the Indian Territory and became the editor of the *Cherokee Advocate* and eventually was elected Principal Chief of the Cherokees.[14]

While the Cherokees, Chickasaws, and Choctaws adopted an Anglo-American form of government and educational system, all of the Five Civilized Tribes maintained their unique system of communal land tenure. A tribal member could hunt, fish, and cut timber anywhere except in places occupied by towns or farms. Open range law prevailed in the Indian nations. Livestock, branded with their owner's mark, were allowed to roam the public lands. In order to keep cattle from damaging crops, cultivated land was surrounded by fences. Most of the tribesmen settled on small farms along rivers and streams, engaging in subsistence farming.[15]

In addition to these Indian farmers, there arose a class of Native American slaveholders who owned black slaves and used them to cultivate large plantations dedicated to growing cotton and corn. The largest plantations in Indian Territory were in the Red River Valley. Robert Love, a Chickasaw, operated two large plantations there and owned two hundred slaves. Robert M. Jones, a

12. Charles J. Kappler, *Indian Treaties, 1778–1883* (New York: Interland Publishers, 1972), 442.
13. Debo, *And Still the Waters Run,* 9–10.
14. Gibson, *Oklahoma,* 84.
15. Gibson, *The History of Oklahoma,* 51–52.

Choctaw planter, owned five Red River plantations, over five hundred slaves, and a number of steamboats. Most of the prominent planters were members of the mixed-blood elite of the Five Civilized Tribes, who sometimes obtained their slaves in exchange for horses, which were scarce in the neighboring slave-holding states.[16]

The presence of slavery led each of the five Indian nations to adopt slave codes to control their black chattel. The Cherokee, Choctaw, Chickasaw, and Creek slave laws were very restrictive; slaves were denied the right to own property, to hold office, or to intermarry with Native Americans. Severe punishments were accorded anyone caught harboring runaway slaves or teaching abolitionism. Just as in the southern states, Indian masters displayed a wide variation in the treatment of their slaves. Some were cruel and physically beat their chattel, while others seldom resorted to violence, preferring to adopt a more "paternalistic" approach to master-slave relations. The Seminoles had an unusual relationship with their slaves. The slaves lived in separate towns apart from their masters, planting and cultivating fields in common. They were also responsible for the upkeep of large herds of livestock, which were allowed free range. The only obligation of the slaves was to furnish their individual masters with an annual tribute of produce or livestock.[17]

By the Civil War, then, the Five Civilized Tribes were developing a distinct slaveholding elite, whose wealth and status in society were built upon their control over their black chattel. Not surprisingly, when the war started, this group sought to support the Confederacy and its dedication to the preservation of slavery. At the same time, many Indian farmers saw the Civil War as an opportunity to vent their disapproval of the emerging discrepancy in power and wealth between planters and farmers by joining the Union forces. So while officially the Five Civilized Tribes concluded treaties supporting the Confederate States of America, in fact, the tribes were bitterly divided in their support for the two sides. A schism between Confederate and Union sympathizers tore the Five Civilized Tribes apart. The physical devastation of the Civil War in the Indian Territory was also abundantly evident. Homes were abandoned, fields lay in ruins, bridges were destroyed, and numerous lives were lost on the battlefields. Having spent the previous decades rebuilding their society after the devastating effects of removal, the Civil War forced the Five Civilized Tribes to once again rebuild their society out of the ashes of despair and destruction.[18]

16. *Ibid.*; Rev. Charles Davis, interview, File 87.53, OHP.

17. Daniel F. Littlefield Jr., *Africans and Creeks: From the Colonial Period to the Civil War* (Westport: Greenwood Press, 1979), 142–48; Theda Perdue, *Slavery and the Evolution of Cherokee Society, 1540–1866* (Knoxville: University of Tennessee Press, 1979), 96–119; Daniel F. Littlefield Jr., *Africans and Seminoles: From Removal to Emancipation* (Westport: Greenwood Press, 1977), 8.

18. W. David Baird, *A Creek Warrior for the Confederacy: The Autobiography of Chief G. W. Grayson* (Norman: University of Oklahoma Press, 1988); Perdue, *Slavery and Cherokee Society,* 119–141.

SINCE THE FIVE Civilized Tribes had officially supported the Confederacy during the Civil War, upon the war's end the federal government included Indian Territory in its Reconstruction policy. Each of the Five Civilized Tribes was forced to sign new treaties in 1866 establishing relations with the United States, treaties in which they were required to sell their "surplus" land to the federal government and to adopt their ex-slaves as citizens or else have them removed from the Indian nations. These demands profoundly affected the future nature of race relations in the Indian Territory.

The Five Civilized Tribes, as part of their agreements to relocate west in the 1830s, had been allotted "surplus" lands to accommodate their future increase in population. Most of this land was located west of the independent Indian nations. The federal government intended to use the land reacquired from the Five Civilized Tribes to settle other Indian tribes relocated from the northern Plains and elsewhere.[19]

Soon after the conclusion of the Civil War, government officials came to argue that the solution to the "Indian question" lay in the consolidation of the scattered Indian tribes. The federal government in 1867, in the aftermath of a series of bloody conflicts, appointed an Indian Peace Commission to suggest solutions to the current crisis. The commission recommended abandoning the policy of scattering the tribes onto small selected reservations spread across the Plains, and proposed in its place to relocate all the Plains Indians in two large reservations—one in Indian Territory and the other in the Dakotas. The secretary of the interior concluded in 1871 that there was enough land in the federally reserved Indian Territory to allot every Native American person 180 acres. This the secretary noted was enough to "afford them all comfortable homes," and furthermore, "such a disposition of the now scattered tribes . . . would release from Indian occupancy 93,692,731 acres of land, and throw it open to white settlement and cultivation." Government agents then cajoled, bribed, and tricked the Plains Indian tribes into relocating to these areas. Many tribes violently resisted relocation. For the next several decades an unofficial state of war existed on the western Plains between the U.S. Army and various tribes.[20]

Many of the relocated Plains tribes experienced the same dislocation and sense of loss as the Five Civilized Tribes had undergone a generation earlier. When the Ponca tribe was relocated from Dakota Territory to the Indian Territory, they, like many other Plains tribes, experienced their own "Trail of Tears." The Ponca chief noted, "our forefathers selected a home as every body ought to do and we obeyed our Great Father's wishes—we made farms—built houses as white people do. We never expected such a thing to happen as that we should have to leave our homes." Another Ponca tribesman complained,

19. McLoughlin, *After the Trail of Tears,* xiii; Kappler, *Indian Treaties.*
20. Columbus Delano, SI, Oct. 31, 1871, in *RSI* 1871, 1:6–7, 562; Ralph K. Andrist, *The Long Death: The Last Days of the Plains Indians* (New York: Macmillan, 1964).

"We did not feel that we had done anything wrong and we felt that he [the government agent] ought to have come carefully and talked to us as reasonable beings—but he came on us by surprise and hurried us down here at the point of a bayonet." A council of the chiefs of the Wyandott, Seneca, Shawnee, Ottawa, Peoria, Quapaw, and Modoc tribes made an impassioned plea to the secretary of the interior of the United States that the relocation of the Plains tribes to the western lands of the Indian Territory give them a permanent home in which they could feel secure from further dislocation as a result of the intrusion of white settlers. For as they noted from past experience:

> As soon as its scenes begin to be familiar, and its surroundings endeared by associations, becoming the last resting place of our departed kindred—the ever reaching and grasping hand of the white man would come again, find us out and seek controll [*sic*] of our homes, and point us to others nearer the setting sun. Where surely we could remain undisturbed and possess our lands forever after in peace—and so it has ever been until today we seem standing upon the last hill left for us, the West of us, like the East, and the North and South is in possession of the white man, and for us no new home can be found—of that vast and almost unbounded country which once was ours.[21]

The introduction of the relocated Plains Indians into the Indian Territory profoundly altered the future course of race relations between whites and Native Americans, for it interjected into the area several tribes dedicated to preserving their culture and traditions in spite of the efforts of white officials and reformers who sought to impose Anglo-American culture and values upon them. This ensured that those full-blood members of the Five Civilized Tribes who opposed assimilation would have a new powerful ally.

Equally important to the future of race relations in the Indian Territory was the question of the rights to be accorded the freedmen of the Five Civilized Tribes. In the immediate aftermath of the Civil War, the Indian nations faced the question of what to do with their freedmen. Many Indians wanted the ex-slaves removed from their nations and settled elsewhere. However, the freedmen were adamantly opposed, and the United States government also refused to discuss the possibility of relocation. The 1866 treaties re-establishing relations between the United States and the Indian nations required the Five Civilized Tribes to protect the rights of their freedmen and give them full citizenship in the nation. Native American governments saw this as punishment for supporting the Confederacy during the war and resented the fact that they

21. Chief of the Ponca Tribe to William Nicholson, SIA, R 674, Ponca Agency, 1876–77, LR-RBIA; Frank Le Flesh to William Nicholson, SIA, R 674, Ponca Agency, 1876–77, LR-RBIA; Council chiefs of Wyandott, Seneca, Shawnee, Ottawa, Peoria, Quapaw, and Modoc tribes to SI, R 709, Quapaw Agency, 1879, LR-RBIA.

were being requested to do more for their former slaves than the former rebel states. Since land in the Indian Territory was held communally, granting ex-slaves tribal citizenship, in effect, gave them equal rights in the ownership of tribal land. While each of the tribes did sign new treaties with the government in 1866 recognizing the rights of their freedmen, they differed in the degree to which they implemented this provision.[22]

The Seminoles had a long tradition of intermarrying with their slaves, and it is generally agreed that slavery in the Seminole Nation was less harsh in comparison with the other Five Civilized Tribes. Thus it is not surprising that the Seminole Nation quickly adopted their freedmen and gave them equal rights and full citizenship in the tribe. The Seminoles lived up to their treaty obligations, and a Freedmen's Bureau agent could conclude in 1866 that "the national laws and customs are sufficient for [the freedmen's] protection."[23]

Allowing their freedmen full civil rights had a positive effect upon race relations between the Seminoles and their ex-slaves. In 1869, the superintendent of Indian affairs for the Southern Superintendency could write, "the Seminoles are living in a state of more perfect peace than any other tribe within the superintendency." As historian Daniel F. Littlefield Jr. has noted, "Only in the Seminole Nation did the blacks have full rights of citizens and enjoy as well a life relatively free of political difficulties."[24]

The Creek tribe, like the Seminoles, quickly moved to adopt their freedmen. In their 1866 treaty with the United States government, they agreed to recognize their freedmen as equal citizens but added the proviso that the freedmen had to be currently living within the Creek Nation or must return to the Creek Nation within one year of the ratification of the treaty in order to qualify for citizenship. This proviso created problems, as many freedmen had fled the Creek Nation during the war and some had been forcibly removed by their masters, who had sought to withdraw their property to safer grounds in Texas or the Deep South states. Many freedmen being absent from the nation, and hence not knowing the provisions of the treaty, returned to the nation after the deadline and were denied citizenship rights. The Creek government regarded such people as intruders and consequently subject to removal by the authorities. Having received numerous pleas for help from freedmen petitioners seeking citizenship rights, the local Creek Indian agent recognized that if they had been "half white in place of half colored and the other half Indian, no objection would be raised to [their] claim to citizenship."[25]

22. John B. Sanborn, Brevet Major General, U.S. Army, to SI, Jan. 5, 1866, in *RSI* 1866, p. 285; Nathaniel J. Washington, *Historical Development of the Negro in Oklahoma* (Tulsa: Dexter, 1948), 21.

23. Sanborn to SI, Jan. 5, 1866, in *RSI* 1866, p. 285.

24. Littlefield, *Africans and Seminoles,* 203.

25. Kappler, *Indian Treaties,* 932–33; Jonathan Tufts to SI, June 10, 1885, Freedmen File, Box 49, RG 48, RDI.

The Cherokees, like the Creeks, signed a treaty in 1866 with the United States government, recognizing the rights of their freedmen to citizenship. Also like the Creeks, the Cherokees added a proviso that citizenship would be bestowed upon only those freedmen living in the nation at the time of the treaty and those who returned within a period of six months. This proviso, too, created all kinds of trouble. The concerned freedmen petitioned the president in hopes that the U.S. government would intervene and deny the Cherokees the right to remove freedmen deemed intruders by the terms of the 1866 treaty. In a letter to President Ulysses S. Grant they wrote:

> Some of us had fled North to get away from slavery, or to take our families away from the horror and sufferings of the War, while we ourselves enlisted in the Union army. Some of us, had been dragged by our owners, to the South to keep us from being freed by the Union army so that we were a long way off from the Cherokee Country when the Treaty was made. We were so far, that we had no way of getting back to our old homes so that we could not possibly have reached there in time, even if we had known what provision was made for us in the Treaty.

The freedmen argued that the Cherokee Nation was the only home they knew, and that they had no desire to be relocated elsewhere. To them it seemed barbarous that after years of toiling for Indian masters as slaves, they were being forced to leave the country "as intruders."[26]

In the years following the Civil War, the Cherokee freedmen were afraid to make great improvements upon the lands they settled for fear the Indians would confiscate their property and remove them from the nation. As one freedman declared, "we hope that the greedy indians will have to be satisfied, with the farmes that we made for them befor the war and not grasp after what we have acculated in days of freedom." One freedman teacher remembered how, whenever an ex-slave had settled land, the local Cherokees would come in and cut down timber and often fence in the area around the black family's cabin, claiming the land was owned by some Cherokee citizen. The freedman was left with little choice but to remove and settle elsewhere only perhaps to see the same sequence of events repeated.[27]

The Cherokees were also reluctant to share their annuity payments, educational subsidies, and orphan-fund payments with their ex-slaves. Many Cherokee leaders argued that by adopting their freedmen and giving them full citizenship rights, their land and monetary grants would be greatly diminished

---

26. Microfilm CHN 8, NRCN; petition from Saline District freedmen to President Grant, Feb. 1872, R 105, Cherokee Agency, 1872, LR-RBIA.

27. Jesse Ridge to the President of the United States, R 875, Union Agency, 1880, LR-RBIA; C. W. Dallas to CIA, R 873, Union Agency, 1879, LR-RBIA.

per capita. Frustrated with their bids to entice Cherokee officials to their side, the freedmen petitioned the United States government to support their bid to be included in tribal funds distribution. In a petition to a joint meeting of the United States Congress, the freedmen argued that "in violation of the Ninth Article of the Treaty of 1866, . . . the Cherokee National Council did enact a law excluding all Cherokee citizens not Cherokee Indians by blood from any pro rata share in the $300,000 paid to the Cherokees . . . in return for lands ceded to the United States government." The freedmen added that "this hardship is the more trying and unjust in view of the fact that as slaves of the Cherokee Indians, the unrequited toil of your petitioners went toward up-building the millions of Cherokee National wealth . . . while your petitioners and their ancestors were totally denied reward." It took several years and numerous petitions and appeals before the United States finally recognized the freedmen's rights to share in tribal payment and paid them the money owed.[28]

Although freedmen citizens did have the vote, and the right to serve on juries and to act as guardians and administrators of estates, and although some freedmen served on local boards as school directors, the Cherokees and their freedmen engaged in a long, bitter struggle which served to factionalize the tribe. By the time most Cherokee freedmen could rest assured that their rights would be protected in the Cherokee Nation, the Cherokee Nation itself was on the verge of extinction.[29]

The Choctaws proved even more reluctant than the Cherokees to give their freedmen membership in the tribe and the civil rights citizenship brought. Immediately following the war, the Choctaws exhibited a profound antipathy toward their former slaves. Many were reluctant to even admit to their slaves that slavery had come to an end. A Freedmen's Bureau agent noted, "one freedman has been killed at Boggy Depot by his former master, and there are rumors of several other cases, and no action has yet been taken by the government to punish the guilty party."[30]

The Choctaws remained divided in sentiment as to whether the freedmen should be removed or their rights accommodated within the nation. The United States commissioners in negotiations with the Choctaw Council proposed two alternatives. The Choctaws could either retain their freedmen and grant them full citizenship rights, or they could opt to have the freedmen removed at the expense of the Choctaw government and relocated in the "Leased District" which the United States had recently purchased. At first, to most Choctaws the choice appeared clear—they wanted the freedmen removed. However, many of the Choctaw leaders asked their fellow tribesmen

28. R. B. Ross and S. H. Mayes, Box M-50, SHMP; Microfilm CHN 81, NRCN.
29. Daniel F. Littlefield Jr., *The Cherokee Freedmen: From Emancipation to American Citizenship* (Westport: Greenwood Press, 1978), 249.
30. Sanborn to SI, Jan. 5, 1866, in *RSI* 1866, p. 285.

not to jump to any rash conclusions about the desirability of removal. The Choctaw chief argued that if the freedmen were removed and settled in close proximity to the Choctaw Nation the result might be worse than allowing the ex-slaves to remain within the nation, for the new settlement might attract a flood of African American migrants from the Deep South states. The chief cautioned his tribesmen about the potential result of a freedmen's colony, noting, "To say the least, they will be anything but desirable neighbors as a separate community. . . . Removed and established as a separate colony, they may do us and our brethern [*sic*] of the other adjacent tribes irreparable injury." After a prolonged battle, the proponents of adoption finally won out. Nearly two decades after emancipation, the Choctaw freedmen were finally adopted into the tribe and given full citizenship rights. In addition, the treaty provided that freedmen were to be guaranteed equality before the law in civil and criminal cases, they were entitled to equal educational facilities, they were permitted to hold any political office in the nation except the offices of Principal Chief and District Chief, and they were to be provided forty acres of Choctaw land upon which to settle.[31]

Of all the Five Civilized Tribes, the Chickasaws were the most resistant to adopting their freedmen and giving them full membership in the tribe. In the aftermath of the Civil War, the Chickasaws were reluctant to even admit the end of slavery. The Chickasaws blamed the freedmen for the failure of the Confederacy, and after the end of the war, "a reign of terror is reported to have set in." On one occasion the bodies of five blacks were found "piled together, killed by Indians."[32]

Almost all contemporary observers throughout the territorial era agreed that the Chickasaw freedmen were treated the worst of all the ex-slaves of the Indian nations. The local Indian agent reported in 1887 that the freedmen lived in "a deplorable condition. They are landless in a territory which has 4,650,935 acres, and where the Chickasaw inhabitants are entitled to 775 acres per capita." The agent continued, "they are recognized neither as citizens of the United States nor as Chickasaws. In fact, they are neither fish, flesh, nor fowl." One agent wrote in 1890, "these Chickasaw freedmen are the worse [*sic*] mistreated and most shamefully abused people on earth today. They are fearfully oppressed, ignorant, distressed, and sorely afflicted."[33]

The Chickasaws signed a treaty with the United States government in 1866

31. P. P. Pitchlynn and Winchester Colbert, Aug. 27, 1873, *Choctaw Nation Papers*, vol. 1 (1872–1937), 9–13, WHC; J. F. McCurtain, in *RSI* 1884, 2:37.

32. Sanborn to SI, Jan. 5, 1866, in *RSI* 1866, p. 285; Kenneth Porter, "Relations between Negroes and Indians within the Present Limits of the United States," *Journal of Negro History* 17, no. 3 (1932): 353.

33. J. D. C. Atkins, CIA, to SI, Sept. 21, 1887, in *RSI* 1887, 2:57; Indian Agent Bennett to SI, Feb. 12, 1890, Indian Territory, Special Files, Choctaw and Chickasaw and Cherokee Freedmen, Box 48 RG 48, RDI.

which declared that if they chose not to adopt their freedmen within two years of the ratification of the treaty, the United States would remove the freedmen and settle them elsewhere. The Chickasaw leaders argued that the tribe would be better off if the freedmen were gone, but the United States refused to hold up its end of the agreement. The Chickasaws argued that the United States had signed the treaty knowing full well it would not live up to its promise to remove the freedmen if the Chickasaws so desired.[34]

The Chickasaws never did agree to adopt their ex-slaves, and thus the freedmen lived for over forty years without civil rights or protection of the law. As historian Daniel F. Littlefield Jr. states, the Chickasaw freedmen were literally "a people without a country."[35]

WHEN THE "surplus" Indian lands were opened to white settlement in 1889, the Five Civilized Tribes with the exception of the Chickasaws, had adopted their freedmen and granted them all the rights of citizenship. This profoundly influenced the course of race relations in the territories, for it meant that most ex-slaves of the Five Civilized Tribes possessed the vote, held a share in tribal lands to be divided according to the dictates of the Curtis Act, enjoyed access to the tribal educational system, and were granted equality in the judicial system. Clearly by the 1890s, then, territorial freedmen enjoyed far more privileges than blacks in the United States proper, either the South or the North. They had every reason to believe they had found "the promised land." To many African Americans, particularly those in the southern states, the newly created Oklahoma Territory also represented a haven wherein they might escape the prejudice and oppression they faced on a daily basis. Many blacks, as a result, began to flock to the new territory hoping to find a place where their civil rights would be respected. However, the exodus of African Americans to the territories created a backlash among white settlers and many mixed-blood Native Americans. Fearful of a massive influx of African Americans, they sought to enact laws which would curtail the civil rights of blacks. By so doing, they hoped to discourage African American immigration.

Hence, the culture of Indian and Oklahoma Territories emerged from a symbiosis of Anglo-American, African American, and Native American influences. From initial contact on the frontier lands of the West, each racial group influenced, and was in turn influenced by, the other groups. All three races proved that their cultures were adaptive to change and input from outside sources. At the same time, each group also demonstrated its own racial preconceptions, preferences, and prejudices. As time passed, however, and as more

34. Jonas Wolf, Oct. 22, 1885, Indian Territory, Special Files, Choctaw and Chickasaw and Cherokee Freedmen, Box 48, RG 48, RDI.
35. Daniel F. Littlefield Jr., *The Chickasaw Freedmen: A People without a Country* (Westport: Greenwood Press, 1980), xi.

and more white settlers entered into the lands previously occupied solely by Native Americans and their former slaves, each group became more ethnocentric—more dedicated to maintaining the distances between cultures than in bridging the gaps. The question of racial separation versus integration became one of the most bitter debates of territorial society and served to factionalize both the Native American and African American communities.

TWO

The One-Drop Rule
Racial Prejudice and Stereotypes

I N THE AFTERMATH of emancipation, the racial attitudes of Native
Americans towards their former African American slaves differed tremen-
dously from tribe to tribe. The Chickasaws, and to a lesser extent the
Choctaws, engaged in mass violence as they blamed the freedmen for the losses
suffered as a result of the Civil War. As historian Nathaniel Washington states,
"it was no disgrace to kill a Negro. . . . [Ex-slaves] were shot down like dogs
by the dozens." As we have seen, the Chickasaws refused to recognize their
freedmen as tribal citizens and thereby excluded them from tribal politics, communal land ownership, annuity payments, and access to the educational system.
On the other hand, the Seminoles quickly adopted their freedmen and gave
them full citizenship rights.[1]

Yet tribal affiliation was not the only factor determining the nature of Native
American–African American relations. Often the degree of Indian blood was
also important. As early as 1872, a freedman named Lemon Butler claimed that
some Chickasaws would eat and drink with the freedmen but others would not.
Butler said that the full bloods did not make as much distinction between
themselves and the freedmen as did the mixed bloods. The full bloods attended
public gatherings and entertainment events with their ex-slaves, but the mixed
bloods refused. They maintained a strict segregation of the races. As a result,
Butler testified, the freedmen much preferred their full-blood neighbors over
the mixed bloods.[2]

Many Native Americans, especially the mixed bloods, came to espouse a
prejudice towards blacks equally virulent to that of their new white neighbors.
They, like their white counterparts, concluded blacks were intellectually inferior and lacking in morality. In 1872, the *Cherokee Advocate* published a mock
"interview" with a supposed survivor of the Fort Donelson battle in the Civil
War. The "interview," partially reprinted below, belittled the contribution of

1. Washington, *Negro in Oklahoma*, 22.
2. Littlefield, *The Chickasaw Freedmen*, 94.

African American Union soldiers and reinforced the popular stereotype of black cowardice and lack of moral and intellectual ability:

> "Were you in the fight?"
> "I had a little taste of it, sah."
> "Stood your ground, did you?"
> "No, sah, I runs."
> "Run at the first fire, did you?"
> "Yes sah, and, would have run soonah had I know'd it was comin.' [*sic*]"
> "Why, that wasn't very creditable to your courage?"
> "Dat isn't in my line, sah—cookin's my profession."[3]

As well, many Native Americans came to accept the white stereotype of African Americans as a group of thieves and criminals. Blacks came to be looked upon as troublemakers. Many Native Americans reportedly thought the freedmen a "very excitable people," who were "governed by passion and temper" and who fought "a good deal among themselves." In the fall of 1876, for example, the *Indian Journal* noted that a camp meeting at the Fountain Baptist Church had "passed off pleasantly." The paper reported, "about fifteen hundred worshippers were present, many sermons were preached, several converts were baptized, one minister was ordained, and *there was no disturbance*" (emphasis mine).[4]

Similarly, the former slaves of the Five Civilized Tribes displayed mixed feelings towards Native Americans. On the one hand, some freedmen were part Indian themselves. They tended to be proud of their Indian heritage. One settler remembered that freedmen did not consider themselves black but rather emphasized their tribal affiliation. According to historian Leonard Bloom, the knowledge of Indian ancestry afforded African Americans "some symbolic escape from the harsh rigidity of American caste boundaries." Even those freedmen who did not have Indian blood in their veins could relate to Native Americans as a fellow oppressed people who faced discrimination and dishonesty from white officials and settlers. The *Boley Progress* warned Native Americans to be skeptical of legal promises and to remember that "the white man had taken the labor of the Negro and the lands of the Indian, under full protection of the law."[5]

At the same time, African Americans were envious of what they perceived as the relatively higher social status afforded Native Americans by white society.

---

3. *Cherokee Advocate*, Aug. 24, 1872.

4. Littlefield, *The Chickasaw Freedmen*, 94; Angie Debo, *The Road to Disappearance* (Norman: University of Oklahoma Press, 1941), 230–31.

5. Davis, interview, OHP; Leonard Bloom, "Role of the Indian in the Race Relations Complex of the South," *Social Forces* 19 (Dec. 1940): 271; Norman L. Crockett, *The Black Towns* (Lawrence: Regents Press of Kansas, 1979), 75–76.

What infuriated African American leaders was that blacks were segregated while Native Americans were invited to assimilate. One contemporary black leader complained in a letter to a Republican congressman in 1883 that blacks were trying to become industrious and to "materially build up themselves and their children and obtain a substantial ownership of the soil." In contrast, he argued, "the Indian goes down showing no longevity to withstand civilization." The stubborn persistance of many of the relocated Plains tribes in the nomadic life-style of the chase despite the depletion of the buffalo herds led one black editor to conclude, "the poor Indians. Some times they do appear pitiable." Hence, African Americans were jealous that many Native Americans were turning down an offer to join Anglo-American society—an offer that was never extended to African Americans.[6]

On the other hand, many white officials and settlers maintained a racial stereotype of Native Americans as wild savages and moral degenerates. From initial contact, white colonists had viewed Native Americans as savages who had a profound propensity toward violence. As one nineteenth-century reformer noted in an address, whites for centuries "had been taught to regard the Indians as exclusively scalpers and murderers." Indeed, the secretary of the interior, who was the person ultimately responsible for Indian affairs in the late nineteenth century, wrote in 1883 that "the highest ambition of an Indian is to own a gun, the next to have an opportunity to use it." The secretary of the interior argued that Indians killed each other on the slightest provocation, "either for gain, to gratify his passion for blood, or to secure the fame that awaits a successful warrior." The secretary concluded, "We wonder at his ferocity, forgetting that he is a savage."[7]

As a result of the wild savage stereotype, white settlers who moved into the lands of the Indian Territory did so with great trepidation. White settlers were particularly fearful of the relocated Plains tribes, who had not adopted Anglo-American traditions and customs to the extent that the Five Civilized Tribes had. One settler remembered that her parents, upon migrating from Nodaway County, Missouri, into Custer County, Oklahoma, in 1898, feared "fresh scalps might adorn the belt of a Plains Indian." The woman reminisced that reports of recent uprisings had implanted a profound fear of Indians. After her family was safely situated on a claim that adjoined the townsite of Thomas, Oklahoma, this mistrust of Indians persisted to the extent "that when Cheyennes approached, I would quit playing in the yard and rush indoors." One Indian agent reported to his superiors back east that several settlers from Kan-

6. Gary R. Kremer, "For Justice and a Fee: James Milton Turner and the Cherokee Freedmen," *Chronicles of Oklahoma* 58, no. 4 (1980): 381; *Langston City Herald,* Nov. 23, 1895.
7. *Cherokee Advocate,* July 30, 1879; Henry M. Teller, SI, Nov. 1, 1883, in *RSI* 1883, 1:v.

sas had written him asking if it would be safe for them to emigrate to the Indian Territory. The settlers wanted to know if they could leave the train in the Indian Territory without an escorted guard, for as the agent noted, "the great majority think of the Cherokee or Choctaw as a copper-colored person in moccasins and breech cloth, eagle feathers, tomahawk, and pistol laying around for a fair chance to kill somebody." Another settler claimed Indians might act friendly but "deep in their hearts they all hated the white people." He warned, "you never could tell their real feelings unless you were married to one."[8]

A missionary woman sent to live among the Kiowas remembered taking four Indians with her on a train trip to Chicago. At their first stop, in Chickasha, Oklahoma, the local hotel manager refused to serve the Indians in the dining room. When the missionary woman explained the Indians were Christians embarking upon a speaking tour to Chicago, the man acquiesced but sat the group at a table of their own at the back of the room. Later, a woman boarded the train at El Reno, Oklahoma, and as the missionary woman related, "she gave the Indians one look, and sped up the aisle as far as she could go, as if afraid of being pursued and scalped alive." Another white woman remembered living in constant fear of Indian attack. She claimed that at night Indians would come and surround a settler's cabin "a whoopin' and a hollerin'," and that sometimes they would break into the cabin and eat everything that was available. The woman remembered that her family used to burn the fire low when they heard Indians in the vicinity so that "they wouldn't think anyone was home."[9]

Sometimes white fears led to panic. One pioneer woman remembered an army officer who upon his return from Washington ran into a group of loud, screaming Indians in Ponca City, Oklahoma. The officer concluded this to be a sign that the Indians were going on the warpath and therefore he hurried to Oklahoma City to warn of the impending attack. The residents began to collect and fortify the town and waited. A couple of days later, the woman recalled, a United States Marshal appeared in town and proceeded to describe a very lavish wedding ceremony and celebration he had seen in Ponca City, "and the Oklahoma City residents soon realized of the army officer's folly."[10]

The savage stereotype of Native Americans was reinforced by one of the most popular forms of mass entertainment in the late nineteenth century—the Wild West show. Advertisements featured Indians in their "traditional buckskin and headdresses." Native Americans who participated in Wild West shows were undoubtedly shocked that they had to wear "Indian costumes" to add an air of

8. Florence Ogden, memoir, Box 0-3, FOP; Robert L. Owen to CIA, Sept. 1, 1887, in *RSI* 1887, 2:196; Walter Pierce, interview, GFPHC, 93:311.

9. Isabel Crawford, *Joyful Journey: Highlights on the High Way* (Philadelphia: Judson Press, 1951), 84; Mrs. Floyd, interview, File 56.33, OHP.

10. Edna Slaughter, interview, File 397, OHP.

"authenticity." Wild West shows depicted Indians as savage beasts intent upon brutally murdering and scalping every white victim they could get their hands on. Buffalo Bill's Wild West Show featured several supposed re-enactments of pioneer life. All of the scenes which included Native Americans were battles between marauding savage Indians and resilient white pioneer settlers. The official program of Buffalo Bill's Wild West Show promised re-enactment of the following scenes:

> *Illustrating a Prairie Emigrant Train Crossing the Plains.* It is attacked by marauding Indians, who are in turn repulsed by "Buffalo Bill" and a number of scouts and cowboys.
> *Indians* from the Sioux, Arapahoe, Brule and Cheyenne tribes will illustrate the Indian mode of fighting, war-dances, and games.
> *Attack on the Deadwood Mail Coach by Indians* repulse of the Indians, and rescue of the stage, passengers and mail, by "Buffalo Bill" and his attendant cowboys.
> *Attack on Settlers' Cabin* and rescue by "Buffalo Bill" and a band of cowboys, scouts and frontiersmen.

Hence, Wild West shows accepted the popular viewpoint of Indians as savages and a threat to white civilization. By glorifying white violence against Native Americans as noble and just, Wild West shows gave cultural sanction to the prevailing racial ideology advanced by many white settlers and officials. For as one Texas bandit who had killed a white posseman near Little Blue River in southwestern Oklahoma, declared, "that was the eighth man I've killed,—niggers and Indians don't count."[11]

In conjunction with the stereotype of the wild savage, white officials and settlers characterized Native Americans as immoral degenerates. Many agents complained that Native Americans were more intent upon drinking, gambling, horse racing, and dancing than undertaking any form of gainful employment. One Indian inspector noted that Indians seemed to have adopted many aspects of the white man, but that it was "usually his vices, seldom any of his virtues." Many of the local newspapers emphasized the supposed moral degeneracy of the Indians in fictional pieces. The *Norman Transcript* ran the following anecdote in an 1891 edition:

THE LAST OF THE MOHICANS

Ugh! grunted the unconquerable red man, turning his eagle eye unflinchingly toward the distant bivouac of the foe, whose camp fires he could see dis-

11. Official Program of Buffalo Bill's Wild West show, Vertical Files—Wild West Shows, OHS; Arthur T. Burton, *Black, Red and Deadly: Black and Indian Gunfighters of the Indian Territory, 1870–1907* (Austin: Eakin Press, 1991), 126.

tinctly from the lone hillock on which he stood. "Does the pale face think he can crush the proud spirit of a descendant of Kicking Steer and Blood on the Moon? Ha! By the bones of my ancestors, never! This trusty tomahawk shall bury itself in his brain and this Arkansaw toothpick shall lift his beastly scalp. That's the kind of Buffalo Bill I am!"

So saying, the fiery, untamed son of the plains, brave Never Washes His Face, gave one last look at the setting sun, took three fingers of fire water from his pint flask, strode with reluctant step down the slope to his own camp and gloomily kicked his oldest squaw out of the tepee.

The commissioner of Indian affairs in 1872 referred to the Indians of the West as "a large gypsy population, which will inevitably become a sore, a well nigh intolerable affliction to all that region, unless the government shall provide for their instruction in the arts of life." During the debate over the annexation of the Philippines in the late 1890s, the *El Reno News* reported that a Kingfisher, Oklahoma, man had come up with the idea of intermarrying the Philippine Islanders and the Arapaho Indians, "holding that it would improve both tribes, on the theory that they couldn't possibly be worse." One settler remembered that it was common for people with questionable character and low morals to be presumed to have Indian blood in them, no matter how "white" they appeared.[12]

Another stereotype popular among local Indian agents sent to work among the relocated tribes was a view of Native Americans as inherently lazy and unwilling to work even in the face of starvation. The Quapaw agent gave a very harsh criticism of the Indians under his charge in 1883. He wrote his superiors in Washington: "The greatest ambition of many is to ride about vestured in garments of barbaric tint, with paint and feathers. The majority are indolent, and will do no work as long as they have a cent in their pockets or a loaf of bread in the house. You can find them almost any day standing around their cabins or leaning around drowsily, like animals who have been hired to personate men and are tired of the job." Another agent noted that there was nothing more monotonous than the life of the Indian. He claimed that "nothing to do and all day to do it in" was their motto, and "lazy idleness is their life."[13]

Many white settlers came to resent that the Indians were seemingly rewarded for their laziness with gifts of government food rations, clothing, agricultural implements, and seed. In addition, of course, the Indian tribes also received their annuity cash payments. This led one rancher to say, "the Indians

12. Indian Inspector Tinker, R 34, Osage Agency, 1896, RIIIA; *Norman Transcript,* Mar. 21, 1891; Francis Walker, CIA, to SI, in *RSI* 1872, p. 400; *El Reno News,* Dec. 23, 1898; Raymond Knight, interview, File 166, OHP.

13. D. B. Dyer to CIA, Aug. 16, 1883, in *RSI* 1883, 2:138; J. Hertford to CIA, Aug. 1, 1879, in *RSI* 1879, p. 185; Franklin Campbell Smith, FCSA, 154.

get everything down here and the whites nothing." White settlers were often upset that Native Americans received all these advantages but supposedly neglected to put them to use.[14]

Another popular stereotype in the territorial press was that Native Americans, being "uncivilized," were unable to express real human emotions such as love, fear, or remorse. One territorial paper reported, "one of the savage sun-worshippers danced himself to death near Ponca City last week. His chums howled and wept for a few hours and then ran a foot race for his blanket." An anecdote from the *Cheyenne Transporter* records how white Americans felt Indians were uninstructed in the true nature of love. The tongue-in-cheek story claimed that "If the Indians could be instructed in the art of kissing and courting in the right way, they would not want to fight. These fighters who are killing people and disemboweling them and braining little children, could be tamed easily by love, the way white people love. Let a buck Indian come off of the war path and get in love with a girl, and go to work to win her the way white folks do, and there would be no room in his mind for thoughts of murder and revenge."[15]

Finally, a few whites saw within the wild savage stereotype a sense of romanticism. Some romanticized the freedom from the constraints of civilization, a nostalgic dream of a past free from the complications of an urbanizing, industrializing America. As one contemporary white settler noted, "There is, for civilized minds, a positive fascination about the Indian. Its foundation seems to be that he awakened in the modern mind an echo of the primitive from which we all spring sooner or later. We sooner, he later." The settler then compared the aura of romance of the Indian to that of a soldier's uniform. He concluded, "So with the Indian. He, like the soldier, is romance stalking out of the pages of the past into modern humdrum life."[16]

SOME WHITES who came west to settle among the Indian tribes of the territory were quite affected by their first sight and interaction with Indians. While most remained fearful of Native Americans, some eventually came to a grudging respect for their new neighbors. One merchant, for example, was surprised to find how trustworthy and honest his Indian customers were. The merchant noted that he seldom had occasion to go into their camps to make collections. He said praisingly that if an Indian died owing a debt, his relatives always paid it. He concluded, "once they gave a promise, its performance was regarded as a sacred obligation."[17]

14. Smith, FCSA, 154.
15. *El Reno News,* Nov. 11, 1898; *Cheyenne Transporter,* June 30, 1885.
16. Smith, FCSA, 150.
17. R. A. Sneed, quoted in Anne H. Morgan and Rennard Strickland, eds., *Oklahoma Memories* (Norman: University of Oklahoma Press, 1981), 63.

Other bureau officials and white settlers wrote of how proud and strong-willed Native Americans were. Their fight to maintain their culture and traditions against the attempts of officials to enforce assimilation evoked a sympathetic response from a few whites. One of the original settlers of Oklahoma Territory composed several short poems in which a romanticized vision of Native Americans is quite evident. Thomas Athey, an original boomer settler, wrote:

The First American

He has left his name behind him
adding rich and barbaric grace
to the mountains and the rivers
to the fertile meadow place

Frank Linderman composed an eloquent poem detailing the fall of the Indian:

Indian Territory Indians
of All States and Their History!

Step by step and ever backward,
Ov'r the ground his Fathers trod,
Fighting ever and ev'r invoking
Strength and Peace from Pagan Gods!
Gone his greatness and his freedom,
Grinning want alone remains
Bison, sculls and wallows mock him
On his own ancestral plains.[18]

The poems, while attempting to evoke a sympathetic response to the plight of the Indians, nonetheless leave no doubt that early white settlers regarded Native Americans as a conquered people.

Those governmental officials and humanitarian reformers who saw admirable qualities in Native Americans argued that the government should use its power over the Indians to enforce cultural assimilation. They argued that the progress of the Five Civilized Tribes in adopting Anglo-American traditions and customs demonstrated that Native Americans had the requisite attributes to be elevated close to the level of the Anglo-Saxon race through education and moral suasion. The Indian reformers accepted the Darwinian concept of the survival of the fittest. They also believed that the only way to ensure the continued existence of "lesser races" was to ensure their cultural advancement

18. Thomas Athey, "The First American," File 82.197, Miscellaneous Poetry, Box 2, TAP; Frank Linderman, "Indian Territory Indians of All States and Their History!" File 82.197, Miscellaneous Poetry, Box 2, TAP.

through a government-led assimilation campaign. As historian Robert Mardock notes, "The new way of life would be based on the values of idealized middle-class, nineteenth century Easterners—law-abiding, morally Christian, and politically democratic. The new Indians would be industrious, self-supporting, landowners who had all the rights and duties of citizenship."[19]

It is important to note, however, that not all white officials and humanitarians were convinced that Native Americans could be educated to a plane close to that of white society. Governmental officials and humanitarians were divided into two basic camps: those who saw Indians as children who needed kind paternalism and Anglo-American education to become civilized, and those who saw Indians as savages incapable of ever becoming civilized. Often white officials and humanitarians held both views simultaneously. Many white officials and humanitarians held high hopes for the Five Civilized Tribes, and in particular the mixed bloods, in assimilating into American society, but few held much faith in the capacity of the relocated tribes of western Indian Territory of ever achieving full integration into American society. So in reality, the offer of assimilation was by and large aimed at the mixed-blood population of the Five Civilized Tribes.

Officials sought to isolate the relocated tribes on reservations in the West where they might be slowly assimilated through the paternalistic guidance of Indian Bureau officials and Christian missionaries. The reservation was to serve as a laboratory in which Native Americans would be not only instructed in the practices of a settled agricultural existence, but also educated in the traditions of Anglo-American culture. It was hoped that under such a rigid system of controlled supervision, full-blood Native Americans would become more like whites. As the commissioner of Indian affairs noted, "Steeped as his progenitors were, and as more than half of the race now are, in blind ignorance, the devotees of abominable superstitions, and the victims of idleness and thriftlessness, the absorbing query which the hopelessness of his situation, if left to his own guidance, suggests to the philanthropist, and particularly to a great Christian people like ours, is to know how to relieve him from this state of dependence and barbarism, and to direct him in the paths that will eventually lead him to the light and liberty of American citizenship."[20]

Most humanitarians and many sympathetic officials in Washington no doubt recognized the whites' treatment of the Indians in the past had devastated them. It was time, they argued, to make up for past wrongs. Many no doubt agreed with a committee report to the United States Congress which stated, "the white man's treatment of the Indian is one of the greatest sins of civilization, for which no single generation or nation is wholly answerable, but which

19. Robert Mardock, *Reformers and the American Indian* (Columbia, Mo.: University of Missouri Press, 1971), 4.
20. J. D. C. Atkins, CIA, to SI, Oct. 5, 1885, in *RSI* 1885, 2:3.

it is now too late to redress. Repentance is all that is left us, restitution is impossible." The words of one Indian agent exemplify the sentiments of many reformers. He stated, "We owe to the Indians of this country some atonement for the past. We owe them a debt that can only be paid by patient, loving and tireless efforts to enlighten, civilize and christianize them. Less than this will leave blackened the fairest page in the history of this age and country." But officials were quick to add that they had determined that Anglo-American civilization ought to take the place of "barbarous Indian habits." Therefore, as the secretary of the interior declared, "we claim the right to control the soil they occupy, and we assume that it is our duty to coerce them, if necessary, into the adoption and practice of our habits and customs." Hence, whites proved willing to accept Native Americans into American society only if the Native Americans were willing to give up their unique customs and traditions and adopt Anglo-American culture as their own—in reality, they would only be accepted when they ceased to be Indians.[21]

NATIVE AMERICANS often stereotyped white settlers and governmental officials as lacking in morals and undeserving of the Indian's trust. One Cherokee argued that the beginnings of the sorrows of Indian people began when "the white man was permitted to invade the Cherokee Nation." He noted, "with the coming of the white man, there came a strange characteristic where they talked out of both sides of their mouth." Another Indian wrote to his uncle that the reason there was "so much wickedness in Blue County is because there are so much bad white people among us." He concluded, "among all the thousands of whites that is sojourning or renting farms, I don't know but only three white men that is honest and good men, just three only, in this country, the balance is what would be termed trash and out scouring of the United States." Henry Starr, a notorious Indian outlaw, concurred, noting, "I had always looked upon the Indians as supreme and the white renters as trash who moved from year to year in covered wagons with many dogs and tow-headed kids peeping out from behind every wagon-bow, and who, at the very best, made only a starving crop." The Ponca Indian agent recognized the distrust the Indians under his supervision held for whites in general. He wrote his supervisors back east that to achieve change in the Indians was a "prolonged, very painstaking, and very patient work," because "small faith in the advice or counsel of the white man remains with the Indian character of today." Two Ponca Indians accused white officials of waging germ warfare by giving their tribesmen blankets laden with smallpox so that the Poncas "died like flies." They argued that the Poncas, who had numbered about 25,000 in 1870, were devas-

21. William J. Pollock, R 55, Union Agency, 1881, RIIIA; R 121, Cheyenne and Arapaho Agency, 1876, LR-RBIA; Columbus Delano, SI, Nov. 1, 1872, in *RSI* 1872, pp. 3–4.

tated by the "white man's disease," until by the late 1880s only 2,000 of them remained.[22]

Many Native Americans as a result of the long heritage of broken promises and violence at the hands of governmental officials and frontier settlers sought to avoid contact with whites as much as possible. One white commented on the aversion of Native Americans to contact with settlers. He argued that Indians would not meet a white man in the road if they could avoid it. He stated, "I have been going along the road and seen one coming when he would sight me he would halt, throw his head up and ride off in the bushes just like a wild animal. Of course the women did that too; they seemed shyer [sic] than the men." Another settler remembered being lost in the woods and stopping to ask a young Indian girl doing the washing near her hut which way he should go. The girl merely grunted, and the settler assumed she could not speak English. The next day, however, he saw the same girl at the local store buying supplies, and he learned otherwise. The settler concluded that Indians "would just not talk to you if they did not know you."[23]

Given that a significant element of Native Americans tried to avoid even the most casual contact with whites, it is not surprising that many full-blood members of the Five Civilized Tribes and certainly the vast majority of the relocated Plains tribes vowed not to accept the offer to join American society; it was not worth giving up tribal sovereignty and Indian culture for. Hence, the degree of acceptance of Anglo-American culture often was related to tribal identification. Not surprisingly, the Five Civilized Tribes tended to be more supportive of the assimilation policy. The relocated Plains tribes were the most hostile towards it. Carl Sweezy, an Arapaho painter, described how hard it was for his people to accept the Anglo-American cultural norms that were being thrust upon them. The ideals of the reformers to make Native Americans into independent farmers promised both an economic and social transformation which many full bloods would find hard to endure. As Sweezy noted:

There was plenty of rich land, and they expected each man to choose ground wherever he wanted it within our boundaries and settle down. But the Arapahoe had always lived in bands, with their tepees side by side, their horses grazing together, and with hunting and fishing and feasting and worship all carried on by the group. It took years to learn to settle down on a farm and work alone

22. Ned Downing, interview, File T-396, B1, p. 1, DDOHI; Calvin Robinson to Peter Pitchlynn, Apr. 29, 1879, Box 4, File 89, PPP; Downing, interview, DDOHI; Robinson to Pitchlynn, Apr. 29, 1879, PPP; Henry Starr, quoted in Burton, *Black, Red and Deadly*, 66; Ponca Indian agent, quoted in Rennard Strickland, *The Indians in Oklahoma* (Norman: University of Oklahoma Press, 1980), 40; William Collins Sr. and William Collins Jr., interview, File 87.179, OHP.

23. Asbury Brannan, interview, GFPHC, 88:124–25; Luther Sharp, interview, GFPHC, 44:236.

and see one's neighbors only once in a while. Neither we nor our dogs nor our ponies understood this new way of white people. To us it seemed unsociable and lonely, and not the way people were meant to live.

Unlike the leaders of the relocated Plains tribes, Pleasant Porter, the chief of the Creek tribe, did not object to the policy of assimilation per se, but rather the pace at which it was expected that Native Americans would give up their traditions and culture. The chief claimed his tribe had been progressing slowly along the path to civilization, but his people found it difficult to adjust to "the civilization which has been so violently and suddenly thrust upon us."[24]

Even so, many Native Americans also recognized that the government held ultimate authority over their lives. As one Ponca full blood noted, "Father in the beginning the Great Spirit made us a different color you white and I red. Of course he made you white—the Great Spirit has given the power to the whites." The blunt acknowledgment that the white authorities increasingly held the reins of power over the lives of Native Americans led some to conclude that resistance to the imposition of Anglo-American culture was futile.[25]

The difference of opinion over the desirability of assimilation was not strictly dependent upon tribal affiliation: often it was also related to the degree of Indian blood. Many mixed-blood leaders came to argue that Native Americans should resist Anglo-American culture no longer, but rather should immediately seek to embrace it. This, they said, would bring about assimilation and the integration of Indians into mainstream American society. The commissioner of Indian affairs noted the difference in attitude between the full bloods and the mixed bloods in his report of 1875. He stated:

> To the more intelligent among them, and especially the mixed-bloods, who are able to see that close contact with the civilization of the whites will help forward rather than retard their own civilization and prosperity, this outlook is not so full of apprehension. Indeed, it is probable that if the question were left to this class among the Indians, with primary reference not only to their own interests, but to the common welfare, they would regard the settlement of families of respectable whites in such numbers as to fairly populate the country as a contribution to the prosperous condition of the Indians, rather than otherwise.

One mixed blood wrote that under government tutelage Native Americans had made tremendous strides towards becoming civilized. The effect of contact with white Indian Bureau officials and missionaries, he claimed, had totally transformed Native society for the better. He concluded that "We cannot for-

24. Carl Sweezy, quoted in Morgan and Strickland, *Oklahoma Memories,* 94; quoted in Debo, *And Still the Waters Run,* 146–47.
25. Debo, *And Still the Waters Run,* 146–147.

get that scarcely a century has elapsed since our ancestors were blanket savages, that war and the chase were their only occupation." Yet he claimed that with the help of all-wise and omnipotent God, "the blanket has been replaced by decent apparel; the tomahawk has been exchanged for the useful axe; the scalping knife for the plow share, and the dismal tone of the warrior's whoop has mellowed into the sacred songs of Zion."[26]

Generational lines also affected the assimilation campaign. Young boys and girls were much more willing to adopt Anglo-American culture than were Native American elders. One Native American woman remembered that tribal elders were disgusted to find that the young members of the tribe "all wanted to be white."[27]

But the relocated Plains tribes and the non-assimilationist full bloods of the Five Civilized Tribes proved resilient in the face of pressure to adopt Anglo-American culture. Thus, ironically, white Americans in attempting to legislate Indian culture out of existence actually helped to preserve it. For in the face of an organized assimilation campaign, many Native Americans banded together, often overcoming inter-tribal hostilities, centuries old in tradition, creating a pan-Indian culture in which differences between tribes were of less consequence than the similarities. Although the Five Civilized Tribes had socially integrated with white society to a far greater extent than the relocated Plains tribes had, a large portion of the Civilized tribesmen, particularly the full bloods, found solidarity with their fellow Indians on the reservations to the west. With their cultural institutions under attack from white officials, many Native Americans came to think of themselves not so much as Chickasaws, Cherokees, Osages, or Poncas, but rather as members of a distinct race—as Indians. As a result, many Native American leaders were able to promote the idea of tribal consolidation unthinkable only decades earlier. The governor of the Chickasaw Nation stated, in 1876, "It further impresses upon my mind that the political, material, and social interests of the Indian race demand their consolidation."[28]

Full-blood Indians also sought to promote their own traditions and customs through the rise of tribal factions such as the Keetoowahs within the Cherokee tribe. The Keetoowah society was dedicated to maintaining tribal sovereignty and resisting the attempt of white officials to transform Native American culture into Anglo-American culture. It was also dedicated to wresting political control of the Cherokee Nation from its mixed-blood leaders, who, it was argued, were too accommodationist with white administrators. But the Keetoo-

26. Edward P. Smith, CIA, to SI, Nov. 1, 1875, in *RSI* 1875, p. 515; I. L. Garvin, Oct. 19, 1879, Box G-25, File 2, ILGP.
27. Julia Edge, interview, File 88.99, OHP.
28. B. F. Overton, annual message, Sept. 5, 1876, Chickasaw Nation Papers, vol. 1, 11–12, WHC.

wah society was also a religious movement. As historian William G. Mc-Gloughlin notes, "its members treasured and sustained many of the ancient ceremonies, ideals, and spiritual aspects of their old religion." In this sense, the Keetoowah society reflected a growing Native American protest movement in the West which sought to promote Indian pride across tribal lines and to develop fierce resistance against white authority.[29]

Perhaps the most dramatic demonstration of full-blood resistance was the rise of the ghost dance movement. The ghost dance was a ceremonial dance which predicted that the Great Spirit would see to it that the white race was wiped off the face of the earth and Native peoples would once more be allowed to roam their ancient homeland in pursuit of the buffalo, which would again frequent the Plains after the whites had disappeared. Adherents wore an elaborate "ghost shirt," which some believed was impenetrable to bullets or weapons of any sort. One contemporary observer claimed the ghost dance replaced hostilities centuries old in tradition with a brotherhood of peace between rival tribes.[30]

Hence by the early twentieth century, many mixed bloods of the Five Civilized Tribes had been assimilated into Anglo-American culture; the other Native Americans—the relocated Plains tribes of the western reservations and many full-blood members of the Five Civilized Tribes—found themselves marginalized.[31]

THE RACIAL STEREOTYPES white Americans held of African Americans in many ways were similar to those they held of Native Americans. For example, many white reformers felt African Americans, like Native Americans, needed the strict moral guidance of a kind authority figure. After the war was over, northern reformers may have been sympathetic toward the plight of the ex-slaves, but they thought African Americans were incapable of looking after themselves. White officials complained of the ignorance of the ex-slaves. They argued that freedmen, like many Indians, did not have any market sense—they had no conception of saving money. One territorial newspaper complained that the Cherokee freedmen were receiving $200 per capita for the lease of the Cherokee strip lands and "still they are starving." In words very reminiscent of how whites described Native Americans, another local newspaper commented that African Americans seemed to live according to the dictum "easy come, easy go." The paper described African Americans as "an indolent people, car-

29. McLoughlin, *After the Trail of Tears*, 156.

30. James Mooney, *The Ghost Dance Religion and the Sioux Outbreak of 1890* (Chicago: University of Chicago Press, 1965), 29, 25.

31. Frederick Hoxie, *A Final Promise: The Campaign to Assimilate the Indians, 1880–1920* (Lincoln: University of Nebraska Press, 1984), 243.

ing for little more than an easy existence," and "unwilling to work as long as food and a place to sleep are even temporarily in sight."[32]

The stereotype of the lazy, ignorant African American was given its most dramatic expression in the proliferation of minstrel shows, which became an important part of popular culture from the middle of the nineteenth century well into the twentieth century. Their popularity extended across America, so it is not surprising that minstrel shows were one of the most celebrated attractions after the coming of the railroad to the territories. As early as 1878, African American minstrel shows were touring the Indian Territory. Local newspapers advertised the shows weeks in advance of the performances. On the day of the show, the troupe gave a free promotional concert or parade to entice crowds for the evening performance.[33]

Minstrel shows were performed usually by white actors, but regardless of whether the actors were white or black, most of the people on stage would be in blackface. In these minstrel shows the essence of the entertainment came from the depiction of supposedly typical African Americans. African Americans were portrayed as lazy, ignorant, and untrustworthy. Yet at the same time they were portrayed as jovial and comical. The gags typically revolved around the idiotic, childlike behavior of stereotypical black slaves. Most of the productions were set on plantations in the antebellum South. "The Romance of Coon Hollow" featured a "steamboat race," a "jolly plantation scene," and a "cotton press tragedy" among its songs and dances. "In Old Kentucky" advertised "50 rollicking, frollicking, comical pickanninies," "six Kentucky thoroughbred horses," and "the famous pickanninny band." The United Minstrel Shows advertisement for the production of "Deacon Rastus and Johnsing's Experiences in Chicken Sandwich Island—We Had a Hot Time at the King's Dance," showed several Africans in tribal attire and had two blackfaced minstrels in a cooking pot over a hot fire. Minstrel shows stereotyped blacks in conventional terms—as lazy, comical children who could never be trusted to act responsibly. Minstrel shows reinforced the notion that it was useless to try and upgrade African Americans' culture—unlike Native Americans, blacks were simply too ignorant and childlike to ever become civilized by Anglo-American standards.

As a result, whites sought to segregate African Americans; assimilation would not be offered to blacks as it was to Indians. De facto segregation existed in the territories from the first massive influx of white settlers when the "surplus" Indian lands were opened up for settlement. In addition, since many of the white settlers who came to settle in both Indian and Oklahoma Territories in the late nineteenth century immigrated from the southern states, they had

---

32. *El Reno News,* July 22, 1898; *Rochester Courier,* undated, Racism—Oklahoma File, Historic Oklahoma Collection, WHC.

33. *Cherokee Advocate,* Apr. 27, 1878; Littlefield, *The Chickasaw Freedmen,* 87.

been used to deference from African Americans and they expected it to continue in their new home in the West. White settlers clearly wanted blacks to "stay in their place." African Americans were expected to show deference to whites in public areas. When they did not, whites became incensed. In 1895, for example, Simon Brown and his wife were arrested and fined ten dollars for "cursing and otherwise abusing some white ladies." Later that same year, some white women were taking a Sunday stroll in a carriage in Pauls Valley, Chickasaw Nation, when another carriage containing a black man and three female companions narrowly missed hitting them on the road. That night, the black driver of the carriage was taken to the town's outskirts, whipped, and warned to leave town. To stress the message, night riders rode through the black section of town and fired shots into his home. Hence, the actions of the massive numbers of white settlers who came to settle in the Indian lands in the late nineteenth century indicated that they had every intention of maintaining the distinction between black and white which had existed for centuries in the American South.[34]

NOT SURPRISINGLY, African Americans objected to the racial stereotypes whites held of them. For example, many black leaders were quick to denigrate the stereotype of African American criminality. Black editorialists in Oklahoma Territory claimed it was no more fair to portray the entire race as thieves and liars than to denounce all whites and Indians as criminals. As one territorial paper queried, "Why make the Negro responsible for the crimes of a few of his race, and make the individual responsible in the white race. We demand measurement by the same standard. Is it not a fact that the Negro learned his first lessons in kleptomania from the white man?" The fact that African Americans had themselves been "stolen" was a fairly common defense enunciated by black leaders when confronted with the accusation that all blacks were thieves, liars, and cheats.[35]

Black editorialists in Oklahoma vehemently denied that their race was ignorant and debased, as many whites claimed. They responded that often such racist remarks arose out of fear from poor whites who saw African Americans as successful competitors in the labor market. One black newspaper noted that it was "the poor and less informed whites" who were against blacks. The editors rationalized that prejudice arose because African Americans were "thrifty, industrious, and intelligent—hence a competitor in the struggle of life." Black leaders also tried to convince government officials and eastern reformers that

34. Philip Mellinger, "Discrimination and Statehood in Oklahoma," *Chronicles of Oklahoma* 49, no. 3 (1971): 340–77; William E. Bittle and Gilbert L. Geis, "Racial Self-Fulfillment and the Rise of an All-Negro Community in Oklahoma," *Phylon* 18, 3rd quarter (1956): 251; Littlefield, *The Chickasaw Freedmen*, 95.

35. *Muskogee Cimeter*, June 22, 1905.

their race was progressing quite dramatically in the wake of emancipation and that all that was necessary to continue this advancement was to ensure African Americans equal access to educational facilities and to economic opportunities.[36]

Thus, not surprisingly, the demands for Jim Crow laws and racial deference met with stubborn resistance from the black community. However, blacks were far from united in their opposition. For one thing, there was a variation in the attitude between freedmen who had lived their entire lives in the Indian nations (who called themselves "natives") and those African Americans who had emigrated to the Indian lands after they were opened up to settlement (referred to by the "native" freedmen as "state negroes"). Initially there was tremendous resentment because "native" freedmen thought that the new settlers showed too much subservience to whites. No doubt, "native" freedmen were cognizant that it was the fear of a massive influx of "state negroes" that lay behind the movement to restrict African American civil rights. As historians William Bittle and Gilbert Geis note: "The freedmen tried to keep their distance from the state Negroes, whom they considered to have a lower status. They called them 'Watchina,' a corruption of Virginia—meaning 'white man'—with the connotation of 'White man's Negro.' . . . they suffered the discrimination imposed upon all Negroes and complained bitterly: 'It was those state niggers from Texas that spoiled it for us, bowing and scraping and scratching the head.' "[37]

Originally there were social sanctions against "native" freedmen and "state negroes" from intermarrying. In part these social sanctions were due to the tribes' concern that "state Negroes" who intermarried with "native" freedmen would claim full tribal rights as intermarried white settlers enjoyed. However, these sanctions broke down in the face of increasing racial prejudice from whites and Native Americans. At times, the tensions between the two groups of blacks led to violence. "Native" freedmen frequently broke up church services and other public gatherings with gunfire and periodically amused themselves by riding through Boley, Indian Territory (settled by "state negroes"), late at night shooting out windows. Mrs. Moses J. Jones remembered that "a burning light in a house served as their target," and therefore her family spent many sleepless and fearful nights sitting in a dark house. A few people on both sides were wounded or killed during such skirmishes, but in time overt violence between the two groups was replaced by complete social separation.[38]

Many black leaders felt that such divisions within the black community

36. *Langston Western Age,* Dec. 6, 1907.

37. Mary Grayson, *WPA,* vol. 6 (St. Clair Shores: Scholarly Press, 1976); William E. Bittle and Gilbert Geis, *The Longest Way Home: Chief Alfred Sam's Back-to-Africa Movement* (Detroit: Wayne State University Press, 1964), 23.

38. Bittle and Geis, *The Longest Way Home,* 43; Crockett, *The Black Towns,* 39–40.

needed to be overcome in order to present a united resistance against white and Native American discrimination. One black editorialist argued, "the reason we are treated so badly by our white friends, is because we as a race stand so far apart, revel in dissension. . . . Now if we would all come together and stick like other races, to each other, we would readily see how quick mob violence and lawlessness would take the flight to oblivion." Despite such warnings the black community remained divided over the question of the desirability of integration versus racial separation from white society. Many black leaders felt blacks were only deluding themselves to think that whites would ever accept them as equal members in American society. The *Langston City Herald* noted, "if we were to say that all the white people of this country are against the Negro we fear that we would say too much, but when we say that there is no white man who wishes to give the Negro an all around equal chance with his white brother, we believe we speak facts." One black resident stated bitterly: "The white man ain't no good. All he is trying to do is to keep us down and no Negro will ever get a break as long as he's in the lead. When a negro does make good, it ain't because the white man helps him, but he has to get what he can get in spite of him."[39]

African Americans who saw little hope of whites ever accepting them as equals pointed to the experience of black professionals in Oklahoma Territory. Black leaders claimed that while whites maintained blacks were morally and intellectually inferior, they did not accept even those black professionals who were well educated and held well-respected jobs. One black newspaper documented the discrimination experienced by African American lawyers. The paper noted, "frequently in the courtroom and elsewhere in performance of his duty he is met with that opprobrious and damnable epithet of 'nigger,' 'slick head,' 'darkey,' 'coon,' etc." In 1904, a black candidate for admission to practice medicine in the territory was reminded by the board of examiners "to play the coon." The doctor, taking offense at the racial slur, scuffled with the president of the board and needless to say was denied his certificate. The white papers came out the next day with the charge that the doctor was "a big, burly Negro" who had attempted to assault the president of the Medical Board.[40]

To many black leaders such events demonstrated that whites would never accept African Americans regardless of their educational backgrounds or occupational position—they would always be "niggers" in the eyes of whites. As a result, many territorial black leaders came to argue that there would never be social equality between the two races. As one editor noted, "there is and can be no such thing as social co-mingling between the whites and blacks of this

39. *Langston City Herald,* June 15, 1893, July 6, 1895; quoted in Mozell Hill, "Basic Racial Attitudes toward Whites in the Oklahoma All-Negro Community," *American Journal of Sociology* 49 (May 1944): 520.
40. *Muskogee Cimeter,* Sept. 15, 1904; *Lincoln Tribune,* Oct. 29, 1904.

country. The whites won't have it, and the Negroes don't want it." Hence, for some territorial black leaders the only answer for the future of African Americans lay in racial separation. Blacks, they said, would only truly be free when they were located securely away from white Americans. It was this sentiment that led to the proliferation of all-black towns in Indian and Oklahoma Territories at the turn of the century.[41]

Many African Americans had migrated to the West in search of a place free from the prejudice and discrimination they faced in the South. Few blacks migrated to the territories from the North. Most of the pioneers came from Texas, Arkansas, Louisiana, Kentucky, South Carolina, Alabama, Mississippi, and Missouri. They sought a place where they would no longer be obliged to be reminded on a daily basis that they were second-class citizens. Booker T. Washington recognized upon his visit to the all-black town of Boley that the town owed its existence to the desire of African Americans to find greater opportunities and more freedom of action than they had in either the North or the South. Washington noted that:

> Boley, like the other negro towns that have sprung up in other parts of the country, represents a dawning race consciousness, a wholesome desire to do something to make the race respected; something which shall demonstrate the right of the negro, not merely as an individual but as a race, to have a worthy and permanent place in the civilization that the American people are creating.
>
> In short, Boley is another chapter in the long struggle of the negro for moral, industrial, and political freedom.[42]

Those African American leaders such as Edward P. McCabe who established all-black towns like Langston believed that racial harmony was best served by "a pattern of avoidance." Most residents felt that it was in the best interest of the community to shun social relations with whites. One prominent citizen of Boley remarked, "I came here when the place was still a territory. I wanted to go to a place where a man could be a man. I came from Arkansas, and I didn't like a white man's civilization where if two people got to fighting, a whole mob would jump on one." An ex-slave who came to the territory with her father claimed blacks "came in searchin' for education and freedom. I mean they come here lookin' for de same things lots of Negroes is goin' North for now." One farmer recalled that living in Texas, he had to "bow down and grin to all the poor white folks. I even had to call little poor white boys 'Mister,' " but in

---

41. *Muskogee Cimeter*, Sept. 15, 1904.
42. Mozell C. Hill, "The All-Negro Communities of Oklahoma: The Natural History of a Social Movement," *Journal of Negro History* 31 (July 1946): 259; Booker T. Washington, "Boley, A Negro Town in the West," *Outlook* 88 (Jan. 4, 1908): 30–31.

Langston, "no matter how little you be here, you can still be a man." One Boley resident asserted that in his town "everybody can be somebody."[43]

Hence the all-black towns were not constituted as racial ghettos as a result of white prejudice against African Americans settling in white towns. Rather, African Americans felt that isolation from whites was a stepping-stone in which the race would progress free from interference. In this sense, the all-black town in some way represented the ultimate fulfillment of Booker T. Washington's self-help philosophy. As historians William Bittle and Gilbert Geis note, "the all-Negro community was in no sense a retreat from American standards and values, and certainly not an anachronistic revival of Africanism, but rather an attempt to develop fully and to exploit thoroughly the American culture." The all-black towns were established with the implicit assumption that at some point in the future, the progress of African Americans would be respected and blacks would be accepted into mainstream American life. Black towns, hence, in their inception were a means to an end. The ultimate goal remained integration into white society.[44]

The response of white Americans to the creation of black towns was generally positive. Some viewed the towns as proof that segregation was not only just, but also that blacks themselves desired it. Yet no white Americans were willing to admit that the success of the black towns undermined the racial stereotype of African Americans as childlike, lazy, and lacking in moral and intellectual capacity. As historian Norman L. Crockett argues: "A viable black town, however, made the white argument for disenfranchisement and segregation seem all the more contradictory. If blacks were excluded from the electorate on the grounds of their inability to make an intelligent decision at the polls, how could one explain their success at self-government in their own community? And if their economic and social behavior inside their own corporate limits contradicted the white stereotype of the race, by what standard could one justify segregation?" Those whites who recognized the contradiction explained it away by claiming the people who resided in the black towns were atypical of the race in general, or they simply refused to comment on the success of the black towns whatsoever. The newspaper at Coyle, Oklahoma Territory, located a scant ten miles from Langston, seldom mentioned its black town neighbor either in its news items or among business advertisements.[45]

THROUGHOUT THE LATTER decades of the nineteenth century, white reformers tried to entice Native Americans to assimilate into Anglo-American

43. Quoted in Joseph H. Taylor, "The Rise and Decline of a Utopian Community, Boley, Oklahoma," *Negro History Bulletin* (March 1940): 91; Crockett, *The Black Towns,* 46–47.

44. Bittle and Geis, "Racial Self-Fulfillment," 248; Crockett, *The Black Towns,* 51.

45. Crockett, *The Black Towns,* 99, 102–103.

culture, even while seeking to segregate African Americans. The level of racial intermarriage in the territories illustrates this difference in dramatic fashion.

The Chickasaws, Cherokees, and Choctaws had rigid regulations concerning intermarriage with African Americans long before the coming of white settlers. A Cherokee law of 1839 prohibited marriages between Cherokees and "slaves or persons of color." Anyone caught violating this law was to suffer corporal punishment not to exceed fifty stripes, though any colored male convicted under this act was to receive one hundred lashes. The Chickasaws passed a law in 1858 prohibiting intermarriage between Native Americans and African Americans. This law also had the proviso that any white man living in the nation who took a black wife was subject to fine and banishment from the nation.[46]

Such restrictions against intermarriage continued after emancipation. The tribes were afraid that blacks who intermarried with Indians would try to claim citizenship in the tribe, just as intermarried whites could do. In 1885 the Choctaws passed a law which prohibited the intermarriage of Choctaws and their freedmen. Anyone breaking the law was to receive fifty lashes on the bare back as punishment. The restrictions imposed by most of the Five Civilized Tribes were apparently rather successful in discouraging intermarriage between tribesmen and their ex-slaves. A delegation of freedmen sent to Washington in 1884 reported, "as a general rule, we of African descent do not intermarry with Chickasaws; we intermarry amongst ourselves." Although the Chickasaws did admit some intermarriages had occurred (for example, Charles Cohee, a prominent leader of the freedmen in the late nineteenth century, was a mixed blood, as was his wife, Mary) they nonetheless insisted a "practical unanimity" of sentiment was against it. As historian Daniel F. Littlefield Jr. notes, "those who ignored the custom were socially ostracized. Their marriages were not considered legal, and their children were considered illegitimate."[47]

Even the Osage, who had never owned slaves, refused to allow blacks to intermarry with anyone living on their lands. One settler remembered that when one old white man brought his African American wife with him into the Osage country, "the full blood Osage Indians took him out and whipped him and ran them both out of the country."[48]

Most of the Five Civilized Tribes also made it difficult for their freedmen to marry blacks from outside their nation, hoping to discourage the immigration of African Americans from the surrounding southern states. For example, if a

46. Laws of the Cherokee Nation, Sept. 19, 1839, Manuscript and Archives Division, OSU; Laws of the Chickasaw Nation, Mar. 16, 1858, Archives and Manuscript Division, OSU.

47. Bill No. 52, Choctaw Nation, Indian Territory, Special Files, Choctaw and Chickasaw and Cherokee Freedmen, RG 48, Box 48, RDI; Littlefield, *The Chickasaw Freedmen*, 92, 92–93.

48. Ben Buckley, interview, GFPHC, 51:110.

Cherokee married a white citizen of the United States, that person received full citizenship rights in the tribe; but if a freedman citizen married a black from the United States or even a freedman from another tribe, that person had no tribal rights and was subject to removal as an intruder. The Choctaws passed a similar law, but also required all freedmen who married outside their group to purchase a permit. As one confused newlywed petitioned the U.S. authorities: "I am a collard man marred a collard woman that belonged to a Choctaw indian and chief has declared them all citzens of the nation but still they want to compell me to pay a permit is this lawfull or not or am I yet a noncitzen shall I still pay a permit you will pleas giv me an ancer soon as posable.[49]

It was only among the Seminoles, and to a lesser extent among the Creeks, that intermarriage was fairly commonplace. One contemporary commentator noted that among the Seminole and Creek tribes, "intermarriage became so common, so that now (I have it on the best authority) there is not a Seminole family that is entirely free from negro blood; and there are but three Creek families, some make it two, that are of pure blood." As a result, the Creeks and Seminoles came to be regarded as the most "primitive" of the Five Civilized Tribes in the eyes of contemporary white settlers.[50]

On the other hand, the degree of intermarriage between white settlers and members of the Five Civilized Tribes was truly astounding. When the Dawes Commission, created in 1893 to investigate tribal ownership of land, had completed its enrollment, the final rolls listed 101,526 persons who qualified for tribal land grants. A mere 26,794 were full bloods; another 3,534 were enrolled as having three-fourths or more Indian blood; 6,859 were listed as having one-half to three-fourths Indian blood; and a staggering 40,934 were listed as having less than one-half Indian blood (a separate roll of 23,405 freedmen completed the final calculation). High rates of intermarriage between white settlers and Native Americans has been a recurring theme on the American frontier, and America's "last frontier" in this sense was no different from its predecessors. General O. O. Howard, Civil War hero and onetime commissioner of the Bureau of Refugees, Freedmen, and Abandoned Lands, wrote in his memoirs with regard to his experience in traveling through the West, "I have seldom visited a tribe of Indians without finding at least one white man married to an Indian woman." As in the past, part of the explanation was simply that many white single males came to settle in the Indian lands, whereas most white females who came west did so as wives and mothers accompanying their husbands and children. One soldier assigned to Fort Sill described it as

49. National Records of the Cherokee Nation, Microfilm CHN 83, OHS; B. E. Gardner to SI, May 14, 1886, Indian Territory, Special Files, Choctaw and Chickasaw and Cherokee Freedmen, RG 48, Box 48, RDI.

50. L. J. Abbott, "The Race Question in the Forty-sixth State," *Independent* (July 25, 1907): 208; Wilton M. Krogman, "The Racial Composition of the Seminole Indians of Florida and Oklahoma," *Journal of Negro History* 19 (1934): 412–30.

"the lonesomest place out of hell." He noted, "thare [sic] is only one white girl in the neighborhood and she is caught and cold weather is coming. What will I do for a bed fellow this winter? Send me one and I will marry her right off." Many such men ended up taking Indian brides because of the lack of white females residing in the territory in the early years of white settlement.[51]

Perhaps even more important, however, were the benefits that accrued from marrying a tribal citizen. If a white citizen of the United States intermarried with a tribal citizen of one of the independent Indian Nations, that person received full citizenship rights in the tribe, including the right to share in tribal lands. This was a significant factor in accounting for the prevalence of white-Indian intermarriage before the Indian lands were opened up to white settlement. For many landless white males, marrying an Indian bride was the quickest way to gain land on the frontier. One white settler noted in 1880 that the government was encouraging this action. He argued the government "gives a good farm to any white man who will abandon his own wife and come in and marry a greasy squaw and raise up a family of half breeds who will spend their lives stealing from the good Indians in the nation and in bushwacking our soldiers."[52]

Many government officials agreed with this assessment. They did not disapprove of intermarriage per se, but rather objected to the prevalence of intermarriage between poor white males and Indian women. The government felt that the men attracted west to secure land through marriage served as poor "cultural ambassadors" and argued that their influence had a retarding effect rather than a positive one on the process of elevating the Indian population. The Sac and Fox agent claimed that the white men who took Indian brides were a "disreputable class." He further noted that such "squaw men," as they were known, "do more real harm against civilization and Christianity in one year than all the Christian ministers in America can counteract in ten years."[53]

Many agents sought to convince the federal government to prohibit intermarriage between white settlers and Indians under their charge, labeling such marriages "an authorized system of prostitution." As the Cheyenne and Arapaho agent noted, "it is not difficult for a white man to secure an Indian wife. The woman's parents treat her as so much property, to be disposed of to the best advantages and the belief is prevalent that by securing for his daughter a white husband, the future sustenance of the family is secured."[54]

51. Strickland, *The Indians in Oklahoma*, 48; Oliver O. Howard, *My Life and Experiences among Our Hostile Indians* (New York: Da Capo Press, 1907), 525; Strickland, *The Indians in Oklahoma*, 33; W. B. Guiderson, Oct. 28, 1877, in SFCTR, vol. 1, p. 8, OHS.

52. Robert L. Owen to CIA, Sept. 1, 1887, in *RSI* 1887, 2:185; Melville D. Landon to President Rutherford Hayes, 1880, R 874, Union Agency, LR-RBIA.

53. Isaac A. Taylor to CIA, Aug. 11, 1884, in *RSI* 1884, 2:141.

54. Jonathan Miles to CIA, July 5, 1878, R 123, Cheyenne and Arapaho Agency, LR-RBIA; Jonathan Miles to CIA, 1879, R 124, Cheyenne and Arapaho Agency, LR-RBIA.

However, Native Americans began to take steps to discourage intermarriage or at least to ensure that those whites who married Indians were respectable members of society. The Cherokees, for example, required that every white person who applied for a marriage license to marry a Cherokee citizen present the clerk a "certificate of good moral character, signed by at least ten respectable Cherokee citizens by blood, who shall have been acquainted with him at least six months immediately preceding the signing of such certificate." One white settler remembered the process claiming, "you had to have so many people say, 'I think you'll be a good man—make him an intermarried member of the tribe.' . . . so you had people sign that your [sic] going to be a good character and they would vouch for you and that you wouldn't be a trouble maker and you weren't a prisoner or criminal of any effect."[55]

Another means of discouraging intermarriage was by increasing the length of time a settler had to have been in the Indian nation before he could be granted a marriage license. The Choctaws, for example, required that a white man be resident for three years before he could apply for a license.[56]

The most prevalent practice, however, was for the Indian tribes to charge a high fee for the issuance of a marriage license to non-citizens. This, tribal leaders argued, would eliminate the most indigent white settlers from intermarrying with Native Americans to secure land for themselves. For most tribes the fee was not prohibitive; the Osage charged $20.00. However, among some of the Indian tribes, the price of a marriage license was astronomical. The Chickasaws, for example, were known to charge upwards of $1,000.00. This clearly meant that intermarriage would only be an option for the most well-to-do white settlers.[57]

These measures, however, were not successful. By statehood, Five Civilized Tribes members with at least some Anglo-American ancestors outnumbered those with none by almost two to one (49,000 to 27,000). In fact, one contemporary observer wondered whether the Five Civilized Tribes were soon to be absorbed into the white race. He acknowledged it was increasingly difficult for full bloods to intermarry (due to their dwindling number), and he found mixed bloods "invariably seek as a life partner a non-citizen; not infrequently some school ma'am or milliner employed in one of the numerous thriving cities of the Territory." This led the observer to conclude, "it will be but a generation or two until there will be no Indians of the Five Civilized Tribes. The Cherokees, Choctaws, and Chickasaws will have lost their identity in the white race."[58]

55. Microfilm CHN 10, NRCN; Jack Gregory, interview, File T-503, p. 20, DDOHI.

56. Jonathan Moore to SI, 1867, R 178, Choctaw Agency, LR-RBIA.

57. Frank F. Finney Sr., "Progress in the Civilization of the Osage, and Their Government," *Chronicles of Oklahoma* 40, no. 1 (1962): 10; *Chickasha Daily Express,* 1901.

58. W. David Baird, "Are There 'Real' Indians in Oklahoma? Historical Perceptions of the Five Civilized Tribes," *Chronicles of Oklahoma* 67, no. 1 (1990): 15; Abbott, "The Race Question," 208.

Of course, the depiction of the ultimate elimination of the Five Civilized Tribes was not true. Even today, almost a century since the passage of the Curtis Act, full-blood Indians still dwell in the lands that used to constitute their exclusive home. But the degree of intermarriage did affect tribal affairs. Interestingly enough, mixed bloods in the Five Civilized Tribes often assumed the leadership of tribal politics and economics. By the end of the nineteenth century, almost every Principal Chief of the Five Civilized Tribes was a mixed blood. The elite status of this group continued after statehood in 1907. Ten mixed bloods were elected to the Oklahoma Constitutional Convention in 1906, including Clem Rogers, the father of humorist Will Rogers. During the first two decades of statehood, mixed bloods constituted 30 percent of Oklahoma's delegation elected to the U.S. House of Representatives. Robert L. Owen, a mixed blood, was one of the state's first U.S. senators.[59]

Throughout the latter nineteenth century, white–Native American relations were characterized by an apparent dichotomy. On the one hand, whites stereotyped Indians as either uncivilized "children" or as savage "beasts." On the other hand, a significant portion of white settlers were willing to intermarry with them. The only hypothesis that seems to account for this perplexing situation is that whites considered mixed bloods for all intents and purposes to be "white." Whites made a clear distinction between mixed-blood and full-blood Indians, and most chose to intermarry with the former rather than the latter (although intermarriage between whites and full-blood Indians became more common after the discovery of oil on Indian lands just after statehood). Mixed bloods were always categorized as morally and intellectually superior to full bloods. In addition, children born unto mixed marriages between whites and Native Americans were socially defined as "white." Whether Native American culture would continue to exist was to be determined by the willingness of Native peoples to intermarry with whites.

While intermarriage was commonplace between whites and Native Americans, the territories, like the southern states, had strict rules prohibiting intermarriage between whites and African Americans. The first miscegenation law was passed in Oklahoma Territory on February 26, 1897. The legislation specified that, "all marriages of persons of the white race with persons of the negro race are prohibited." Just after Oklahoma statehood, a new law was passed which prohibited the marriage of whites and blacks, violation of which was a felony punishable by a fine of $500 and imprisonment from one to five years. A minister who performed a wedding ceremony for an interracial couple was also to be held guilty of committing a felony and fined.[60]

Just as in the American South, miscegenation legislation did not prove suc-

59. Baird, " 'Real' Indians in Oklahoma?" 16.
60. Arthur L. Tolson, *The Black Oklahomans: A History, 1541–1972* (New Orleans: Edwards, 1972), 127; *Shawnee Daily Herald,* May 6, 1908.

cessful in completely eliminating interracial relationships between whites and African Americans. Despite the rhetoric concerning racial purity, numerous social and sexual liasions between the races existed. The following examples give proof to the assertion of one black newspaper "that legislation will not prohibit intermarriage. Love is always blind—can see no law nor penalty thereto." One Kansas white man created a sensation in Guthrie, Oklahoma Territory, when he asked local authorities to aid him in recovering his wife, who had run off with a married black man. The wife of the Guthrie African American also begged for assistance, claiming her husband had deserted her and their nine children, leaving them with no means of support. Another white woman raised tremendous controversy when she sued her black lover for breach of contract when he reneged on his promise of marriage. The black man, who was a waiter, claimed in defense that he "could not afford to marry a white woman." One black man who had legally married a white woman in the United States and had then moved to the Indian Territory with her was arrested so often for breaking the miscegenation law that he had to carry his marriage license from out of state with him at all times.[61]

The repercussions of racial intermarriage could be significant. The son of a local Republican United States district court judge married a well-educated Indian girl. The judge was reportedly proud of his new daughter-in-law until it was discovered that some of her ancestors had been African American. The judge immediately ordered his son to leave the girl and procure a divorce, which the young man resisted. When one citizen of the Creek Nation appealed to the courts to be included in the tribal allotments according to the provisions of the Dawes Commission, the investigation revealed the man was one-sixteenth African American, and had no Indian blood whatsoever. According to a contemporary observer, "his business was ruined, he was a marked man. . . . immediately his wife left him. . . . as it was her children had a stain that soap could not wash out, nor society forgive."[62]

When interracial relationships led to children, those children were socially defined as being black. The one-drop theory predominated in the territories as it did throughout the United States. Mulattoes were not granted the intermediate racial categorization that Native American mixed bloods were. However, most whites did believe that they were more intelligent than pure blacks. One settler referred to a mulatto family that lived close by as "clean colored folks, you know, they wasn't . . . real dark. They . . . weren't niggers you know. Just mulattos." The same theory applied to children of mixed Native American–African American parentage. While in the early years of settlement the Indians generally regarded these mixed bloods as superior to blacks, whites were not

61. *Langston Western Age*, Dec. 13, 1907; *Indian Territory Sun*, May 20, 1905, Dec. 22, 1904; Edna Slaughter, interview, File 397, OHP.
62. *Guthrie Daily Leader*, July 29, 1893; Abbott, "The Race Question," 206–207.

inclined to make distinctions. Most whites felt mixed Native Americans–African Americans were "niggers just like the rest of them." The theory most closely observed by white Americans was that "in any mixture nigger blood will dominate and show out."[63]

Hence, white Americans came west with a fervent belief in their own cultural superiority. Whites considered Native Americans "primitive" and "savage." Nonetheless, many humanitarian reformers in the East and governmental officials in Washington believed Indians could be elevated closer to the level of the Anglo-Saxon race through education and moral guidance. Officials then proceeded to invoke policies designed to assimilate Native Americans into Anglo-American culture. Conversely, in the decades following the Civil War, white officials in Washington gradually lost interest in advancing and protecting the civil rights of African Americans. In a quest for sectional reconciliation and with the pressing issues of economic recession and political scandals raising the ire of northern voters, the Republican Party was content to allow white southerners to deal with the "race question." Hence, most officials back in Washington were willing to acquiesce to the desires of white settlers emigrating to the Indian lands from the South who demanded restrictive laws be passed to segregate African Americans. For African Americans the overwhelming racial problem was segregation, not assimilation.

The essence of race relations in the Indian and Oklahoma Territories resided in the difference between the tripartite racial categorization that was made with respect to white–Native American relations and the one-drop theory that applied to African Americans. Because whites were willing to recognize mixed-blood Indians as partially white, there existed the possibility of ultimate assimilation over time—a possibility that was never extended to African Americans. The fact that through intermarriage and miscegenation Native Americans could be absorbed into white society while African Americans could not meant that the government and white settlers themselves adopted very different attitudes and proposed very different answers to race relations in the West in the late nineteenth century.

63. George M. Fredrickson, *The Black Image in the White Mind: The Debate on Afro-American Character and Destiny, 1817–1914* (New York: Harper and Row, 1971), and Joel Williamson, *The Crucible of Race: Black-White Relations in the American South Since Emancipation* (New York: Oxford University Press, 1984); Frank Castro, interview, File T-377-3, p. 14, DDOHI; quoted in Crockett, *The Black Towns*, 100.

THREE

The Fight for the Promised Land
The End of Indian Sovereignty

PRESIDENT JACKSON moved the Five Civilized Tribes to the Indian Territory in the 1830s ostensibly to protect them from unscrupulous whites, who, it was argued, would cheat the Indians out of their valuable homelands in the East. The Five Tribes received land in the West with the understanding that this was to be their perpetual home. One Creek leader noted: "He told me that as long as the sun shone and the sky is up yonder these agreements will be kept. . . . He said as long as the sun rises it shall last; as long as the waters run it shall last; as long as grass grows it shall last. . . . He said, 'Just as long as you see light here, just as long as you see this light glimmering over us, shall these agreements be kept, and not until all these things cease and pass away shall our agreement pass away.' "[1] In their new home, the Five Civilized Tribes flourished. Under the guidance of Indian Bureau officials, Christian teachers, and missionaries, the tribes established successful, agriculturally based economies, representative governments, judicial systems, and educational systems. After the Civil War, the success of the Five Civilized Tribes served as a beacon of hope to concerned humanitarians who sought to elevate all the Native American peoples.

Anglo-Americans, convinced of their cultural superiority, sought a way to inculcate their values and traditions into Native Americans. This, they argued, was the only way to save them from extinction. As early as 1866, the commissioner of Indian affairs noted that the white population was crowding westward into Indian lands, with the result that "the people who have held these lands are compelled to give way before the advancing tide." He noted, "wandering bands, subsisting upon game or the products of the forest, . . . must submit to see their resources grow yearly less as the white population advances; while, if they have become so far civilized as to be willing to till the soil, a class of settlers too often gathers around them who regard but little the rights of the red men." The commissioner predicted that the situation would only get worse as the

---

1. Chitto Harjo, quoted in Debo, *And Still the Waters Run*, 55.

years progressed. He concluded, "it is the law of nature and of progress of mankind, and its operations cannot be stayed." Most government officials and concerned humanitarian reformers recognized that Anglo-American civilization was "aggressive" and that Native Americans had a "natural distrust" of whites. This, they claimed, was the reason for the long history of hostility and violence between the two groups. It also convinced them of the need "to separate Indians from the whites by placing them on suitable reservations as fast as circumstances will permit to avoid such collision in the future."[2]

Hence, given the shining example of the success of the Five Civilized Tribes in the Indian Territory, governmental officials and humanitarian reformers became convinced that the answer to "the Indian question" lay in the isolation of the reservation system. The result was what became known as the "peace policy." The peace policy had five central tenets. First, the Native Americans would be relocated to reservations as quickly as possible, where they would be provided instruction in agriculture and Anglo-American education. Being removed from the vicinity of white settlers, the acculturation process could occur without the frequent disturbances that had traditionally arisen between white settlers and their Indian neighbors. Second, any tribe that refused to settle on their assigned reservation and instead continued their nomadic lifestyle would be punished and forced to abandon the chase by the U.S. Army. Third, all reservation supplies distributed to Native Americans were to be procured at reasonable prices. Fourth, the government must act in conjunction with religious groups to secure the spiritual and moral elevation of the Indians. Fifth, the government and religious orders would establish churches and schools to teach Native Americans Anglo-American beliefs, values, and customs. Such a program reflected the Republican belief in an active, intrusive, strong federal government. The commissioner of Indian affairs felt this was justified, given the nature of the "Indian question." He argued, "such a use of the strong arm of Government is not war, but discipline."[3]

Most Anglo-Americans supported the peace policy, not so much out of a desire to see the Indians become civilized, but because they favored any policy which advocated the end of the nomadic lifestyle of the chase. They felt that land which could be used for agricultural production was allowed to lie uncultivated because of the wanderings of buffalo herds. As historian Rennard Strickland notes, "the Plains Indians['] roaming hunter culture with the seasonal migration patterns following the herds was marked for extinction on both economic and moral grounds. The goals and values of white and Indian civilization were incompatible." Most white settlers would have agreed with the

2. CIA to SI, Oct. 22, 1866, in *RSI* 1866, p. 2; Columbus Delano, SI, Oct. 31, 1873, in *RSI* 1873, p. ix.

3. Columbus Delano, SI, Oct. 31, 1873, in *RSI* 1873, pp. iii–iv; Francis Walker, CIA, to SI, in *RSI* 1872, pp. 393–94.

sentiment of one Indian inspector who reported, "this is a fine country and it is a shame that such a worthless set of vagabonds are the possessors of it." One settler expressed a belief no doubt shared by many white pioneers when he stated, "I have no sympathy whatever with the long-range complaints of . . . robbing the Indians of his ancestral lands. It is inconceivable that the progress of civilization in the expansion of this country would have left in the possession of roving bands of savages, much of its fairest portions. This has never been the history of mankind, right or wrong."[4]

Government officials quickly recognized that the end of the buffalo chase would work to their advantage in confining Native Americans to reservation lands and thereby forcing them to adopt a settled agricultural existence. As the secretary of the interior noted in 1872, "the rapid disappearance of game from the former hunting-grounds must operate largely in favor of our efforts to confine the Indians to smaller areas, and compel them to abandon their nomadic customs, and establish themselves in permanent homes. . . . When the game shall have disappeared, we shall be well forward in the work in hand." Officials argued that as Native Americans came to realize that they could no longer rely upon the supply of game for their subsistence, they would turn to the support of the reservation agencies. The result, officials concluded, would be "that a few years cessation from the chase . . . and they will be more readily led into new directions, toward industrial pursuits and peaceful habits."[5]

As early as the 1850s, white migrants to the West had been killing buffalo to provide themselves with food and supplies. After the Civil War, white demand for buffalo hides increased dramatically. Professional hunters swarmed into the plains to gather hides they could sell in the East. Amateur hunters traveled to the plains to shoot buffalo for sport. Railroads organized large shooting expeditions to thin the herds, which were responsible for a large portion of railway accidents. The army and the local agents of the Bureau of Indian Affairs condoned and even encouraged the killing, realizing the destruction of the economic lifeblood of the Native American groups forced them to accept relocation as the only alternative to starvation. General Philip Sheridan of the U.S. Army noted, "let them kill, skin, and sell until the buffalo is exterminated, as it is the only way to bring lasting peace and allow civilization to advance." Sheridan even suggested that the Texas legislature strike medals honoring the hide hunters for destroying the Indian food supply. The result of such sentiment was a slaughter of unprecedented scale. So great was the destruction of the buffalo herds between 1872 and 1874, that 1,378,359 hides, 6,751,200 pounds of buffalo meat, and 32,380,650 pounds of bones were shipped eastward to market over the Santa Fe Railroad. In 1865, there had been at least 15 million buf-

---

4. Strickland, *The Indians in Oklahoma*, 33; Morris Thomas, R34, Osage Agency, 1888, RIIIA; Smith, FCSA.

5. Columbus Delano, SI, *RSI* 1872, pp. 5–6, 7.

falo; a scant decade later, fewer than a thousand of the great beasts survived. One Kiowa Indian informed his local Indian agent, "the Great Spirit beyond the sun gave us the buffalo and the creation of our people and told us when the buffalo were dead we should die too, just as two brothers die. We want you to send this paper to Washington, that he may know that his red children are soon to be no more."[6]

Some officials in Washington were sympathetic to the plight of the Indians in the wake of the end of the buffalo, but the overwhelming majority of white settlers in adjoining lands were not. They were not convinced of the need for the entire Indian Territory to be reserved for the exclusive settlement of Indian tribes and their freedmen. White observers felt that the reservations were far larger than they needed to be, given the rudimentary subsistence agriculture being practiced by the tribes. As historians H. Wayne Morgan and Anne H. Morgan note: "The Indians' calmness toward nature often seemed apathy to those imbued with a different work ethic. And a willingness to take what nature gave without destructive effort seemed 'lazy' in the eyes of many whites."[7]

White settlers in the late 1870s and early 1880s, particularly those from the surrounding states of Arkansas, Kansas, and Texas, began to petition local politicians and newspaper editors in an effort to put pressure on Washington to open up what they deemed "surplus" Indian lands. As one contemporary settler noted, "there were 27,974,400 acres in all in the territory, occupied by less than seventeen thousand Indians who at best could make use of but a fraction of it." He argued that it was unreasonable to expect that such land should remain uninhabited when surrounded by settled states where land was at a premium. The settler concluded, "it was inevitable that its settlement and development should be immediate and rapid." Officials in Washington refused to open the lands to white settlers, however, and remained steadfast that the Indian Territory was to remain the exclusive home of the Native Americans and their freedmen.[8]

The Native tribes of the Indian Territory also made their desires quite clearly known to officials in Washington. They wanted white settlers kept out of the Indian lands. As early as 1869, a Cherokee delegation wrote, "to mingle the Cherokees and white men together in the same community would result in the white men soon owning everything, the Indian nothing; and he becomes a worthless outcast in the country which was once all his own—his home." The

6. Quoted in Leonard Dinnerstein, et al., *Natives and Strangers: Blacks, Indians, and Immigrants in America* (New York: Oxford University Press, 1990), 202; Carl C. Rister, *No Man's Land* (Norman: University of Oklahoma Press, 1948), 28; Crow Lance, 1878, R 383, Kiowa Agency, LR-RBIA.

7. H. Wayne Morgan and Anne H. Morgan, *Oklahoma: A Bicentennial History* (New York: W. W. Norton, 1977), 11.

8. Carl C. Rister, *Land Hunger: David L. Payne and the Oklahoma Boomers* (New York: Arno Press, 1975); Smith, FCSA.

superintendent of public schools for the Choctaw Nation pleaded for "a few years of rest from these surrounding land-hunters." He argued that the intrusion of whites was a great hindrance to the education and civilization of his people. He stated, "if we could only be let alone, so we could in quietness seek to have our children educated, so that they may not be crushed in the tide of immigration."[9]

Lewis Downing, the Principal Chief of the Cherokees, noted in 1870 that the Five Civilized Tribes had accumulated property, adopted the Christian religion, had built churches and schools, and established printing presses and agricultural societies, all without the interference of white authorities. Downing warned that "the very foundations of our National and individual existence are threatened." The chief noted, "demand is made in influential quarters, that the Government of the United States shall disregard its sacred pledges and raise the flood gates, and let in upon us a stream of immigration to overwhelm us." He concluded, "viewed in every light, and from every stand point, our situation is alarming. The vortex of ruin, which has swallowed hundreds of Indian nations, now yawns for us."[10]

While officials in Washington seemed to take the pleas of Native tribes to remain isolated from white society to heart in the 1870s and early 1880s, white settlers paid little heed. An increasing number of whites simply crossed over the Indian Territory border and took up residence as illegal squatters. Although demands for opening up the Indian lands to white settlement came from many sources, commercial interests in the surrounding states were the most vigorous supporters. Merchants argued that the settlement of whites upon the Indian lands would open up a lucrative market for locally produced goods. Railroad companies were also staunch supporters of opening the Indian lands to white settlers. They looked forward to seeing a land filled with small farmers who would need their produce shipped on railway lines rather than a land inhabited by bands of semi-nomadic Indians. The leader of the movement to open up the territory to white settlement, Elias C. Boudinot, represented the interests of major southwestern railroad companies. In 1879, Boudinot published an article in the *Chicago Times* which claimed that fourteen million acres of Indian land was eligible for white settlement according to the dictates of the Homestead Laws. His argument appeared in newspapers in Wichita, Kansas City, and other towns bordering the Indian Territory, which were all anxious to increase their trading areas.[11]

Editorialists in the early 1880s began to describe the Indian Territory as a

9. Delegation of leading Cherokees, quoted in Littlefield, *The Cherokee Freedmen*, 39; Forbis LeFlore to T. D. Griffith, Aug. 19, 1871, in *RSI* 1871, p. 988.
10. Lewis Downing, *Cherokee Advocate*, Oct. 22, 1870.
11. Danney Goble, *Progressive Oklahoma: The Making of a New Kind of State* (Norman: University of Oklahoma Press, 1980), 4.

promised land. In an era when civic boosterism was coming in vogue, the Indian lands were described as a veritable Eden containing an unsurpassed wealth of virgin land and bountiful resources. As historian Carl C. Rister relates, "Here were the brightest skies, the grandest sunsets, the softest twilights; and the most brilliant moon and glittering stars, smiling their welcome to visitors . . . and God had reserved it as man's paradise on earth." The sensational reports of the Indian Territory as a promised land touched off a decade of agitation in which expectant settlers "boomed" the opening of the Indian lands to white settlement. Groups of white "boomers" gathered in Kansas border towns like Independence, Baxter Springs, and Arkansas City, awaiting the federal government's decision to open the Indian lands to white settlement. David L. Payne, a failed politician and farmer, but an energetic promoter, soon took the lead of the boomer cause.[12]

Payne had migrated to Kansas from Indiana in 1857, seeking to make his fortune out of the expanding frontier. Inspired by Boudinot's assertions, he contacted representatives of the Santa Fe Railroad, and with the help of financial backing from Wichita merchants, he organized "the Oklahoma Colony." Payne sold investors in the colony membership certificates for $2.50 each. These certificates supposedly guaranteed their purchasers preemption rights to 160 acres of Oklahoma land when it was opened to white settlement. Payne promised his investors that the organization would stake claims for its members, distribute the land, and defend investors' property against rival claimants.[13]

To dramatize what Payne and his followers felt was the injustice of allowing fertile farmland to lie uncultivated, he led a group of colonists into the Indian Territory to begin preparations for establishing permanent settlement. Payne felt a direct challenge to federal policy leading to his arrest would allow him the opportunity to seek vindication in court. Payne led his band of devoted followers into the Indian Territory seven times, and each time he and his men were rounded up by United States soldiers and dragged out of the territory, sometimes in chains, and then thrown into jails. Habeas corpus proceedings were always successful in liberating the boomers from prison, as there was no law upon the statute books making it a crime for men to settle upon public lands. Each time Payne and his followers were liberated, they immediately began to organize for another movement into the disputed territory.[14]

Adding fuel to the fire was the fact that often the boomers were removed by Indian police and African American troops. As early as January 1882, Company F of the all-black 9th Cavalry was assigned to escort illegal squatters out of the

12. Rister, *Land Hunger*, 76; Goble, *Progressive Oklahoma*, 4–5.
13. Goble, *Progressive Oklahoma*, 5–6.
14. Unidentified newspaper clipping, April 22, 1905, File 82.197, Statehood File, Box 3, TAP.

territory. Not surprisingly, the boomers objected strongly to being subjected to what they felt was an obvious indignity. W. L. Couch, one of the original boomers, claimed the whole affair was not only frightful but disgraceful. Why, he asked, "should a mob of negro soldiers and blanketed Indians thus attack with arms a party of peaceable and unarmed citizens, cursing, and swearing that they would blow their —— brains out?" It was bad enough, boomers claimed, to be removed from land which they considered was rightfully theirs to settle upon, but to be driven back across the line by black troops added insult to injury. One must wonder whether the use of Indian police and African American soldiers was merely a coincidence. It might have reflected a conscious decision on the part of the government to evoke even greater outrage among white settlers so that the opening of the Indian lands to settlement would seem the only way of pacifying an angry frontier electorate.[15]

Although the boomers may have had their reasons to be upset, it was Native Americans who were the most infuriated with the situation. They argued that the United States had promised to remove all white intruders by the treaties of 1866. The Cherokees pointed to Article 26 in their treaty, which specified, "they shall also be protected against interruptions or intrusions from all unauthorized citizens of the United States who may attempt to settle on their lands or reside in the territory." As early as 1870, the Cherokees petitioned the secretary of the interior, noting the presence of intruders from the state of Kansas. They claimed the settlement was "a lawless experiment, intended to feel the temper of the government." They maintained that if the intruders were allowed to remain, it would be the precursor to more extensive settlement, and so they requested that the government promptly remove the squatters.[16]

Throughout the 1870s and into the early 1880s the United States government diligently tried to remove as many illegal white squatters from Indian lands as possible. One Indian remembered seeing a white family which had decided to squat on land near his parents' cornfield. When his parents mentioned this at church, the next day U.S. Marshals arrived to escort the white family out of the territory. The Cherokee agent noted in 1872 that "great wrath and indignation was expressed by these removed intruders . . . for maintaining the rights of the Indians."[17]

In response to Native American petitions, in April of 1879, the United States government issued a proclamation warning all persons not to enter the

15. W. Sherman Savage, "The Role of Negro Soldiers in Protecting the Indian Territory from Intruders," *Journal of Negro History* 36 (1951): 32; W. L. Couch, quoted in Rister, *Land Hunger*, 149.

16. Microfilm CHN 83, NRCN; Lewis Downing to SI, 1870, R 792, M 619, Letters Received, Office of the Adjutant General, RG 94, Records of the Adjutant General's Office, 1780–1917, National Archives, Washington, D.C.

17. Davis, interview File 87.53, OHP; John B. Jones to CIA, Sept. 1, 1872, in *RSI* 1872, p. 618.

Indian lands without proper authorization. The proclamation warned that all intruders found in the territory without a legitimate permit would be removed, if necessary by military force. The leaders of the Indian Nations took actions of their own to curb the problem of intrusion. The Chickasaws, for example, passed a law which required all non-citizens to pay a $25.00 fee in order to remain in the nation. They also enacted a law to collect a tax of $1.00 per head per month on cattle owned by white men. They organized a large force of Indian police to round up all the cattle and hold them until the owners claimed them by brand and paid their tax.[18]

Such measures, however, did little to discourage white settlers from settling in the Indian lands, and simply too much territory existed for the federal authorities to cover. Boomers returned to the territory often. As the 1880s wore on, intrusion became a chronic problem which the United States government seemed unable or unwilling to stop.[19]

The primary reason the federal government became less interested in removing intruders from Indian lands was that a profound transformation occurred in federal policy with respect to the reservation system. Many governmental officials and humanitarian reformers in the 1880s began to question the wisdom of separating Native Americans from Anglo-American society on reservations, feeling that isolation had tended to reinforce and perpetuate Native American culture rather than promote assimilation. Merrill E. Gates, the president of Rutgers College and a member of the U.S. Board of Indian Commissioners, declared in an address given in 1885 that

> While we profess to desire their civilization, we adopt in the Indian reservation the plan which of all possible plans seems most carefully designed to preserve the degrading customs and the low moral standards of heathen barbarism. Take a barbaric tribe, place them upon a vast tract of land from which you carefully exclude all civilized men, separate them by hundreds of miles from organized civil society and the example of reputable white settlers, and having thus insulated them in empty space, doubly insulate them from Christian civilization by surrounding them with sticky layers of the vilest, most designingly wicked men our century knows, the whiskey-selling whites and the debased half-breeds who infest the fringes of our reservations, men who have the vices of barbarism plus the worst vices of the reckless frontiersman and the city criminal, and then endeavor to incite the electrifying, life-giving currents of civilized life to flow through this doubly insulated mass.[20]

18. Carl Schurz, SI, Nov. 15, 1879, in *RSI* 1879, pp. 14–15; Parthena L. James, "Reconstruction in the Chickasaw Nation: The Freedman Problem," *Chronicles of Oklahoma* 45, no. 1 (1967): 76–78; Box P-15, p. 10, JFPP.
19. Jonathan Tufts to CIA, Sept. 1, 1882, in *RSI* 1882, 2:149.
20. Merrill E. Gates, in *RSI* 1885, 1:782.

What was needed, reformers stressed, was for Native Americans to become individual landowners. Emphasis came to be placed on the civilizing influence of the homestead. Each Native American family should be given title to its own tract of land. Communal tribal land ownership, centuries old in tradition, should give way to individual land grants. The commissioner of Indian affairs noted in 1881, "I am very decidedly of opinion that ultimate and final success never can be reached without . . . the location of every family, or adult Indian who has no family, on a certain number of acres of land which they may call their own and hold by a title as good and strong as a United States patent can make it." J. D. C. Atkins, the commissioner of Indian affairs in 1887, wrote to the secretary of the interior extolling the virtues of the homestead, arguing, "The homestead to-day is the greatest bulwark of American progress and liberty."[21]

The issuance of individual land grants to tribe members would also, of course, mean that "surplus" lands (when each Indian had accepted his allotment of land, the remaining acreage was to be deemed "surplus") could be opened to white settlers as public domain. Officials and reformers argued that the presence of white settlers in close proximity to Indian farmers would have a civilizing influence on the Indians. Anglo-Americans would have the opportunity to lead by example. As one member of the Board of Indian Commissioners argued, "guard the rights of the Indian, but for his own good, break up his reservations. Let in the light of civilization. Plant in alternate sections or townships white farmers, who will teach by example."[22]

Native Americans generally opposed the idea of individual land ownership, seeing the policy as nothing more than a subterfuge to disguise the government's desire to yet again take more land from them. As one disgruntled Native American argued:

> Here was a proposal which paralyzed the Indians for a time with its bold effrontery. Here we, a people who had been a self-governing people for hundreds and possibly a thousand years, who had a government and administered its affairs ages before such an entity as the United States was ever dreamed of, are asked and admonished that we must give up all idea of local government, change our system of land holding to that which we confidently believed had pauperized thousands of white people—all for why; not because we had violated any treaties with the United States which guaranteed in solemn terms our undisturbed possession of these; not because of any respectable number of intelligent Indians were clamoring for a change of conditions; not because any non-enforcement of law prevailed to a greater extent in the Indian Territory than elsewhere;

21. Hiram Price, CIA to SI, Oct. 24, 1881, in *RSI* 1881, 2:2; J. D. C. Atkins, CIA, to SI, Sept. 21, 1887, in *RSI* 1887, 2:12.
22. Merrill E. Gates, in *RSI* 1885, 1:784.

but simply because regardless of the plain dictates of justice and a [C]hristian conscience, the ruthless white man demanded it. Demanded it because in the general upheaval that would follow the change he, the white man, hoped and expected to obtain for a song, lands from ignorant Indians as others had done in other older states.

Another Native American agreed with this assessment. He noted that with the opening up of "surplus" lands it would be easy for capitalists and monied men to become enriched at the expense of the Indian. But, he questioned, "what about the other side? What about our people, who are now, the legal owners and sovereigns of these lands?" He answered his own question, predicting, "he [the Indian] will be crushed to earth under the hoofs of business greed . . . for business has no moral consciousness; when a statute comes in its way, it will invoke the aid of a 'higher law' and grasp the Indian's property anyway."[23]

Throughout the 1880s delegations of Native Americans were sent by their tribes to plead with officials in Washington not to force the Indians into accepting individual land grants. One delegation of the Five Civilized Tribes petitioned the federal government, arguing that "the opening of said lands to homestead settlement would be in conflict with the uniform policy of the Government in reference to the Indians of this Territory, and its solemn pledges that the lands of the Indian Territory shall not, in all time to come, be included within the limits of any State or Territory without their consent." Nonetheless, despite the protest from Native Americans, the federal government remained determined to end tribal sovereignty and integrate Indians into American society as individual landowning citizens.[24]

The end of the reservation, the foundation of American Indian policy for generations, was put forth under the proposal of Massachusetts senator Henry L. Dawes. The Dawes bill proposed that the Indians' best interest would be served by breaking up the reservations, thereby ending all recognition of tribal authority, and propelling Native Americans, as individuals, into mainstream society. The bill provided for the distribution of 160 acres of reservation land for farming, or 320 acres for grazing, to each head of an Indian family who accepted the law's provisions. The remaining reservation lands (often the richest) were to be sold to settlers, and the income thus obtained was to go toward the purchase of farm tools for the Indian tribes. Under the Dawes Act, passed in 1887, Native Americans were declared citizens of the United States with all the rights and responsibilities that attended such status, including the protection of federal laws and the requirement to pay taxes.[25]

23. Chief G. W. Grayson, quoted in Baird, *A Creek Warrior,* 164; quoted in Debo, *And Still the Waters Run,* 29–30.

24. Julius C. Fulsom, quoted in Robert L. Owen to CIA, Sept. 20, 1886, in *RSI* 1886, 1:377.

25. Francis P. Prucha, *The Great Father: The United States Government and the American Indians,* vol. 2 (Lincoln: University of Nebraska Press, 1984), 659–87.

Interestingly, the Five Civilized Tribes and other Native Americans resident in the Indian Territory were exempt from the provisions of the Dawes Act. Since the tribal lands of the Indian Territory were not regarded as reservations, they did not fall within the parameters of the Dawes Act, and therefore, Native Americans were allowed to continue to hold their lands in the territory under communal tenure. However, this exemption did not last long. In March of 1893 the Dawes Commission was created to investigate the allotment of tribal lands in the Indian Territory in fee simple to tribesmembers. The commission submitted its first report on November 20, 1894. It was critical of the effects of communal land tenure and Native self-government and strongly recommended that Congress amend the Dawes Act to include Indian Territory in its allotment policy. On June 28, 1898, Congress passed the Curtis Act, which authorized the Dawes Commission to draw up rolls of tribal citizens and allot land in fee simple to each qualified applicant. With the passage of the Curtis Act, Native American self-government in the Indian Territory came to an end. On March 3, 1901, Congress passed a law granting American citizenship to all Native American inhabitants of the Indian Territory.[26]

The first report of the Dawes Commission also raised the question of freedmen rights. By 1894, all but the Chickasaws had adopted their freedmen as full tribal citizens. This meant that freedmen had an equal share to tribal lands under the communal tenure practiced by the Five Civilized Tribes. The federal government thus had to decide if the former slaves of the Five Civilized Tribes were entitled to individual allotments according to the terms of the Dawes Commission. Native Americans vehemently denied that their freedmen should receive land allotments. Chitto Harjo, the most outspoken critic of allotments in general, claimed that "I hear that the Government is cutting up my land and is giving it away to black people. I want to know if this is so. . . . These black people, who are they? They are negroes that came in here as slaves. They have no right to this land. It never was given to them. It was given to me and my people and we paid for it with our land back in Alabama. . . . Then can it be that the Government is giving it—my land—to the negro?"[27]

The freedmen adamantly believed they deserved inclusion in land allotments to the Five Civilized Tribes because they were tribal citizens with all the responsibilities and privileges that that status conferred. They claimed that their years of toil as slaves for Indian landowners earned them the right to a fair share in the allotments. Most of the freedmen had lived their entire lives among the Indians in the Indian Territory—it was the only home they knew. As one freedman put it, "You talk about adoption; we are not of that class of people; we never came here from Kansas, Missouri, or Texas, to be adopted into this na-

26. Prucha, *Documents,* 171–74, 190–95.
27. Chitto Harjo, quoted in Debo, *And Still the Waters Run,* 135.

tion. We were born here; this is our birthplace and I think it would be a hard matter for the Cherokees to adopt one of their own family."[28]

The federal government concurred with the ex-slaves of the Five Civilized Tribes who claimed that their tribal citizenship entitled them to individual land allotments. Even the Chickasaw freedmen who had not been adopted as members of the tribe were given grants of land. Hence, ironically, the concept of communal land ownership present in the Indian Nations for generations enabled the freedmen of the Five Civilized Tribes to obtain land that former slaves of white southerners never received. The freedmen of the Indian Territory received the "forty acres and a mule" their fellow bondsmen of the South had fought so hard for twenty-five years earlier.[29]

Congress established a Land Commission Board (the Dawes Commission), whose job it was to go to the Indian Nations and review applicants making claims for allotments under the terms of the act. Successful applicants had their names placed on what became known as the Dawes Roll. A separate roll was compiled consisting of freedmen applicants. The process was painstakingly slow, as many of the applicants were illiterate and others were so adamant in their opposition to individual allotment of land that they refused to put forth a claim before the commission.

What was not slow was the progression towards opening up "surplus" Indian land to white settlement. (The western portions of Indian Territory which had not been settled by relocated tribes were deemed to be "surplus.") The government decided to open the so-called "Unassigned Lands," which the government had purchased from the Five Civilized Tribes in the treaties of 1866. President Benjamin Harrison announced that the nearly two million acres was to be settled by the unprecedented method of a land run. At noon, April 22, 1889, thousands of men, women, and children, on buggies, wagons, horses, bicycles, and even on foot, lined up to make the mad dash to claim their piece of the promised land. Lots had been surveyed and each lot was marked with a stake claim. The settler who removed the stake claim and replaced it with his own marker, then simply had to go to the local land office and receive his land title.

Needless to say, the process was fraught with problems. Despite the effort of the United States Army to keep settlers from entering the lands before the official noon opening, many so-called sooners had secretly invaded the lands early to stake their claim. When settlers entered the lands on April 22, and found sooners already plowing the fields, violence often broke out. As well, violence often occurred when more than one person tried to claim the same piece of land. In the wake of the land run it was not necessarily the person with the quickest horse who got to claim the land but often the person with the quickest

28. *Vinita Indian Chieftain*, May 28, 1891.
29. Theda Perdue, *Slavery and Cherokee Society*, 143.

shot. It is interesting to note that by the terms of the land run, the boomers (members of David L. Payne's Oklahoma Colony) received no recognition for their land certificates. They, like all the others, had to run to stake their claims, since the proclamation opening up the lands to settlement recognized no pre-emption rights for these old squatters. Even more ironic was the fact that David L. Payne, the leader of the boomers and the most active force in pressuring the government to open the lands to white settlement, did not live to see his dream fulfilled. One historian has argued that the Oklahoma land run was the ultimate symbol of the American frontier—"a frantic rush for economic opportunity."[30]

Despite the problems of the initial land run of 1889, the government continued the trend as more Indian lands opened for settlement. Land runs were held in the early 1890s to settle the Cherokee Outlet, the Cheyenne and Arapaho reservation, and the Iowa and Kickapoo lands. By the late 1890s and early 1900s the federal government decided to settle the remaining Indian lands through a more civilized manner—first, the lottery system and then through sealed bid. With all these land openings, the former Indian Territory (the lands opened under the runs and lotteries became known as Oklahoma Territory after 1890) began to look more like a white man's country than the "land of the red man."

WHITE SETTLERS were not the only ones to seek their future in the promised land. African Americans also saw the free land of Oklahoma as offering them an escape from the oppression they faced in the South from sharecropping and indebtedness to merchants. Many African American leaders sought to entice blacks to head for the promised land. Some African Americans staked claims in the original run of 1889. It is estimated that at least 43 African Americans laid claim to land in the April 1889 land run (of whom 36 later acquired title to their homestead). As many as 90 percent of the black claimholders in Oklahoma County and 80 percent in Logan County were located in the eastern region known as the "blackjack," which was considered the poorest agricultural land. As one historian has noted, "the Negro in the rush stood but little show and only secured the portions refused by white men as unfit for claiming, a small tract of land known as the blackjack region." The *Oklahoma Capital* noted in August 1889, "one remarkable feature about them [the black settlers] is that they are content with land that a great many homeseekers will not have and they are taking this land and improving it rapidly."[31]

30. Stan Hoig, *The Oklahoma Land Rush of 1889* (Oklahoma City: Oklahoma Historical Society, 1984); John Thompson, *Closing the Frontier: Radical Response in Oklahoma, 1889–1923* (Norman: University of Oklahoma Press, 1986), 7.

31. John Womack, "Statistics on Blacks in Oklahoma—The First Year," June 1982, File 81.114, JWP; Tolson, *The Black Oklahomans*, 53; *Oklahoma Capital*, Aug. 31, 1889.

White prejudice played a large role in African Americans having to claim the poorest land. One settler remembered that during the Cherokee Outlet Run, a band of pioneers boasted of frightening any African Americans from claiming land in their vicinity with the threat of lynching. Their new neighbors endorsed the act with cries of "that's right; we don't want any niggers in this country." One black settler remembered that blacks often did not get the claims they had settled on and had to accept land which had gone unclaimed: white officials in the land offices would not accept their claims immediately and made them wait, meanwhile letting a white claim and receive title to the land the black applicant was claiming. Many blacks also lost their claims because they arrived with no provisions and no money to help them make it through the difficult first year. A federal officer wrote to the secretary of the interior in August 1890 that a house-to-house inspection of predominantly black settlements had revealed "fully one-third of the people need aid and two-thirds of [the] farmers need seed wheat. Many more [are] in want of food. No money. Nothing to sell. Prospects gloomy."[32]

Despite the hardships faced by African Americans who came to Oklahoma Territory in the first few years of settlement, newspaper editors and black leaders continued to agitate for African Americans to move to the West and stake their claim to free land. One historian estimates that black newspapers in Oklahoma Territory were the primary force behind the 7,000 to 8,000 African Americans who emigrated west during the ten land openings in Oklahoma. An editorial in the *Langston City Herald* admonished blacks to buy land. It noted that "nothing makes a colored man feel prouder than to stand on his own property, and call it home."[33]

No African American leader was more influential in enticing blacks to settle in Oklahoma than Edward P. McCabe. McCabe had moved to Kansas and was an important figure in the founding of the all-black colony of Nicodemus. While in Kansas, he was elected state auditor—the first African American to achieve such a high office outside of the South. However, as racial hostilities increased in Kansas as a result of the mass exodus of southern blacks to that state in the 1870s and 1880s, McCabe was defeated in his third attempt at becoming auditor. He, like many other black leaders, soon came to advocate that the future of the African American race lay in the newly formed Oklahoma Territory. As a result, he took a leading role in advocating the colonization of Oklahoma by African Americans. McCabe went to Washington to seek support from federal Republicans for his colonization plan. He was given an interview

32. Quoted in Morgan and Morgan, *Oklahoma: A Bicentennial*, 55; Happy Davis, File 625, OHP; quoted in Goble, *Progressive Oklahoma*, 125.

33. Nudie E. Williams, "The Black Press in Oklahoma: The Formative Years 1889–1907," *Chronicles of Oklahoma* 61, no. 3 (1983): 311; *Langston City Herald*, Nov. 17, 1892.

with President Harrison, and he reported to the chief executive the rationale behind his proposal. McCabe argued that "We desire to get away from the associations that cluster about us in the Southern states. We wish to remove from the disgraceful surroundings that so degraded my people, and in a new territory in Oklahoma, show the people of the United States and of the world that we are not only good, loyal citizens, but that we are capable of advancement, and that we can be an honor to those who broke down the barriers of slavery."[34]

McCabe helped to establish an all-black town in Oklahoma Territory in 1890, which he named Langston. He was successful in gaining the financial support of William Waldorf Astor, who pledged $500,000 to support the construction of Langston University so black students could have access to higher education. In addition, he oversaw the establishment of the *Langston City Herald,* which was used as an organ to entice African Americans to leave the South and its racial and economic oppression for the supposed racial freedom of the West. One editorial admonished its readers:

FREEDOM, PEACE, HAPPINESS AND PROSPERITY—DO YOU WANT ALL THESE? THEN CAST YOUR LOT WITH US & MAKE YOUR HOME IN LANGSTON CITY

Do you ask why? We will tell you. Langston City is a Negro city, and we are proud of the fact. Her city officers are all colored. Her teachers are colored. Her public schools furnish thorough educational advantages to nearly two hundred colored children. The country is as fertile as ever was moistened by nature's falling tears, or kissed by heaven's sunshine. Here too, is found a genial climate— about like that of southern Tennessee or northern Mississippi—a climate admirably adapted to the wants of the Negro from the southern states. A land of diversified crops, where there need be no such thing as a total failure. A land where every staple crop of both north and south can be raised with ease.

. . . Remember it is not a picnic we are inviting you to, but to join hands with us in an active and earnest effort to better our conditions and to open to the race new avenues through which they may obtain more of the good things of life.

Another black newspaper advised its readers that "the door of hope for the Negro" had once again been closed in the South, and yet blacks were still standing outside vainly rapping for admittance. The editor queried, "why not go to a country where the door still stands open and where you can enjoy all the rights and privileges as a citizen of this country?"[35]

34. Arvarh E. Strickland, "Toward the Promised Land: The Exodus to Kansas and Afterward," *Missouri Historical Review* 69, no. 4 (July 1975): 376–412; Jere W. Roberson, "Edward P. McCabe and the Langston Experiment," *Chronicles of Oklahoma* 51, no. 3 (1973): 345; unidentified newspaper clipping, File 82.89, FBP.
35. Roberson, "Edward P. McCabe," 348, 349; *Langston City Herald,* Nov. 17, 1892; *Boley Progress,* Mar. 23, 1905.

McCabe sent agents throughout the South to try and induce blacks to settle in Oklahoma. Black newspapers constantly alluded to a sort of unannounced race between whites and blacks for Oklahoma land. As the *Boley Progress* declared: "If you will come out here now and get a good location *before this country gets settled up by the caucasian race* we will be able to demand our rights and they will be respected when this shall come a state. Every Man's vote will count. Every man will be privileged to vote if he desires. Every man will get a fair trial and impartial. No man's life will be ruthlessly taken from him" (emphasis mine).[36]

McCabe's activism in promoting African American colonization in Oklahoma led white editorialists to warn readers that he intended to make Oklahoma an all-black state. Such reports were given national coverage in newspapers across the country, including the *New York Times*. White editors claimed McCabe had influence in Washington with Republican leaders and that he was trying to have himself installed as governor of Oklahoma Territory. White editors predicted that Oklahoma would soon be overcome with a massive influx of African Americans seeking a place where their civil rights would be respected. They pointed to the comments of some of the leaders of the First Grand Independent Brotherhood (an organization formed in 1889, in Nicodemus colony, devoted to enticing black settlers to come to Oklahoma and agitating for black civil rights within the new territory), who argued in 1890:

We do propose to not only have a majority of the voters in Oklahoma, but we propose also to have nearly the entire population. There are many now there who will not live in a "nigger" state. These we will help move out. We will not want the mass of white people with us, but will welcome those whites who have money and who are willing to come among us for purposes of trade. If they wish to make their homes there, and will make our customs their customs, our people their people, we will be glad to have them with us. But when the time comes we will welcome only those who will make themselves of us and for us.[37]

On the other hand, African American leaders, including Edward P. McCabe, took great pains to deny that they wanted to create an all-black state. Rather, they argued, they hoped to create a state in which all residents regardless of color or nationality would prosper. The black editorialists of Oklahoma Territory released a proclamation on April 8, 1890, stating, "We do not wish to be misunderstood. We would not, if we had the power, bar any class of citizens; far from it; we desire to go with our white fellows hand in hand; to aid them and they us in building the Territory up to a grand and properous commonwealth."[38]

36. *Boley Progress,* Sept. 7, 1905.
37. *Ibid.; Topeka Republic,* Mar. 1, 1890.
38. *Topeka Republic,* Apr. 8, 1890.

White Oklahomans were not convinced by such proclamations, and they pledged to do all they could to prevent the expected massive influx of black settlers. One Republican resident warned that if McCabe was appointed governor, "I would not give 5 cents for his life." He predicted that if blacks moved into Oklahoma and tried to assert their political rights it would lead to racial violence, and he threatened, "dead niggers make an excellent fertilizer and if the negroes try to Africanize Oklahoma they will find that we will enrich our soil with them."[39]

White editors constantly played upon the fear of a massive migration of blacks to Oklahoma Territory by exaggerating the numbers of blacks in the territory. One territorial paper noted, "at the present writing there are seven large colonies of negroes in Oklahoma, and within the next sixty days there will be upwards of sixty more colonies established." The paper warned, "there are said to be 200,000 negroes in the South organized for settlement in Oklahoma. A few years may see two negro Senators at Washington."[40]

White newspaper editors also tried to discourage African American immigration directly by manufacturing all kinds of absurd stories aimed at scaring African Americans. As one contemporary commentator noted, articles would appear about centipedes "as large as a man," tarantulas, tornadoes, and savage Indians with tomahawk and scalping knife in hand. White editors also made sure that all racial atrocities committed in Oklahoma Territory received widespread coverage. They hoped to discourage blacks from immigrating by noting the prevalence of lynching, race wars, and the practice of whitecappers running blacks out of towns at gunpoint.[41]

However, it was not the threats from whites that kept large numbers of African Americans from immigrating en masse from the southern states to Oklahoma, but rather their destitution. Most poor sharecroppers in the South simply did not have the provisions necessary to undertake the long journey westward. Most of the newspapers like the *Langston Herald* warned impoverished sharecroppers not to make the trip unless they had proper provisions. African Americans contemplating coming to Oklahoma were warned to come with sufficient money to take care of themselves until they could raise a crop or enter into business. One editorial warned: "We especially invite people of our race who have some means to come; we warn those who have nothing, that, this being a new country, peopled by strangers, with no ready employment, and everybody husbanding what little cash and effects he or she may have until conditions change, that they will surely suffer by the change. So come prepared to care for yourself and family by all means, and you will make no mistake; if

39. *Republican Bureau*, Mar. 2, 1890.
40. Unidentified newspaper clipping, File 82.89, FBP.
41. C. Douglas Clem, *Oklahoma: Her People and Professions* (Kingfisher: Constitution Publishers, n.d.); *Globe-Democrat*, Mar. 14, 1890.

you come penniless you must expect to get it rough, as you ought to do."
Hence black editors demonstrated that they only wanted African American settlers who believed in hard work as the key to economic advancement to come
to Oklahoma. Here again the fundamentally assimilationist goals of the black
leadership are demonstrated.[42]

WHILE WHITE and African American settlers poured into the new territory
of Oklahoma, the distribution of the tribal lands of the Indian Territory proceeded very slowly. When the Dawes land commissioners arrived in the territory in early 1894 to negotiate allotment agreements, they found the
procedure fraught with problems. Many of the full bloods were illiterate and
some could not speak any English, which made the application procedure all
the more difficult. In fact, after the Cheyenne and Arapaho lands were allotted
in 1892, some Indian Bureau officials argued that the government should "rename" the Indian applicants found on the rolls, since in their opinion some Indian names were "silly or disgusting." One observer noted of the efforts to
enroll the Cheyenne in 1903 that, "the ones working on the rolls are revising
from the white man's point of view with a feeling that the names ought to be
as nearly Anglo as possible. My notion is to treat them as we would Polish or
Russian names—retain as much of the Cheyenne as we can easily pronounce."
Commissioners also had to deal with the problem of settlers who preyed upon
illiterate Indians and freedmen by posing as representatives of the Dawes Commission who, for a small fee, would ensure that their claims were processed. A
further problem was determining the accuracy of claims. Each applicant had to
have sworn witnesses as to their residency in the Indian nation. Many questions
were raised about the validity of witness testimony. Some Cherokees claimed
that several freedmen had acted as witnesses in from two hundred to four hundred cases. Such witnesses, they argued, gave perjured testimony, appearing before the commission, "with their pockets full of bribes and their mouths full of
lies."[43]

However, the most enduring difficulty of the Dawes commissioners was to
convince Native Americans of the need to apply for title to land that they already considered theirs. Even though the enrollment process was not yet finished, the Curtis Bill of 1898 finalized the allotment of lands in severalty to
members of the Five Civilized Tribes (though the rolls were not officially closed
until 1914). However, some conservative full bloods refused to recognize the
legitimacy of the new order. The largest outbreak of resistance arose in 1901
with a group of Creek full bloods under the leadership of Chitto Harjo (Crazy
Snake). Harjo was described by his contemporaries as "a Northern Creek and

42. *Langston City Herald,* Nov. 17, 1892.
43. Quoted in Strickland, *The Indians in Oklahoma,* 37–38; *Woodville Beacon,* Sept. 28,
1906; Littlefield, *The Cherokee Freedmen,* 229.

a member of the ancient line of Creek royalty. He was a typical defender of the old order. He lived in a little log cabin in a clearing and plowed a little patch of corn." Harjo and his followers came to be known as the "snakes," and they warned all Creeks not to accept their allotments, rent land to non-citizens, or employ white labor. They formed their own "light horsemen" who arrested and whipped Creeks who violated these orders. Such actions were justified, according to Eufaula Harjo, because "the half breeds and the negroes are the ones that have taken all the land, and there is nothing left for the full blood Indian at all." Chitto Harjo demanded that all Creeks who had received their allotment certificates from the Dawes Commission, surrender them to him so he could return them to the United States government. Eufaula Harjo refused to accept his certificate and encouraged others to do the same. He gathered up hundreds of certificates and returned them to the local Indian agent.[44]

In November 1900, Pleasant Porter, the elected Creek chief, appealed to U.S. authorities for assistance to put down the "insurrection." In January 1901, a troop of cavalry was dispatched from Fort Reno, and in conjunction with United States Marshals and Indian police, the soldiers rounded up Chitto Harjo and his followers and placed them in jail in Muskogee. While Harjo was jailed, Alexander Posey, a full-blood-Creek poet, wrote a poem in reverence of Harjo. Posey wrote:

> Down with him! chain him! bind him fast!
> The one true Creek, perhaps the last,
> To dare declare, "You have wronged me!"
> Defiant, stoical, silent,
> suffers imprisonment!
> Such coarse black hair! such eagle eye!
> Such stately mein [*sic*]!—how arrow straight—
> Such will! such courage to defy
> The powerful makers of his fate!
> A traitor, outlaw—what you will,
> He is the noble red man still.
> Condemn him and his kind to shame!
> I bow to him, exalt his name!

After a short imprisonment, Harjo and the rest of his "snake" followers were paroled under the provision that they accept their allotments and live according to the terms of the Curtis Act.[45]

However, the problems surrounding the allotment of lands to Native

44. Goble, *Progressive Oklahoma,* 75; Smith, FCSA; quoted in Debo, *And Still the Waters Run,* 128, 57–58.
45. Smith, FCSA.

Americans in severalty continued. Governmental officials had been concerned that Native Americans would quickly lose their newly acquired title to their lands to unscrupulous whites. Therefore, the Curtis Bill of 1898 dictated that land allotments in the Indian Territory were to be inalienable for a period of twenty-five years. However, these restrictions were slowly lifted over a period of several years for intermarried white citizens, freedmen, and mixed-blood Indians. By 1908, as historian Angie Debo notes, "allottees were divided into three classes: whites, freedmen, and mixed bloods of less than one-half Indian blood were released from all restrictions; mixed bloods of one-half or more and less than three-fourths Indian blood were free to sell their surplus, but their homesteads remained inalienable; and Indians of three-fourths or more Indian blood were restricted in all their holdings."[46]

Not surprisingly, most full bloods in the territory objected to being denied the ability to manage their own affairs. What was truly appalling to them was that the restrictions applied only to those Indians designated as full bloods by the Dawes Commission rolls; they argued that all allottees should be treated the same. As one editor noted, "The amount of blood does not in any way determine the amount of sense an Indian may have."[47]

Despite the intentions of governmental officials to protect Native Americans in the possession of their lands, unscrupulous whites were still able to find ways to circumvent the law and thereby engage in speculation of Indian lands. White grafters got full bloods to lease their lands to them at ridiculously low rents. Entire allotments might be leased for as long as ninety-nine years and for as little as ten or fifteen dollars. These lands were then subleased at enormous profits. Often the speculators had the full support of local Indian officials, who were often themselves involved in plundering Indian lands. Tams Bixby, the chair of the Dawes Commission, for example, was a shareholder in numerous speculative land companies in the Indian Territory and in fact owned one outright himself. Among the Creeks, one land company held 80,000 acres under lease and paid annual rent sometimes as low as one dollar per allotment. As historian Angie Debo explains: "In their poverty and bewilderment it is not strange that the Indians were glad to earn a few dollars by the simple process of making their mark on a paper. Usually they had no idea of the commitments they made. In other cases they realized they had leased or sold their land, but they had no use for it, they knew nothing of real estate values, and the pittance they received seemed like a great windfall."[48]

Some white land speculators were willing to use the most underhanded tricks imaginable to get their hands on Indian land. For example, one Cherokee full blood was "befriended" by a group of white land speculators who took

46. Debo, *And Still the Waters Run*, 179–80, 179.
47. *Kingston Messenger,* Apr. 20, 1906.
48. Goble, *Progressive Oklahoma,* 78; Debo, *And Still the Waters Run,* 130.

him to Kansas City by train. They then refused to pay his fare back home. Stranded in a strange city, not knowing any English, and without the means to get back home, the Cherokee sold his allotment for a mere $20.00. Other speculators were able to secure power-of-attorney papers over full-blood landowners. One Kansas-based firm reportedly secured hundreds of these documents. The full bloods were paid a dollar each to sign papers which the firm's agent told them would raise the rents paid for their surplus land. In reality, these signed power-of-attorney forms gave the firm complete control of the allotment.[49]

Perhaps the most prevalent and certainly the most despicable form of land fraud occurred with respect to the land allotted to Indian orphans. In a society whose people had a short life-expectancy and in which accidental death was common, there were so many orphans that their care became a big business for white entrepreneurs. As a result of the Curtis Act, each child whose name appeared on the tribal rolls was granted an allotment for future use. Hence, minors' estates came to be regarded by the unscrupulous as a sort of natural resource. If the child was an orphan or if the parents were full bloods, then the consent of a legal guardian was required to lease a minor's land. As a result, a whole class of professional guardians arose. Some white speculators would amass dozens, sometimes even hundreds of guardianships. In Antlers, Choctaw Nation, in 1906, one speculator applied for the guardianship of 161 children at once. Horror stories of the abuse of guardianship abound, none more poignant perhaps than that of three children who lived in a hollow tree and foraged for food while their guardian enjoyed the returns from their property. One historian has summarized the exploitation of Native Americans in the wake of the distribution of land in severalty by stating, "what earlier generations had seized with sword and rifle, these men took with paper deeds and conveyances."[50]

Native Americans were not the only targets for unscrupulous whites. Speculators also took advantage of illiterate freedmen, whose land was particularly valuable in that after 1904 it was not subject to any restrictions in terms of resale. One contemporary observer noted that one of the most common practices of land grafters was to loan a freedman money and in return to secure a five-year lease from him, and in the transaction to slip in a deed to the land. The freedman often would not find out about the fraud until he tried to sell his allotment. Another favorite trick of grafters was to purchase a portion of a freedman's allotment, often forty acres, and have the deed made out with a complicated wordy clause which conveyed the remaining eighty acres for no

49. Goble, *Progressive Oklahoma*, 80, 79.
50. Thompson, *Closing the Frontier*, 39; *Daily Oklahoman*, July 25, 1905; Goble, *Progressive Oklahoma*, 81; Theda Perdue, *Nations Remembered: An Oral History of the Five Civilized Tribes, 1865–1907* (Westport: Greenwood Press, 1980), 199; Goble, *Progressive Oklahoma*, 78.

extra cost. Many illiterate and barely literate freedmen could not understand the legalese in which the contract was written, and could not afford the cost of a lawyer to safeguard their interests. As a result, they lost their land for a mere pittance.[51]

White speculators also tried to get themselves appointed guardians over freedmen children so as to gain control over the estates. In the Creek Nation, a white man appeared before the courts seeking to be named the guardian of two African American twins. The man claimed he was the father of the children. The clerk reportedly took one look at the man and asked, "you are a white man, do you mean to tell me your children are Negroes?" The claimant then tried to deny he was white but was rather a light-skinned mulatto. However, no evidence of his parentage could be provided, and his application was denied. The local paper quipped, "The Indian Territory is the only place on earth where the white man has tried to prove himself a Negro. When it comes to getting land the white man can accommodate himself to any and all circumstances."[52]

The extent of freedmen's losses was staggering. J. Coody Johnson, a freedman member of the Creek National Council, told a congressional committee in 1906, only two years after removal of restrictions upon the sale of freedmen lands, that nearly two-thirds of the Creek freedmen had lost their allotments to white speculators and had received next to nothing in return.[53]

BY STATEHOOD in 1907, many Native Americans and freedmen had been cheated out of their allotments. The former Indian lands now contained over a million white settlers. Both Native Americans and their ex-slaves had reason to feel strangers in their own land. A minority of each group was ready to abandon their historic roots and home in the Indian lands and search for yet another promised land elsewhere.

African Americans emigrated West from the Southern states during the 1890s seeking a place where their civil rights and security of property would be respected. For a brief period Oklahoma did present African Americans with opportunities such as political participation and land ownership denied them elsewhere. But in response, white settlers became alarmed, fearing a massive influx of blacks. They moved to restrict the civil rights afforded African Americans, and it soon became apparent that Oklahoma would not be a racial Utopia. Faced with segregation, disfranchisement, racial violence, and dispossession of their land and dwellings, many African Americans came to the conclusion that Oklahoma would never be a peaceful home for them. Hence, paradoxically, during the same years when thousands of African Americans

51. Untitled newspaper clipping, Indians File, Box 2, TAP.
52. *Muskogee Cimeter*, Aug. 17, 1905.
53. Goble, *Progressive Oklahoma*, 131.

were coming into Oklahoma from the South seeking a new life, thousands of Oklahoma blacks were looking for a new promised land. Despairing of ever finding freedom and security in the United States, many sought refuge in Africa and Canada. Throughout the 1890s, small organizations were formed in the territories with the express desire to move to Liberia on the west coast of Africa. As early as 1894, the International Immigration Society based in Birmingham, Alabama, had agents in the Indian Territory seeking to recruit colonists with the promise of twenty-five free acres of land and the necessary implements to till it awaiting settlers in Liberia. Such promises were attractive to individuals such as P. S. Meadows, who wrote the secretary of the interior, noting, "Sir the feeling has become so bitter it is getting worse all the time between the whites and blacks in this country that it is not best for us to try to stay here any longer."[54]

Others sought their freedom in the vast plains of the Canadian West. Many Oklahoma blacks saw the Canadian West "as an opportunity to have both land and liberty, without restrictions." One spokesman for a group that entered Canada through British Columbia stated, "the people of Oklahoma treat us like dogs. We are not allowed to vote and are not admitted to any of the theatres or public places. They won't even let us ride the streetcars in some towns." Historian R. Bruce Shepard notes a direct relation between the rise of segregationist sentiment and black migration to the Canadian Plains.[55]

Some Native American leaders also petitioned the government to have their tribes removed from the Indian lands and colonized elsewhere in complete isolation from white society. One Choctaw proponent of emigration proclaimed, "Our educated people inform us that the white man came to this country to avoid conditions which to him were not as bad as the present conditions are to us; that he went across the great ocean and sought new homes in order to avoid things which to him were distasteful and wrong. All we ask is that we may be permitted to exercise the same privilege." He claimed the Indians expected no financial support from the United States government, but demanded that they be allowed to sell their lands without restrictions to raise the money required to settle elsewhere. Mass emigration, the Choctaw noted, was not only in the interest of the Indians. He reasoned such an emigration was also in the interest of white Americans, noting, "He [the white American] does not want the Indian any more than we want him, and by carrying out this plan he will get that which he wants—the Indian land."[56]

54. Strickland, "Toward the Promised Land," 404; *Daily Ardmoreitte,* Sept. 24, 1894; P. S. Meadows to SI, Sept. 10, 1902, Indian Territory, Special Files, Choctaw and Chickasaw and Cherokee Freedmen, RG 48, Box 48, RDI.

55. R. Bruce Shepard, "The Origins of the Oklahoma Black Migration to the Canadian Plains," *Canadian Journal of History* 23 (April 1988): 2, 22, 10.

56. Quoted in Debo, *And Still the Waters Run,* 59–60.

THE NINETEENTH CENTURY was indeed dominated by the notion of Manifest Destiny—that it was the divine right of Anglo-Americans to extend their culture across the North American continent. Having annexed Texas, California, Oregon, Alaska, and Hawaii, Americans now began to ponder the wisdom of allowing a vast tract of land to remain sparsely settled in the midst of the continent. From the end of the Civil War onwards, whites came to debate the future of the last frontier on the North American continent—the lands known as the Indian Territory. The existence of vast acreage of virgin lands in the territory led many observers to see it as a "promised land"—a haven for small farmers where they could escape the overcrowding and soil exhaustion besetting the East. As a result, the Indian Territory became a battleground in the late nineteenth century, as whites, African Americans, and Native Americans sought to ensure their foothold in "paradise."

Interestingly, in the decades immediately following the Civil War, the United States government firmly dedicated itself to maintaining the Indian Territory as the exclusive home for Native Americans and their freedmen. Government officials and concerned humanitarians argued that Native Americans had to be isolated from white society until such time as they could be properly indoctrinated with Anglo-American values and traditions. Under the paternal guidance of Indian Bureau officials, Christian teachers, and missionaries, Native Americans would slowly be prepared for ultimate assimilation into Anglo-American society. But white settlers in the surrounding states had a very different viewpoint. To them, Indians were savages, obstacles to opening up vast acreages of fertile lands. They repeatedly petitioned the government to make Indian lands available to white settlement. When the government refused to do so, they circumvented the law and squatted on Indian lands illegally. For years, the government was forced to send federal troops to remove these settlers known as "boomers." The boomers were able to capture the sympathy of many editors in the East, and eventually their perseverance paid off. In 1889, President Harrison announced that surplus Indian lands would be made open to settlement in a land run. In the years to follow, several other tracts of land were declared surplus and opened to settlement through land runs and later through a lottery system. The transformation of the Indian Territory was completed when the Curtis Act of 1898 ended Indian communal land ownership and replaced it with individual land title.

When the new state, in 1907, was named Oklahoma—"the land of the red man"—it was in obvious reference to its historic traditions, not its contemporary nature. For in 1910, out of a total state population of 1,657,155 citizens, 1,444,531 were classified in the census as white, 137,612 as Negro, and 74,825 as Indians. Clearly "the fight for the promised land" was won by white Americans. Oklahoma, like much of the West, was "won" through a combination of determination, hard work, government assistance, graft, fraud, chicanery, and violence. To officials in Washington and humanitarian reformers, this was a victory of progress and civilization over savagery and barbarism. For Native Americans, the imposition of individual land ownership according to the dictates of the Dawes Commission was complicated, disappointing, frustrating, and tragic. It ended a lifestyle centuries old in tradition. As the *Daily Oklahoman* noted in 1907, "The uniting of Indian Territory with Oklahoma Territory in statehood removes the last particle of that vast domain, which in the early part of the last century was set aside by Congress as an eternal home for the red man." To many Native Americans the loss of sovereignty over the last piece of territory in a continent which was once their own was a tragic experience. As Chief Gotebo of the Kiowas declared: "Oh, you paleface! You go to church and tell the Great Spirit how good you are and in your pockets you have the Indian's money. You walk down the street smoking a cigar, and your kind say 'good man, plenty money,' and it is the Indian's money that you have. Oh you white man; the Great Spirit knows and he will not forget." All could relate to the sense of loss, the feeling that somehow life would never be the same for Native Americans again. One Cherokee woman married to a white man could not bring herself to attend the statehood ceremonies with her husband. He returned and said to her, "well, Mary, we no longer live in the Cherokee Nation. All of us are now citizens of the state of Oklahoma." Tears came to the woman's eyes thirty years later as she recalled that fateful day. She remembered, "It broke my heart. I went to bed and cried all night long. It seemed more than I could bear that the Cherokee Nation, my country, and my people's country, was no more."[57]

Yet for the former freedmen of the Five Civilized Tribes, the Curtis Act represented a victory. Unlike their fellow ex-slaves in the South, they received their "forty acres and a mule" (although a generation later than proposed). Clearly in terms of land policy in the late nineteenth century, it was Native Americans who were the biggest losers.

57. Though Oklahoma was numerically dominated by whites it had by far the greatest number of Indians of any state in the Union. In fact, one-fourth of the total U.S. Native American population in 1910 resided in the state of Oklahoma. Population density studies done in 1910 indicated Oklahoma had 108.7 Indians per 100 square miles, which was more than four times higher than Arizona, its closest competitor in this regard. Bureau of the Census, *Indian Population of the United States—1910* (Washington, D.C.: Government Printing Office, 1910), 12–14; Bureau of the Census, *Thirteenth Census of the United States—1910* (Washington, D.C.: Government Printing Office, 1910), 461; *Daily Oklahoman,* Jan. 27, 1907, Apr. 14, 1912; quoted in Strickland, *The Indians in Oklahoma,* 54.

FOUR

Teaching the Four *Rs*
Reading, 'Riting, 'Rithmetic, and Racism

T HE HISTORY OF EDUCATION in the Indian Territory begins with the rebirth of Native American culture in the West. Some of the Five Civilized Tribes had missionary schools in their homeland in the Southeast long before the Trail of Tears. Not surprisingly, then, after their forced relocation to their new home in the West, the Cherokees, Choctaws, and Chickasaws immediately set out to establish a school system there. By the end of the Civil War, these tribes had an extensive educational system in place to guarantee learning for future generations. The Cherokee Nation's educational system was the most extensive. By the 1880s the Cherokees had one hundred public and private elementary schools, plus male and female seminaries, which were housed in "two large well-furnished buildings, each costing nearly $100,000." Control over the education of the Five Civilized Tribes was in the hands of the governments of the independent Indian nations.[1]

White governmental officials were encouraged by the actions of the Five Civilized Tribes. They concluded education was responsible for the tribes' sophistication. As one official put it:

> For your present advanced condition, in all that pertains to civilization, you are indebted chiefly to the wisdom, courage, patience and forbearance of your noble, brave, and worthy ancestors, who . . . adopted a system of educating the most prominent and promising of their young men, thus bringing their native talents and genius in direct contact with the development of their white brethren and opening up to their minds and understandings the superior advantages of educated industry, a knowledge of arts, sciences, and the peaceful pursuits of civilized life.[2]

1. Foreman, *The Five Civilized Tribes,* 35–59; John B. Riley to SI, Nov. 1, 1886, in *RSI* 1886, 1:147.
2. Address of Hon. W. W. Willshire of Arkansas at the 8th Indian International Fair, Muskogee, Indian Territory, R 55, Union Agency, 1881, RIIIA.

There was no reason to believe, officials argued, that the salubrious effects of education upon the Five Civilized Tribes would not have a similar impact on the other relocated tribes. Reformers were convinced that by giving those tribes an Anglo-American education, the tribes would thereby become more civilized and hence closer to the final step of accomplishing cultural assimilation into white society.

By the latter half of the nineteenth century, most Americans were firm believers in the power of education. They saw education as intimately linked to American ideals of freedom and liberty. Education was considered the great emancipator, freeing all from the chains of ignorance. Most officials would have agreed with L. J. Miles, Indian agent for the Osage, who asserted that if a policy of educating the relocated tribes were conducted, "in one generation, Indians would be an English-speaking people, acquainted with the labors, habits, and means of [a] self-sustaining, self-governing race." Miles would then concede Indians would be ultimately "ready for citizenship." To him, as to many officials back in Washington, this was the only way to solve the "perplexing Indian problem."[3]

Anglo-Americans assumed that, given the proper education and role models, the Native American population would integrate well into white society. Milton W. Reynolds, editor of the *Edmond Sun*, succinctly put forth this optimistic view when he declared: "The West should now revise its shibboleth that there is no good Indian but a dead Indian and admit that the Indian may be civilized and the cheapest way to do it is to corral the children and young warriors in the schools. Let the Eastern spelling book go with the Western engine and the Indian problem can be solved."[4]

THE TASK of assimilating Native Americans into Anglo-American culture fell to three basic types of schools: religious schools, manual labor schools, and boarding schools. Many of the first schools established by whites in Indian Territory were religious schools and almost all denominations were represented, the Baptists, Methodists, and Catholics being the most prevalent. Most of these schools were located in the western lands of the Indian Territory and were specifically intended to instruct the relocated Plains Indian tribes, since many of those tribes had not yet adopted Christianity. In these schools, the task of Christianizing the Indians was paramount. One Mennonite missionary believed that the teaching of the Christian religion was "the most important branch of training in our school." He maintained that a true and permanent

3. James D. Anderson, *The Education of Blacks in the South, 1860–1935* (Chapel Hill: University of North Carolina Press, 1988), 1; L. J. Miles to CIA, Aug. 20, 1885, in *RSI* 1885, 2:316; Finney, "Progress in the Civilization of the Osage," 8.

4. D. Earl Newsom, *Kicking Bird and the Birth of Oklahoma: A Biography of Milton W. Reynolds* (Perkins, Okla.: Evans Publications, 1983), 98.

civilizing of the Indians would never be accomplished without the religion of Christ. He declared, "show me an Indian who has accepted Christ as his personal Savior to a change of heart, and I will show you a civilized Indian with a radical change of life." Native Americans were regarded as a religious people; religion permeated their daily life. According to white observers, almost every act that they did was connected with a religious meaning, scrupulously inculcated into the child from infancy. All that was necessary, therefore, in the minds of white missionaries was to give Indians "a higher, the only true religion, that of Christ."[5]

Secular education, it was argued, could not affect the transformation required to assimilate Native Americans into white society. Advocates of religious schools pointed out that denominational schools had the power to appoint their own teachers according to their own criteria, whereas public school teachers were appointed through patronage or, by the 1890s, selected through competitive exams. Hence, advocates of religious instruction argued that only true Christian representatives should be appointed to instruct the Indians. One missionary argued that "we may teach the Indian child all the arts of our civilized life," but "without a living Christ in the heart of such a child, returning as a young man to his people, [he] will soon fall back into the old superstitious customs and habits of his race."[6]

While denominational schools taught students to read, write, and do basic arithmetic, they also emphasized Christian morality. The denominational schools used textbooks that stressed "kindness, truthfulness, temperance, modesty, and goodwill," while denouncing "profanity, gambling, intemperance, and vice." The books hoped to shape Indian behavior by exalting "thrift, industry, hard labor, and economic individualism," as well as praising the virtue of "regular religious habits."[7]

What is indeed ironic is that while professing these noble aims, many of the denominational schools fell into bitter sectarian disputes over the right to bring the light of God's truth to the Indians. The Osage, for example, were innocent victims in the struggle between Quaker and Catholic missionaries, both anxious to save their souls. The principal of the Quaker-run school wrote agent Miles to inform him that the Catholic brothers from the Osage Mission in Kansas had been trying to lure students to come to their school by making "false statements" against the Quaker-run school. The government caused part of

5. Robert H. Keller, *American Protestantism and United States Indian Policy, 1869–1882* (Lincoln: University of Nebraska Press, 1983); S. S. Haury to Agent Miles, Aug. 15, 1883, in *RSI* 1883, 2:127.

6. Meyer Weinberg, *A Chance to Learn: The History of Race and Education in the United States* (Cambridge, Eng.: Cambridge University Press, 1977), 207; S. S. Haury to Agent Miles, Aug. 15, 1883, in *RSI* 1883, 2:127.

7. Christopher J. Huggard, "Culture Mixing: Everyday Life on Missions among the Choctaws," *Chronicles of Oklahoma* 70, no. 4 (1992): 439.

the problem by reassigning tribes to various religious sects according to the terms of Grant's peace policy. However, some government officials did their best to try to discourage such internecine warfare. Secretary of the Interior Enoch Hoag, while recognizing the need "to impress upon their youthful minds the importance of sound morals and Christian virtues," argued these virtues were recognized by "all Christendom." Thus it appeared to him that it did not "seem practicable or allowable that any interference should be permitted" by those seeking to influence the Indians for or against any particular denomination.[8]

Manual labor schools set up in the Indian Territory had a much more secular goal—instilling in Native American children the value of work. White officials believed that many of the Indian tribes (particularly the relocated Plains tribes) felt they were above manual labor and agriculture, having been at one time fierce warriors and brave hunters. Hence, they felt it was necessary to teach Native Americans what was termed the Protestant work ethic. Teachers developed lessons which emphasized the value and positive rewards of hard work. Teachers in the Indian Service were instructed that "the most important part of an Indian child's education is the art of making a living. If we can teach lessons in economy and industry with reading and writing, and also numbers, we are working to a greater advantage." One agent plainly stated that "industry is of more importance in civilizing the Indian than the study of books and sightseeing."[9]

In fact, one of the manual labor schools in conjunction with the academic year arranged summer employment programs for their Indian students called "outings." The students worked for white families, the boys assisting in farming, gardening, and repairing tools, while the girls performed housework, cooked meals, and sewed clothes. There were several supposed benefits for the Native American students partaking in this program: "a practical experience with an employer; opportunity to live in a Christian household; and the possibility of earning money."[10]

8. Benjamin Miles, Principal Osage School, 1876, Letters Received, R 72, M 856, RG 75, Record of the Bureau of Indian Affairs, National Archives, Washington, D.C.; Enoch Hoag, SI, to E. P. Smith, CIA, 1875, R 634, Osage Agency, LR-RBIA.

9. Hoxie, *A Final Promise*, 197; "Lessons for Use by Teachers in the Service," *Indian School Journal* (1903): 44; J. M. Lee to CIA, Aug. 31, 1886, in *RSI* 1886, 1:335.

10. The "outing" system was devised by Richard H. Pratt, superintendent of the Carlisle Boarding School in Pennsylvania. See Richard H. Pratt, *Battlefield and Classroom: Four Decades with the American Indian, 1867–1904* (New Haven: Yale University Press, 1964); Abraham Makofsky, "Experience of Native Americans at a Black College: Indian Students at Hampton Institute 1878–1923," *Journal of Ethnic Studies* 17 (fall 1989): 39. Summer "outings" did not always have assimilation as their ultimate goal. Many "outing" programs became a way of providing cheap domestic labor to white householders. See Robert A. Trennert, "Educating Indian Girls at Nonreservation Boarding Schools, 1878–1920," *Western Historical Quarterly* 13 (July 1982): 271–90.

While on these summer "outings," as well as at school during the regular academic year, Native American students were subjected to firm lessons not only in the value of labor but in the strict division of labor according to sex. White observers had long criticized Indians for subjecting their women to cruel treatment and excessive labor. Most of the relocated Plains tribes still saw agricultural labor as women's work. According to ancient tradition, women farmed while the men hunted and were warriors. This contrasted sharply with the established practices of the white population, who saw a woman's proper place as being the home and a man's role as the provider.[11]

A key element in education was to foster a change in thinking with respect to gender roles. Many of the schools, particularly those set up especially for Indian students, had adjacent farms where the boys were to learn all about the planting and care of a farm. In addition, boys were to be taught how to build houses; make clothing, boots and shoes; construct wagons and do the work of a blacksmith; and to butcher cattle. In sum, the Indian boy should be taught "all the trades that the farmer and the herdman patronize," since farming and grazing "were the two great industries which the Indian of the future must follow."[12]

Girls, on the other hand, in each of the reservation manual labor schools, were given instruction in all branches of household industry as well as the making and repair of garments. The commissioner of Indian affairs noted that girls were taught the "work of the kitchen, laundry, dining-room, dormitory, and sewing-room," and he reported that "it is expected that they will receive as thorough and constant instruction in the art of homemaking as in reading and writing the English language." The teachers were diligent in their efforts, as the superintendent of education for the Arapaho Manual Labor School reported that "the girls have been drilled in all the different branches of house work until they have become . . . finally fit for the practical duties of the housewife." To ensure that Anglo-American gender roles were learned, the instructors often resorted to separating the children into male and female schools.[13]

While white officials and advocates of Indian education were pleased with the efforts of religious and manual labor schools, they argued the best possible solution to civilize the relocated Indians was to remove them from the "backward" environment of the of the tribe and immerse them in Anglo-American culture at boarding school. For officials thought it was "just as necessary to teach Indian children how to live as how to read and write." The boarding school, it was argued, surrounded the student with an English-speaking com-

---

11. Trennert, "Educating Indian Girls," 271–90.

12. E. H. Rishel, interview, GFPHC, 69:3–7; John H. Oberly to SI, Nov. 1, 1885, in *RSI* 1885, 2:112.

13. Hiram Price, CIA, to SI, Oct. 10, 1882, in *RSI* 1882, 2:26; J. H. Seger to CIA, Aug. 15, 1881, in *RSI* 1881, 2:131; Huggard, "Culture Mixing," 436.

munity, "giving him instruction in the first lessons of civilization, which can be found only in a well-ordered home." This contrasted with the experience of Indian children attending day schools. Advocates of boarding schools claimed that education of Indian children thus far had brought forth "but little good fruit." The reason they argued, was clear:

> The barbarian child of barbarian parents spends possibly six of the twenty-four hours of the day in the school room. Here he is taught the rudiments of the books, varied, perhaps, by fragmentary lessons in the "good manners" of the superior race to which his teacher belongs. He returns, at the close of his school-day, to eat and play and sleep after the savage fashion of his race. In the hours spent in school he has not acquired a distaste for the camp-fire, nor a longing for the food, the home-life, or the ordinary avocations of the white man. In a restricted sense the day-school gives to the Indian child useful information, but it does not civilize him, because it does not take him away from barbarous life and put him into the enjoyment of civilized life—does not take him from the tepee into the house, and teach him how to appreciate, by experiencing them, the comforts of the white man's civilization.

Not so with the boarding school experience. Here, the Indian child was removed from the "perverting environment of the Indian camp," and put under the influence of the methods of civilized life. The child was instructed in personal cleanliness and proper hygiene. He was clothed in the "garments of civilized men and taught how to wear them," and given a bed and instruction on "its usage." In addition, the child learned proper table manners, including "how to use a knife and fork, how to eat at a table," and proper nutrition.[14]

IN RELIGIOUS, manual labor, and boarding schools, the emphasis was upon assimilating Native American students into white society. In reality what whites strove for was the annihilation of Indian culture. Richard H. Pratt, the founder of the Carlisle Indian Industrial School, located in Carlisle, Pennsylvania, declared, "We accept the watchword. There is no good Indian but a dead Indian. Let us by education and patient effort kill the Indian in him, and save the man." Educational officials then designed curricula, instituted rules and regulations, and instructed teachers, all in an effort to destroy Native American culture and replace it with Anglo-American culture. Apparently Indians would only be acceptable to white society when in fact they had ceased to be Indians. However, while whites hoped that cultural assimilation would be entirely one way, the reality of frontier life necessitated cultural interaction between whites and Indians. While missionaries and teachers tried to impose their culture upon

14. Carl Schurz, SI, Nov. 1, 1880, in *RSI* 1880, 1:7; Edward P. Smith, CIA, to SI, Nov. 1, 1873, in *RSI* 1873, 1:377; John H. Oberly, to SI, Nov. 1, 1885, in *RSI* 1885, 2:111–12.

their students, they invariably adapted to some of the Indians' ways themselves.[15]

As contemporary research in education shows, one of the most powerful tools in the educational process is the determination of curriculum. White officials and missionaries were quick to develop a curriculum which would emphasize the accomplishments and sophistication of white society and minimize the contribution of other cultures. Students were taught that whites had been responsible for the advancement of mankind while Native American cultures had been retarding influences which had to give way before the onslaught of a superior civilization. The textbooks used by white schools to teach Indian children were full of descriptions of savage Indian fighting and displayed pictures of naked forms with ugly features proudly displaying their scalp locks. The *Cherokee Advocate* noted, "The books that show us up for what we are NOT, show up the pale face for what he is, and these books are in use in the schools of both races alike." Native Americans were taught in school and inundated in the print media with a very culturally biased view of history and race relations.[16]

In the systematic campaign to annihilate Native American culture, educators attacked Native language with the greatest tenacity. The commissioner of Indian affairs directed his subordinates to force Indian children to speak English. He declared, "The language which is good enough for a white man or a black man ought to be good enough for the red man. It is also believed that teaching an Indian youth in his own barbarous dialect is a positive detriment to him." This policy remained in effect long after Oklahoma statehood. Only when Indian friends visited or during the first few weeks at school were Indian children allowed to speak their Native language. During school hours the students were required to speak only English. Those who did not adhere to this regulation faced a variety of often inhumane punishments.[17]

White educators and missionaries attempted to further influence Native American behavior through a series of rules and regulations regarding behavior on school property. For example, they enforced a strict dress code and Anglo-American hairstyles upon Indian students. Boys were given jeans and cotton shirts to wear, while girls were issued calico dresses. Moccasins and bare feet were forbidden, shoes and boots were required. Punishment awaited any transgressors of appropriate fashion. Male students were given crew cuts, and younger female students lost their braids, while more mature girls were forced to wear their long hair up in a bun. Educators took it upon themselves to rename Indian children with Anglo-American names for children's Indian names,

15. Captain Pratt, founder of Carlisle Indian Industrial School, quoted by Merrill E. Gates, president of Rutgers College, member of U.S. Board of Indian Commissioners, 1885, in *RSI* 1885, 1:775.

16. Michael C. Coleman, *American Indian Children at School, 1850–1930* (Jackson: University of Mississippi Press, 1993), 206; *Cherokee Advocate*, Feb. 4, 1880.

17. Strickland, *The Indians in Oklahoma*, 42.

which were often related to animals or events in the young child's life. In all these ways then, white educators attempted to destroy Indian culture and impose Anglo-American culture in its place.[18]

Native Americans had a mixed response to the actions of white educators. Most of the mixed-blood members of the Five Civilized Tribes located in the independent Indian Nations embraced Anglo-American education. Many of the white Americans sent to settle among the Five Civilized Tribes as Indian agents, missionaries, and teachers constantly wrote back east of their amazement at the diligence of Indian students and the enthusiasm with which they undertook their studies. The superintendent of the Tallahassee Manual Labor School, for example, boasted "The interest of the Creek people in the education of their children seems undiminished; and the children themselves manifest a readiness and aptitude in learning which is rarely, if ever, surpassed by white children." He then added that students "advance in their studies at a rate which is truly astonishing." Some Indian leaders were quick to recognize and point out the benefits of education to their respective tribe members. The Principal Chief of the Creeks encouraged his people to seek a formalized education, noting that "The most prosperous and happy nations on the earth are those who are educated, enlightened, industrious, economical, and who fear God and obey him."[19]

On the other hand, most full-blood leaders, particularly those of the relocated tribes in western Indian Territory, but also some of the leaders of the Five Civilized Tribes, resented the intrusion of white-led schools. However, some were convinced that Indians could use Anglo-American education as a defense mechanism, a form of self-protection against the menace of white aggression. Wilson Jones summarized this view in a message to his tribe, claiming "We are surrounded by the restless and jealous white race, and are daily brought more and more into competition with its members. In this struggle we must be well armed in order to hold our own. Our best weapon, our surest defense is education." Native Americans realized that if their children "could read and write English, they could use the words of the white man's wisdom against him" in an attempt to protect their own culture. Survival seemed to dictate that Native Americans learn to deal with and communicate with whites on their own level. Native Americans wished to avoid the circumstance of naive Indians being cheated and exploited. White settlers, intent on swindling Indians out of their rightful possessions, were warned they would find acumen rather than ignorance awaiting them in Indian Territory.[20]

18. Huggard, "Culture Mixing," 437.
19. Leonard Worchesterr to Major F. S. Lyon, U.S. agent for the Creeks, 1871, in *RSI* 1871, 1:994; Principal Chief of the Creeks to SI, R 235, Creek Agency, 1874–76, LR-RBIA.
20. Foreman, *The Five Civilized Tribes,* 422; Wilson N. Jones, Annual Message, Nov. 1, 1890, WNJP; Smith, FCSA.

However, most full bloods of the relocated tribes, and many of the Five Civilized Tribes, had no use for Anglo-American education at all. These tribesmen resented the intrusion of professional teachers—invariably white—into an area once controlled by tribal elders. They preferred the old tradition of oral education passed from generation to generation. This created a schism in Native American society, not only between tribes, but often directly linked to the degree of Indian blood. Mixed-blood leaders were resentful of what they saw as unreasonable intransigence on the part of the full bloods. One mixed-blood chief declared, "The people seemed to have lost the interest they had formerly taken in education—I speak of our people who are full Indians and whom [*sic*] of all others of our citizens needs educating the most." Hatred, antagonism, and suspicion of whites were part of the objection of full bloods. But in addition, full bloods saw schoolhouse learning as capitulation to Anglo-American culture. They saw no cultural relevance for textbook learning, nor did they see much practical application for higher education. However, one old full blood, when asked for his views on sending one of the tribe's girls to the Carlisle Indian Industrial School, said he "thought it was a fine thing to send a girl to learn to read and write, sew, cook, and keep house," and whereas in the old days wives were worth "only two or three ponies, this higher education might increase their value to eight or ten ponies."[21]

Not surprisingly, what upset full-blood Native Americans most about Anglo-American schools was the systematic attempt to annihilate Indian culture. Interviews conducted with Native Americans as part of a Works Progress Administration program in the 1930s revealed a profound resentment against the attempt of white educators to impose their own culture upon Indian students. One woman remembered that she did not know Native societies had chiefs "because they didn't teach us about that in the white school." Another woman reminisced that "the white man took away all the old ways and now the young children don't want to know about them"; the result of this, the woman continued, was "now the young ones want to be white." Finally, one woman claimed white schools "just flat knocked the Indian out of them . . . they never taught them anything 'bout the Indian heritage or anything." Even in the Cherokee Female Seminary, which was run by the Cherokees themselves, not by the federal government, there were no courses which focused on tribal history, religion, or culture.[22]

Many Native Americans remembered being subjected to cruel and inhumane punishments while attending white schools. One Choctaw woman re-

21. Smith, FCSA; Principal Chief of the Creeks to SI, R 235, Creek Agency, 1874–76, LR-RBIA; Smith, FCSA .
22. Annie Thompson, interview, File 85.74, OHP; Julia Edge, interview, File 88.99, OHP; Mrs. Kelley, interview, File T-114, p. 16, DDOHI; Devon A. Mihesuah, *Cultivating the Rosebuds: The Education of Women at the Cherokee Female Seminary, 1851–1909* (Urbana: University of Illinois Press, 1993), 56.

membered being whipped for speaking her native language. At the New Hope Seminary any Choctaw girl caught speaking her own language was forced to swallow a teaspoon of red pepper. A Comanche man remembered being sat on a chair in the middle of the room and flogged with a stick while the teacher told him "he would never be civilized and ready to join society if he didn't learn how to speak English." A Ponca father and son recalled children being forced to eat a bar of lye soap or sit in their school seat for three days without speaking if caught speaking their native language, and the same men also remembered that children were whipped if they mispronounced an English word. Other Native Americans related stories of less drastic abuse. One woman remembered that if you were caught speaking your native language you were given five demerit points and had to perform odd jobs around the school to work them off (such as washing the windows after school), because if you had outstanding demerit points at the end of a semester you were not allowed to go home. One school superintendent decided to use the "carrot" instead of the "stick." He divided the male students into four military style "companies," each having a sergeant and a corporal who were appointed the prestige of being "officers" because of their proficiency in the English language. By so doing, the superintendent noted, "we found that there was soon considerable rivalry among them as to who should speak the best English." The use of "military" appointments was not all that unusual. Many Native American schools were organized along military lines. Often this reflected the background of the school principals, many of whom were former army officers. The use of military terminology and punishments also reflected the belief of white educators that obedience was foreign to the Indian mind and that discipline was a corollary to civilization.[23]

The whole issue of corporal punishment became a battleground between school administrators and concerned Native American parents. Educators deemed corporal punishment necessary to maintain discipline in the schools. Culturally disposed to see Indians as wild savages, white educators argued that physical coercion was the only way to control behavior. Native American parents, however, did not believe in corporal punishment. One concerned parent wrote:

> I am repeatedly informed by parties who have taken their children from your school, that our children are very inhumanely treated by Mexican overseers or

23. Roxie Crews, interview, File 85.161, OHP; Huggard, "Culture Mixing," 439; William Karty, interview, File 88.75, OHP; William Collins Jr. and William Collins Sr., interview, File 87.179, OHP; Bessie Sorethumb, interview, File 85.154, OHP; Trennert, "Educating Indian Girls," 271–90; J. H. Seger to CIA, Aug. 15, 1881, in *RSI* 1881, 2:131. Edward Gansworth has an interesting insight into this, arguing that many Indian students at meetings with officials spouted rehearsed words and didn't know what they meant. (Daniel F. Littlefield Jr., personal communication with author.) Gansworth's records are at the Buffalo and Erie County Historical Society, Buffalo, N.Y.

Captains who strap them over a chair and apply the lash just as they did to the Negro in the South in anti [*sic*] bellum days.

We have tried to raise our children after the fashion of Christian people and are not willing to subject them to such treatment.

To such objections, parents often received curt replies insisting that "anyone intelligent enough to know" would realize that a government school subjected to "rigid inspection" would not do anything to harm its students. But usually such rebukes contained warnings that as long as the child endeavored to do his best, he would not be harmed. But "if he does not he will have to be disciplined." Over time apparently Indian parents became more accepting of corporal punishment, for the Kiowa and Comanche superintendent noted in 1881 that in the past year, "there were indications that before a great while the parents might submit to a more rigid discipline." The superintendent reported that on several occasions punishments had been inflicted "without complaint or protest of any kind from the parent, and such as two years ago would have caused trouble and very probably the withdrawl [*sic*] of the child from the school."[24]

Many Native American parents were opposed to the practices of white boarding schools. Most of these detractors were parents who objected to the fact that most boarding schools accepted only those students who agreed to stay on a minimum of three or sometimes even five years. These parents often felt that the boarding schools were getting away with kidnapping. In the wake of one such attack in the local press by a Mrs. Hahn, one superintendent of education replied in a very condescending manner:

And what is the average Indian "home," which Mrs. Hahn talks about, like? A tepee or wigwam not high enough to stand within, a fire burning inside on the ground, filling the "home" with stifling smoke (sometimes there is a stove, but oftener not), a pile of filthy quilts, a few dishes and cooking utensils, and over all and about all the vilest, most disgusting filth. The parents in these "homes" live in unspeakable degradation. Their ideas of morality are seldom higher than those of their canine friends, which help to fill the "home" and sometimes the dinner kettle.

Blessed is the child "kidnaped" [*sic*] from such "homes" and such parents as this.

Educators such as the one above believed that whatever sacrifices Indians had to make, the end result—undertaking a civilized lifestyle—was worth it.[25]

24. B. McIntosh to S. M. McGowan, Nov. 11, 1903, Microfilm CHL-20, NRCIS; Superintendent of Chilocco Indian School to David Perea, Microfilm CHL-20, NRCIS; George W. Hunt to P. B. Hunt, Indian Agent, 1881, in *RSI* 1881, 2:142.

25. Unidentified article, *Indian School Journal*, n.d., File Box 2, TAP.

Not surprisingly, Native American parents were not convinced by such defenses of boarding school practices. Most objected to the fact that students were not allowed to go home even during the summer vacation for fear of relapsing into "barbarous ways." Parents who wanted their children sent home due to illness in the family, need for extra labor, or even simply because they missed seeing them were usually given curt reprimands. School administrators simply reminded them that they had agreed to a contract which guaranteed the school the child would remain on campus for a specified length of time. One Indian parent who had evidently heard that his child was not well wrote asking for her to be sent home. The superintendent replied that "Eliza looks well, feels well and is well." He continued, "As Eliza entered for a number of years, you know I cannot return her home, without consent of Department, if you desire to make this request of the Department and it is willing I shall send her home." Another parent whose child was allowed to return for the summer was chastised by the Chilocco Indian School superintendent for keeping his daughters home after the beginning of school to partake in a Native feast and dance. The superintendent bemoaned that "You are an intelligent man and know perfectly well that I am right in being annoyed when your children or others are not sent back for the beginning of school. The schooling your girls are getting is worth a dozen times more than to stay at home for a payment, a feast or a show. Instead of thinking that I do not want your children you should feel that your children are in good hands and that I want them or I wouldn't care a continental whether they missed school or not."[26]

Faced with few alternatives, many Native American children simply chose to run away from school to escape the constant supervision and rigid controls. Often this was a difficult task, since officials in anticipating this problem had purposely located many Indian boarding schools a long distance away (Pennsylvania, South Dakota, and Kansas, for example). Even if the escapees made the difficult journey back home, some were frustrated because they were arrested by truant officers employed by the local Indian agent and forcibly returned to school. The Cheyenne and Arapaho Indian agent found that a successful way to keep the children in school was to withhold the issue of government rations of beef and other foodstuffs until the physically able children were all in regular school attendance. Many full bloods were unconvinced of Anglo-American benevolence in educating Native American children when governmental officials were willing to starve those who opposed the system.[27]

WHILE MANY Native Americans were justly skeptical of Anglo-Americans' intentions in education, the ex-slaves of the Five Civilized Tribes fought to be

26. Superintendent of Chilocco Indian School to William Wetenhall, Dec. 11, 1905, Microfilm CHL-20, NRCIS; Superintendent of Chilocco Indian School to James Murie, Microfilm CHL-20, NRCIS.
27. Finney, "Progress in the Civilization of the Osage," 8; G. D. Williams to CIA, Aug. 22, 1887, in *RSI* 1887, 2:159.

included in any territorial school system. Having been denied permission to learn how to read or write by the strict slave codes of the Indian nations, the freedmen were anxious to exercise their newfound freedom by attending territorial schools. In the immediate aftermath of the Civil War, workers from the Freedmen's Bureau sent to the Indian Territory, as well as Indian agents in western districts, marveled at the enthusiasm with which freedmen sought education for themselves and their children. As J. W. Dunn, Indian agent for the Creeks, declared soon after the conclusion of the Civil War, "the freedmen, particularly, are anxious that their children shall be educated. Hitherto the customs of the country have prevented their enjoying the benefits of the schools, but now that they are placed on an equality with their former masters, they are determined to profit by the position." The agent noted that in several districts the freedmen had formed their own schools, anticipating the financial assistance of the government.[28]

While the freedmen immediately upon the conclusion of the Civil War petitioned to have access to Indian schools to end the imposed ignorance they had suffered as slaves, Native Americans just as quickly united to deny freedmen access to their schools. Since most of the Five Civilized Tribes in the immediate aftermath of the Civil War, with the exception of the Seminoles and the Creeks, denied their freedmen citizenship rights, the freedmen were consequently denied access to educational facilities which were set up for citizens only (even whites living in the Indian Nations under permits had been denied access to these national schools). The question of educational rights hence became engulfed in the debate over citizenship.

Freedmen petitioned their Native governments to be included in the school system, but received little satisfaction. Therefore, they turned to petitioning the United States government, hoping for a more sympathetic response. Numerous letters were sent to Washington from barely literate freedmen begging for pressure to be brought to bear upon the Native governments to incorporate them into their schools. The following excerpts from freedmen's letters give testimony to their desperate desire to ensure education for their children. One Choctaw freedman wrote: "I went to the council to try to git the privilege of sending a couple of our boys to school to the state and I could not. The choctaws have a catamy to send their children to but they wont alow us the privilege to send our children to their catamy now we wants to no if we is not allowed the privilege to have wone of our own. United States when turned the darkeys loose she mad them equal sitizens with them. Is the choctaw any better than the United States." Another Choctaw freedman wrote "I think we are in a mighty bad condishion. Havin got no school. Just growin up ignerent for the want of schooling." A Cherokee freedman wrote President Ulysses S. Grant:

28. Wyatt F. Jeltz, "The Relations of Negroes and Choctaw and Chickasaw Indians," *Journal of Negro History* 33 (Jan. 1948): 31; J. W. Dunn to Colonel Elijah Sells, SIA, Oct. 1866, in *RSI* 1866, 1:319.

pleas give me a litle information what the dark popution is to doo about that school funds to have our children educated are we to stay here and rais them up lik hethens we have bin deprived of five years school the rebels took our books and even acordin to the sixty six trety we want u say so what to doo if it is lefte to the Cherykees we never will have nothing done. . . . the Cherykees is down on the darkeys the Cherykees says they ainte in favor of the blake man havin any classes that they had rather any body else have a rite than us pore blakies. . . . we donte thinke it rite we have made them rich and bulte his land doo you thinke it rite

But in the immediate aftermath of the Civil War, the Choctaws, Cherokees, and Chickasaws proved intransigent, adamantly refusing to allow their ex-slaves to attend their schools.[29]

Undeterred, the freedmen sought to create their own schools. They did this by undertaking a collection from the local black inhabitants and then using this money to entice a teacher to come West and settle among them. Sometimes they were offered aid by the federal government, other times not. Hence the comment from the Choctaw agent, A. Parsons, that "about two hundred [freedmen] met here today to make prepatory arrangements for the schools" shows a concern common to many black communities in the Indian nations. Parsons continued, "they all seem very highly pleased that you [the government in Washington] are so much interested in them, and they all agreed to do all they could to prepare the buildings and complete everything needed for schools except teachers and books." The freedmen displayed such enthusiasm that they often constructed their own schools and then petitioned the federal government for teachers and books. In this case the Choctaw freedmen must have been successful, for two years later Frank Howard, a teacher sent by the government, said, "The freedmen are fond and grateful for the help which the U.S. government has extended them and there is an universal desire to attend school. Every family will make sacrifices to enable them to send their children regularly." Howard went on to say that the freedmen were "doing the best they can in the way of clothing their children fit to attend school," and he further noted that the local freedmen were "building a good hewed log house for the school, and a house of two rooms for myself and family to live in." Hence freedmen, in their desire to gain access to education, were willing to undergo any personal or financial sacrifice. Excluded from most schools in the Indian

29. Toney Henderson to SI, Indian Territory, Special Files, 1898–1907, Choctaw and Chickasaw and Cherokee Freedmen, RG 48, Box 48, RDI; Simon Love to SI, Indian Territory, Special Files, 1898–1907, Choctaw and Chickasaw and Cherokee Freedmen, RG 48, Box 48, RDI; Louis Rough to President Grant, R 105, Cherokee Agency, 1872, LR-RBIA.

nations, the ex-slaves did all they could to ensure learning for future genera-tions.[30]

These so called "subscription schools" often led to problems between the teachers and the local inhabitants. Most of the teachers who came west to teach at subscription schools were white. Many were very dedicated to their work and provided essential instruction to their eager students. However, some of the teachers abused the system to their own advantage. Teachers compelled the pa-trons of the school to either board them, or pay for their board, and if this crite-rion was not met, they sometimes threatened to close the school and move on. Complaints abound from disenchanted parents whose children were barred of any chance of going to school because they could not afford the monthly fee. One former student reminisced that "my parents didn't have the dollar [the subscription school fee], consequently, those months I missed school." Simon Love, a freedman whose children attended a local subscription school, wrote to the secretary of the interior, telling him that the local teacher was demanding an extra two hundred dollars salary above and beyond what the government had agreed to pay him. Love inquired, "We asked for a free school and they proposed to give it to us and now we are haveing [*sic*] to pay two hundred dol-lars out of our own pocket. This is not what we calculated on having this to pay and we are not prepared to pay it. We don't wish to be swindled out of any money if we are negros [*sic*] but if it is right and just we will pay it without a word."[31]

Even subscription schools for freedmen proved contentious in the early years after the Civil War. The Cherokees, Chickasaws, and Choctaws objected to freedmen gaining access to any school, even a racially separate one. When the Cherokees passed a law authorizing the construction of a separate school exclusively "for the education of children of citizens of this nation, of African descent," the building and the local Indian agency were destroyed by fire a year later, a fire that the agent claimed was "the work of those persons who endeav-ored to stop the school last June." When a faction of the Cherokees attempted to open the Male Seminary to a Baptist freedman, Chief D. W. Bushyhead in-terceded, and it was found out later that the Indian students had procured one hundred feet of one-inch rope and had stashed it in the attic, admitting freely that they would have lynched any blacks attempting to attend their school. In the Choctaw Nation the local agent reprimanded the residents for interfering with the right of the local black inhabitants to have a school. The Indians had

30. Littlefield, *The Chickasaw Freedmen,* 112; A. Parsons to SI, R 180, Choctaw Agency, 1872–73, LR-RBIA; Frank Howard to G. W. Ingalls, R 182, Choctaw Agency, 1875, LR-RBIA.

31. Wiley Loring to SI, R 874, Union Agency, 1880, LR-RBIA; Sally Nash, interview, GFPHC, 37:444; Simon Love to SI, Indian Territory, Special Files, 1898–1907, Choctaw and Chickasaw and Cherokee Freedmen, RG 48, Box 48, RDI.

made threats of personal injury to the teacher, and interrupted services by the local preacher who supported black education. The agent related that the disruption of the church service at Boggy Depot was "simply an attempt to show a disapproval of Mr. Rogers connection with the Day School for Colored people." He wrote that the teacher was a "very worthy young man," who was in the Rebel Army all through the war. "He is a Southern white man and the charge he was a Northern Yankee could not be used against him as it might be in the case of the preacher." U.S. agents did as much as they could to discourage these acts of violence and intimidation, but they lacked sufficient force to protect adequately the rights of freedmen.[32]

However, the agitation of black parents, newspaper editors, and politicians who consistently lobbied for the freedmen to have access to schooling eventually paid off. Washington was able to use its power to coerce Indian leaders into providing education for their freedmen by threatening to withhold government rations and annuity payments made to the Five Civilized Tribes as a result of the 1866 treaties, which specified that the tribes had to adopt their freedmen as citizens. With the exception of the Chickasaws, the Five Civilized Tribes by the 1890s had grudgingly adopted their freedmen and hence allowed them the privilege of attending schools.

The emphasis of the debate then shifted from whether or not freedmen were entitled to an education to what kind of education they would receive. There was a difference of opinion between white officials and concerned humanitarians as to what sort of education was appropriate for African Americans. As with Native Americans, most reformers advocated instruction that emphasized manual labor skills. One concerned observer declared, "Manual training ought to be introduced into every school, even into the theological seminaries. I would put it into every school from the university up to the kindergarten, and I would include women as well as men, girls as well as boys."[33]

Unlike manual labor schools for Native Americans, which were designed to make Indians independent yeomen farmers, those designed for the ex-slaves of the Five Civilized Tribes emphasized unskilled physical labor to prepare blacks to work as hired labor on the farms of white and Indian landowners. Advocates of manual labor schools for the freedmen argued that blacks were only suited to pursue physical labor, lacking the intellectual capacity for more advanced learning. Some humanitarians at the time disagreed, and argued for a classical education for African American students emphasizing reading, writing, and arithmetic. The benefits and drawbacks of industrial education became a heated debate between reformers throughout America.[34]

32. G. W. Ingalls to SI, R 865, Union Agency, 1875–76, LR-RBIA; M. L. Butler, interview, GFPHC, 17:500; G. W. Ingalls to SI, R 865, Union Agency, 1875–76, LR-RBIA.

33. J. L. M. Curry, "Industrial Education for Everybody," *Independent* 52 (Feb. 8, 1900): 357–58.

34. The question of the suitability of manual labor is addressed in E. Franklin Frazier, "The Negro in the Industrial South," *Nation* 125 (July 27, 1927): 259–60.

There was also a debate over the merit of sending freedmen children to boarding schools. This debate included freedmen themselves, some of whom believed that their race, like the Indians, could use education in "morals, good habits, and manners." Like white officials, they argued that this could not be done in secular elementary schools. One preacher noted that "unless the children can be taken from the immediate influence of their parents and homes, they may get the shadow but never the substance of elevation." This was necessary in the preacher's estimation, for "as a rule, my race here are most lamentably devoid of good habits in morals and industry."[35]

The most vigorous debate over freedmen education, however, was centered on the question of separate or mixed schools. In the Seminole Nation, all the schools were racially integrated, and in the Creek Nation, most schools were. On the other hand, in the Cherokee and Choctaw Nations, segregated facilities predominated. The Chickasaws did not provide their freedmen with access to any schools. Hence tribal affiliation was the decisive factor in determining freedmen's access to education.

When freedmen finally did gain access to some of the national schools, they were still victimized by their former owners. One Native American student who attended a racially mixed school remembered that the two races "could never get along." He complained "there was always a fight and it come to where they got to stabbing each other with knives and so on." Trouble between the races finally compelled him to run off from that school.[36]

Attitudes seemed slow to change. Indians still regarded their former slaves as inferior and hence saw their education as unnecessary and a waste of public funds. To them, proof was in the fact that when the Cherokees did finally open a high school for colored citizens on January 1, 1890, it temporarily closed not long after due to a lack of attendance. The *Vinita Indian Chieftain* did admit that the reason for this was mostly that black parents could not afford to pay the high tuition fee of five dollars per month, a price that was prohibitive for most of the freedmen.[37]

Some Native Americans maintained that the two races should not be mixed, arguing that blacks were inferior and would not make good role models for Indian students. An eastern editorial criticized the bringing of Indian students to the all-black Hampton Institute proclaiming, "The Indian is the noblest of savage races. We would not break his spirit and subdue the manhood of his nature

35. Reverend G. W. Dallas to SI, R 875, Union Agency, 1880, LR-RBIA.

36. Billy Spencer, interview, T-48, 6, DDI. Not all experiments in integrating Native American and African American students were failures. Makofsky, in his study of Native American students sent to Hampton Institute, found among Native students that "the dominant note is one of respect for black students." See Makofsky, "Experience of Native Americans at a Black College," 31–46.

37. Makofsky, "Experience of Native Americans at a Black College," 42; *Vinita Indian Chieftain*, Apr. 24, 1890.

by bringing him to an alliance with no valuable quality." In fact, the founding of Carlisle Indian Industrial School had its genesis in the debate over black and Indian students attending Hampton. Richard H. Pratt, who held authority over the Native American students, decided it would be better to educate Indians apart from black students. He then petitioned the government for funds to establish a school of his own in Pennsylvania.[38]

Other Native Americans objected to racial mixing of any sort at school, arguing that Indian children should not attend school with white children either. The Chickasaws, for example, believed that the money appropriated for them by the U.S. Congress as part of its treaty obligations should be spent entirely on the education of Chickasaw tribal citizens, and that white children should not be allowed to share in the benefits. Therefore they opposed allowing white children to attend their national schools. When control over Indian education was placed in the hands of the federal government as a result of the Curtis Act of 1898, many of the full bloods of the Five Civilized Tribes were upset over the loss of control over the education of their children. Many would have agreed with the sentiment espoused by Eufaula Harjo, who argued that

> There has always been lots of schools among the Indians ever since we came here, and we were proud of our schools, and our children went to them until the white man came in and crowded us out and took our schools away from us, and it seems to me that the little white children and the little negro children should not be made to go to the Indian schools that the Indians made with their own money. . . . Now, when I take a little Indian child to school the white man and the negroes will go before me to school with their children and they will put their children first and they will push mine out of school, and that is the way it will go.

Harjo apparently did have some justification for his concern, for the *Western Age* reported that "all manner of ill treatment is said to have been used on the Indian children, especially the full bloods," by a group of twenty-five white students, who drove the group of Native American students out of a school near Coweta. The school had originally been established for Creek Indians, but after the Curtis Bill of 1898, whites had been allowed to attend. The superintendent claimed that there "has been a tendency for some time to crowd the full bloods out of white schools . . . and this will bring about trouble between the races."[39]

WHILE WHITES and Native Americans may have objected to attending mixed schools together, it must be kept in mind (and was later specified in the

38. *Richmond Times Dispatch,* Apr. 27, 1878; Robert A. Trennert Jr., *The Phoenix Indian School: Forced Assimilation in Arizona, 1891–1935* (Norman: University of Oklahoma Press, 1988), 6.

39. *Purcell Register,* Sept. 24, 1904; Debo, *And Still the Waters Run,* 71; *Langston Western Age,* Nov. 1, 1907.

state constitution passed in 1907) that the term "colored children," for the purpose of segregated facilities, was construed to mean children of African descent. The term "white children" was used to include "all other children." Hence for the purposes of segregated-school legislation, Indian children were considered to be "white." Interestingly, there was never a movement to have Indian children segregated and put into separate schools with the blacks. Segregation in the Indian and Oklahoma Territories did not imply facilities were for "whites only."[40]

The incendiary territorial debate over mixed schools, however, was not between white and Indian students but rather the fight to separate black and white students. With an ever increasing migration of both blacks and whites into Indian and Oklahoma Territories, this was bound to happen. Many of the white immigrants who settled in the territories had come from the surrounding Southern states—Texas, Arkansas, Louisiana, Mississippi, and Alabama. Hence white immigrants came to the territories with not only a firm anti-black racial attitude but also a profound faith in the necessity of racial segregation. They maintained whites were superior to blacks and therefore the races had to be separated from each other.[41]

In the early territorial days, schools were simply too few and far between to have a comprehensive segregated system. Hence in its infancy, Oklahoma Territory, like Indian Territory, had racially integrated schools. In the first few years after the opening of Oklahoma Territory in 1889, the black population was rather small and heavily concentrated in certain counties. But by the mid-1890s, African Americans began to leave the oppression of the South to seek opportunity in the frontier West. With the influx of black settlers, objections to mixed schools reached epidemic proportions among whites. Hence segregation came to Oklahoma Territory schools as a result of the fear of white settlers that if black civil rights were not curtailed, a flood of African American immigrants would inundate the new territory.

White settlers quickly demonstrated that they would use all means at their disposal to oppose integrated schools. At one school the only black student was jumped on his way back home from school after being defended against protesting white students by his white teacher. White students whipped and stoned a black student and "wrote offensive words on his blue military cape, and sent him home crying." One principal was forced to retire because he compelled several white girls attending a racially mixed school to kiss the black girls, with whom the former had quarreled. The newspaper reported the action of the principal "caused much indignation among the parents of the white pupils." One white woman remembered how the drinking water was passed in a bucket, with one

40. Oklahoma Territory Laws, art. 11, "Separate Schools of 1901," R 4, M 828, RDI.
41. Frank A. Balyeat, "Segregation in the Public Schools of Oklahoma Territory," *Chronicles of Oklahoma* 39, no. 2 (1961): 184.

tin cup for everyone to drink from. She recalled if the water was passed to the black boy before it came to her, she would not drink, so sometimes she had to go without. Another woman reminisced how her family had wanted to relocate from Catoosa to Tulsa, but when a cousin returned and notified them that white and colored children attended school together, her family stayed in Catoosa, because there were "no colored children in Catoosa at that time."[42]

In 1893 an interesting attempt at mixed education occurred in an abandoned farmhouse. The house contained two rooms separated by a hallway. The white children sat in one room and the black children sat in the other, with the teacher standing in the hallway in between. The playground supposedly had a furrow drawn in the middle of it, with each race playing on its respective side of "this unique Mason and Dixon line." One day a ball rolled over the line, and when a student crossed the line to retrieve it, a racial clash broke out. The teacher disciplined the white children, which provoked resentment from the white parents, and the next autumn there were two buildings for the two races.[43]

Such racial encounters provoked the issue of segregated schools to become a hot political debate. Newspaper editors and local politicians began a campaign to entice supporters. The separate-school question became one of the most bitterly fought issues dividing territorial Democrats and Republicans. In the early years of Oklahoma Territory, the Republican Party, true to the desires of its black constituents, opposed separate schools. The Democratic Party, as racist in Oklahoma Territory as in the South, bitterly denounced mixed schools. Republicans argued that separate schools meant greater expense, and that mixed schools would lead to a better understanding among the races. They also argued that the tide in education was in breaking down distinctions, as was evidenced in the late 1880s and early 1890s, when schools increasingly admitted students of both sexes. Republicans queried that if boys and girls could go to the same schools, why should separate schools be maintained with respect to race?[44]

However, by the mid 1890s, as members of their party became dedicated to the principle of "lily-whitism," some Republican politicians began waffling on the question, trying to persuade whites that blacks in fact agreed with the policy of separate schools and desired them themselves. One Republican paper claimed in 1897 that "ninety percent of both races, in the territory are opposed to mixed schools." Arguing that both blacks and whites recognized the need for separate schools, the editorial declared "if the present legislature is seeking to do the most unpopular act possible, it would pass a mixed school bill." The editor concluded "all alike recognize that any attempt to adopt a mixed school

42. *Ibid.*, 190; *Oklahoma Guide*, Sept. 25, 1902; Nora Eades, interview, GFPHC, 23:177; Ella Morrison, interview, GFPHC, 26:303.
43. Balyeat, "Segregation in the Public Schools," 191.
44. E. J. Giddings, "New State Negro Question Address," File 82.97, FBP.

system would work an injury to both races." The *Woodville Beacon,* a staunch Democratic paper, remained skeptical of the new conservative stance of the Republicans. The editor reminded readers that a Democrat was the author of the separate-school law of Oklahoma Territory, and that every Democrat in the legislature had voted in favor of the bill, whereas a majority of the Republicans had opposed the measure.[45]

It did not take the segregationists long to win their first victory and make the first step towards segregated educational facilities in Oklahoma Territory. Although the first territorial governor, Republican George W. Steele, personally favored integrated schools, segregationists were successful in getting Council Bill No. 2 passed by the Republican-dominated assembly on December 4, 1890. Enough Republicans broke rank and voted with the Democrats to ensure the bill's passage. The measure basically provided for "local option of segregation." Section 113 stated "it would be incumbent upon the County Commissioners to provide for and hold an election in each county of the Territory to determine if there should be separate or mixed schools." The first election was to be held on the first Tuesday of April, 1891, and every three years after that. The first separate school was established under the auspices of this law in 1892 at Kingfisher, Oklahoma Territory. In each of the counties that reported in April of 1891 and 1894 (as per the instructions of the local option law of 1891), there was a majority in favor of organizing separate schools. The minority school was to be financed by a property tax administered by the county commissioners. This created some difficulties in certain counties that had a high black population. In one county there were ten black children for every white child. The local government was by the terms of the bill bound to provide a school for the majority race (the blacks) but claimed not to have enough money to support a separate school for the whites. The whites petitioned to gerrymander the district lines so as to separate themselves from the black population, claiming if their demands were not met, they would sell out and leave the district rather than submit to having their children attend racially mixed schools. A black newspaper found the situation "absurd." This scenario was the reverse of the norm. Most districts had a much higher percentage of whites than blacks, and so in all but a few cases it was the black schools which were designated the separate schools. The problem was that the Republicans had been correct, maintaining two school systems was expensive, and consequently what usually happened was that either very poor facilities were provided for black students, or in more cases, no facilities whatsoever were provided. As late as 1894, the superintendent of education had to admit that in most districts black children "had no school privileges."[46]

45. Howard N. Rabinowitz, "Half a Loaf: The Shift from White to Black Teachers in the Negro Schools of the Urban South, 1865–1890," *Journal of Southern History* 40, no. 4 (Nov. 1974): 564–94; *El Reno News,* Feb. 19, 1897; *Woodville Beacon,* Sept. 28, 1906.

46. Tolson, *The Black Oklahomans,* 125–26; Balyeat, "Segregation in the Public Schools," 183; *Oklahoma State Capital,* Aug. 5, 1893.

The election of November 1896 saw a fusion slate of Democrats and Populists sweep the Republicans out of the legislature, and thus provided an opportunity to write a new, more strict segregation law. This law, passed in April 1897, specified that "it shall hereafter be unlawful for any white child to attend a colored school or any colored child to attend a white school." It was specified that the two schools "should" have terms of equal length and "equal facilities." Under the new law more buildings were built for black students, and school opportunities for blacks slowly improved. But still blacks living in predominantly white areas had to go to schools located well outside their own district, and some still had no school opportunities at all.[47]

Mixed schools, however, still continued to exist even into the twentieth century until the Separate School Law of 1901 strictly forbade them. The new law set the stage for the segregated-school laws which the new state would adopt in its constitution in 1907. The 1901 law declared, "In all counties separate schools for white and colored children are hereby established. . . . no white child shall attend a colored school or colored child attend a white school." Between 1890 and 1901 the tone of the laws became more rigid, changing from separate schools "may" be established in 1890, to "should" be established in 1897, to "must" be established in 1901.[48]

By the early twentieth century, the segregation of African American children from white and Indian children was evident at all levels of education. Segregated schools were set up for freedmen who were deaf, dumb, or blind. With the aid of black leaders such as Edward P. McCabe, and money from white philanthropists, the all-black town of Langston, Oklahoma, received funds to set up a university for African Americans. A Colored Normal School was also established to provide teachers for the segregated school system, as the shift in colored schools was towards employing African American teachers. From the first day of school to graduation, African American children were set apart and forced to attend schools designed for their race only.[49]

Not surprisingly, African Americans in Oklahoma Territory, like those in the Southern states, did not passively accept these actions to restrict their civil liberties. They fought back in the courtrooms and on the streets, determined that the education they received be of the same quality as that of the rest of society. The perseverance and tenacity with which some African Americans fought for their children's rights is clearly identified in historical records. A Mr. Peck was the only black man living in District No. 2 of Lincoln County, Oklahoma Territory, and his three children were refused admittance to the neighborhood school in 1891. Peck petitioned the county school board, which promptly

47. Balyeat, "Segregation in the Public Schools," 183–84, 188.
48. *Ibid.*, 189; Oklahoma Territory Laws, art. 11, "Separate Schools Law of 1901," R 4, M 828, RDI; Balyeat, "Segregation in the Public Schools," 192.
49. *Oklahoma Safeguard*, Sept. 7, 1905; Roberson, "Edward P. McCabe," 354.

voted to detach him from his own district and attach him to a neighboring district (No. 3), which had a colored school. Peck objected to his children having to attend a school so far from home. In addition, the colored school had not even been constructed at the time of his petition. An appeal to the superintendent of public instruction brought forth an acknowledgment that "the children of Mr. Peck have been deprived unlawfully of the school advantages of his district," and the teacher of the school who had denied the children admittance was fired. Similarly, another African American petitioner, John Thomas, wrote to the secretary of the interior, "One of the School Board of Dist 77 said that my children had no right to go to school with the whites. And said that they would kill them if they went there again. I writen [*sic*] to the Territorial Supt at Guthrie, OK. And he said it was all right the way they were doing. Is it law for them to keep my children out of that school house. We are U.S. citizens and has a perfect right to all school Public are we not." Thomas refused to accept the school board's decision that his children would have to attend a separate school, vowing "I will not send my children to a separate school." But an appeal to the superintendent of public instruction proved fruitless. The Superintendent responded: "It thus appears that the authorities, under the law, have agreed to furnish proper school facilities for the children of Mr. Thomas. He pointedly refuses to permit his children to attend said separate school. Mr. Thomas is in error and cannot send his children to the white school under the circumstances. We have no compulsory education law, and it is with him as to whether he will send them to the separate school especially provided for them or keep them at home."[50]

In 1895 the black citizens of Guthrie held a meeting and passed a set of resolutions setting forth the injustice of the separate-school system. They also petitioned the Territorial Assembly to repeal the segregation law. Several months later, in Perry, blacks threatened to petition the Republican territorial government to order the arrest of the members of the board of education for refusing to admit black children to the white schools.[51]

Frustrated with the lack of results forthcoming from the legal battles, African American protest became more militant. On numerous occasions African American students forced the issue by attending the local schools in direct violation of the separate-school legislation. In one district in Indian Territory where the colored school was not finished and ready for attendance the black students came to the white school. A young female teacher on her first teaching assignment faced this difficult situation with confidence and conviction. She kept the black students out of the school and instructed a couple of small white children to run to the nearest farmhouse and tell what was happening. Soon a

50. J. H. Lawhead to Frank Terry, 1891, R 1, M 828, RDI; John Thomas to SI, 1906, R 4, M 828, RDI.
51. Tolson, *The Black Oklahomans,* 126–27.

mob of white parents assembled at the schoolhouse, dissuading the black students from further action and encouraging them to await the completion of their building.[52]

Protest could become violent. In 1901 at Wilburton, Choctaw Nation, the school board had to call in the help of the local marshals. The freedmen threatened that unless satisfactory school facilities were provided, "they would force a place for their children in a white school." A party of deputies, heavily armed, went to Wilburton, and the "trouble quieted down on their arrival." In Edmond, Oklahoma Territory, a quarrel over the admission of black children into the white school district led to a fatal shooting when a white school director killed a black teacher. The director claimed that the act was self-defense.[53]

In a few cases, African American agitation was successful. In Woodville, Chickasaw Nation, blacks had petitioned the school board and brought a legal suit against the district. The case was tried in the district court and led to a decision that until arrangements were made to ensure that a separate colored school having an equal school term to that of the white school was completed, the African American children could attend the white school. Sometimes, however, these could be Pyrrhic victories. In Perry, Oklahoma Territory, when the courts ordered the school board to allow black children to attend the local white schools, the board ordered the schools discontinued. Similarly, Arapaho, Oklahoma Territory, was reported "without schools . . . as a result of the trouble about allowing negroes to attend school with white scholars."[54]

Sentiment ran so strong in the white community behind rigid enforcement of the segregation laws that even black teachers teaching in all-black schools were shunned in integrated associational meetings. In Perry, the local teachers association planned a night of entertainment. However, the six black members of the association demanded a place on the program, "which caused quite a row." Though some of the white teachers defended the right of the black members, others did not. The superintendent finally decided the show would go on but without the performance from the black teachers. A respected black professor from Langston University was asked to address the state teachers association on the topic of "Negro Education in Oklahoma." The invitation was denounced by some white members, who objected to having a black lecture a white audience. Some wanted the invitation rescinded, while others merely asked that the speaker be given a separate rostrum to speak from. The professor responded that "When I accepted the invitation it did not occur to me that my presence at the meeting for the purpose announced would be regarded by any one as a social matter." But the matter did attract wide attention, which led the embattled pro-

---

52. Balyeat, "Segregation in the Public Schools," 190–91.
53. *Beaver Journal*, Sept. 27, 1905; *Edmond Sun-Democrat*, July 10, 1896.
54. *Woodville Beacon*, Nov. 16, 1906; *Stillwater Gazette*, Jan. 2, 1896; *El Reno News*, Dec. 14, 1899.

fessor to decline his invitation. He wrote, "While I am thankful to the Executive Committee for the honor which has been conferred upon me by extending this invitation, and for the confidence which this act implies, I deem it my duty to ask that my name be removed from the program." The segregation of the races within the field of education extended from the young school child to the academic professional. In the eyes of white society they were all "just Negroes."[55]

HENCE, the educational experience of Native Americans varied according to tribal affiliation and degree of Indian blood. Many mixed-blood members of the Five Civilized Tribes embraced the opportunities afforded by Anglo-American schools. Many of these Native Americans proved more than willing to adopt Anglo-American culture, and they looked back upon their years in Indian boarding schools with fond remembrance. The education of these Indians was undertaken by white missionaries and teachers firmly entrenched in a paternalistic view of Native Americans. They viewed Indians as children, who needed the guidance of a kind but just father. These educators believed the power of education was to transform these Indian "children" into adults. One official summarized the transformation resulting from education: "The years of contact with ideas and with civilized men and Christian women so transform them that their faces shine with a wholly new light, for they have indeed 'communed with God.' They came children; they return young men and young women; yet they look younger in the face than when they came to us. The prematurely aged look of hopeless heathenism has given way to that dew of eternal youth which marks the difference between the savage and the man who lives in the thoughts of an eternal feature." In effect, supposed "paternalistic" white educators sought to annihilate Native American culture and replace it with Anglo-American culture. To a small extent, they were successful. Some mixed-blood members of the Five Civilized Tribes got jobs in towns, intermarried with whites, and became fully assimilated.[56]

Conversely, most full-blood members of the Five Civilized Tribes and the relocated Plains tribes proved unwilling to surrender ties to their unique traditions and culture. Wanting to be accepted for who they were, Native Americans found whites only wanted them when they ceased to be Indians. In approaching education from a paternalistic philosophy, white educators denied what the full-blood Indians had been seeking all along—man-to-man respect. Therefore, most full bloods proved intransigent, refusing to adopt Anglo-American culture as their own. Whites saw this as a rejection of American society and therefore as justification for the marginalization of Native peoples.

The educational experience of the freedmen of the Five Civilized Tribes was

55. *Guthrie Daily Leader*, Aug. 26, 1894; I. E. Page to Professor L. J. Abbott, Nov. 20, 1909, File 82.97, FBP.

56. Merrill E. Gates, president of Rutgers College, member of the U.S. Board of Indian Commissioners, 1885, in *RSI* 1885, 1:783.

TABLE 1
Percentage of Population Illiterate
(Population 10 Years of Age and Over, 1910)

	Total Number	Illiterate Number	Percentage
U.S. Population—Indians	188,758	85,445	45.3
Males	96,582	40,104	41.5
Females	92,176	45,341	49.2
Oklahoma Indians	48,886	12,297	25.2
Males	24,580	5,399	22.0
Females	24,306	6,898	28.4
U.S. Population—Blacks	5,812,313	1,910,820	32.9
Males	2,941,656	951,074	32.3
Females	2,870,657	959,746	33.4
U.S. Population—Mulatto	1,505,609	316,911	21.0
Males	695,730	144,926	20.8
Females	809,879	171,985	21.2
Oklahoma Blacks	73,254	14,186	19.4
Males	39,791	7,069	17.8
Females	33,463	7,117	21.3
Oklahoma Mulattoes	27,903	3,672	13.2
Males	13,895	1,733	12.5
Females	14,008	1,939	13.8
Oklahoma Whites	1,197,026	67,567	5.6
Males	648,116	35,876	5.5
Females	548,910	31,691	5.8

Sources: U.S. Bureau of the Census, Abstract of the 13th Census of the United States, 1910 (Washington, D.C.: Government Printing Office, 1910); U.S. Bureau of the Census, Indian Population of the United States, 1910 (Washington, D.C.: Government Printing Office, 1910); U.S. Bureau of the Census, Negro Population of the United States, 1790–1915 (Washington, D.C.: Government Printing Office, 1915).

also significantly influenced by tribal affiliation. The Chickasaws, for example, never did provide their freedmen with a system of schools. This had significant repercussions for the Chickasaw freedmen, as noted by historian Daniel F. Littlefield Jr.: "Except in isolated communities, where missionaries maintained schools on limited budgets, the blacks received no formal schooling, and as the decades passed, their ignorance became more costly to them. They could do little on their own to change their economic or legal status or to acquire education. More importantly, their ignorance and illiteracy made their struggle for rights in the Chickasaw Nation more difficult."[57]

57. Littlefield, The Chickasaw Freedmen, 112.

On the other hand, by the 1890s the Cherokees, Seminoles, Creeks, and Choctaws had adopted their freedmen as citizens, thereby entitling them to send their children to school. Integrated schools predominated in the Seminole Nation and were common in the Creek Nation, whereas segregated facilities were dominant in the Cherokee and Choctaw Nations. The fact that most freedmen had access to schooling had significant results. By 1910, Oklahoma, had the best rate of literacy for African Americans in a former slaveholding state, and its illiteracy rate was two-thirds the national average for African Americans. Interestingly enough, the African American illiteracy rate was below that of Native Americans because of the presence of the relocated Plains tribes in the western portion of the new state (for comparison of white, African American, and Native American illiteracy rates in Oklahoma see Table 1).[58]

The educational experience of African Americans who migrated to Oklahoma Territory also varied. In the early years, some African Americans were able to send their children to integrated schools. However, many black children were located in rural areas that did not have any schools at all. Hence, when white settlers from the South poured into Oklahoma Territory and demanded that Jim Crow laws be passed and African Americans be segregated into separate school facilities, for some blacks this was a step backward from integration; for others, it was a step forward from exclusion.

But while access to education helped give African Americans a sense of self-worth and self-respect, it did little to alter the perception of whites in territorial Oklahoma, who still regarded blacks as inferior. In fact, a year after statehood, when the legislature was debating a $10,000 appropriation for a black industrial school, two legislators stood up and announced they were opposed "to giving one cent to educate the negro" for "negro education had proven a fallacy." While admitting they would not give a cent to provide blacks with education, the two members declared they would be willing to spend money "to ship him from the country." Both members declared they would rather see an effort to repeal the Fourteenth Amendment than "worry about educating the Negro." For African Americans, their educational experience in the territories was merely another example of the "indelible mark" of their black skin.[59]

58. Bureau of the Census, *Negro Population of the United States, 1790–1915* (Washington, D.C.: Government Printing Office, 1915), Table 33, p. 231.

59. *Shawnee Daily Herald,* May 9, 1908. For most African Americans, education was not undertaken to make oneself more acceptable to white society but for its own personal reward. Ironically, segregated instruction had important positive repercussions for African Americans. Clement argues segregated schools had significant positive effects on African Americans: they taught race pride by including African Americans in the teaching of history and literature; they were training centers for black leadership, since schools were led by black teachers and principals; schools became important centers in maintaining black culture; and they were centers for independent racial thought, freed from the supervision of white leaders. See Rufus E. Clement, "The Church School as a Social Factor in Negro Life," *Journal of Negro History* 12, no. 1 (Jan. 1927): 5–12.

FIVE

Teaching the Value of Labor
Planters, Yeomen, and Entrepreneurs

IMMEDIATELY FOLLOWING the Civil War, officials in Washington concluded that the policy of the federal government with respect to the nomadic Plains tribes of the West would be to establish the tribes upon reservations in the lands of the western portion of the Indian Territory. There they would be protected and given government rations of food and provided with agricultural tools until they were taught to cultivate the soil and sustain themselves. The secretary of the interior noted in 1866 that this "is no doubt the best, if not the only, policy that can be pursued to preserve them from extinction."[1]

Officials concluded that the Plains tribes could only become civilized when they abandoned the nomadic lifestyle of the buffalo chase. As the secretary of the interior argued in 1872, "little progress could be made in the work of civilization while the Indians are suffered to roam at large over immense reservations, hunting and fishing, and making war upon neighboring tribes." He concluded that only when the Indians had been taught habits of industry and the advantages of labor could anything be done to elevate them. The secretary claimed that "Industry is the great civilizer; without it no race can be permanently benefited." Policy-makers in Washington recognized the importance of teaching Native Americans the value of labor. They hoped that the former Plains tribes would accept the Protestant work ethic as had the Five Civilized Tribes generations earlier. As one official concluded:

> When the Indian can be compelled or persuaded to give up his gun, he will be ready to devote his energies to earning a living, instead of wasting them in the chase or in raids on the frontier settlements. Give him a plow in place of his gun and a hoe in place of a tomahawk, and impress on his mind that he is now with them, in part at least, to earn his own support, and an important step has been

1. O. H. Browning, SI, in *RSI* 1866, 1:6.

taken towards his civilization; for labor has been, and ever will be, the great agent of civilization of the human race.[2]

Reformers felt that the reservation could serve as a laboratory in which the "savages" could be transformed into civilized beings under the paternal care and guidance of local Indian agents. Officials argued that the Indians had to be taught that "if they want to eat they must also work." As one official related, the government had to "extend over them a rigid reformatory discipline, to save them from falling hopelessly into the condition of pauperism and petty crime." In the absence of this policy, the official warned, "the now roving Indians will become simply vagabonds in the midst of civilization, forming little camps . . . which will be festering sores on the communities near which they are located; the men resorting for a living to basket-making and hog-stealing; the women to fortune-telling and harlotry."[3]

In Indian Territory the government provided the Indians with the essential agricultural tools, including hoes, plows, and wire to construct fences to protect their crops from damage. Local Indian agents were instructed to hire assistants whose function it was to instruct the Indians in the methods of agriculture by teaching them how to plant, till, and harvest crops. Most of the white farmers undertook their job of instructing the Indians with dedication. Some, however, did not. The report of an inspector who had visited the Otoe Agency declared, "The farmer is a gentleman who puts in his time making love to the female school employes [*sic*] and occasionally rides around the settlement. He is entirely ornamental, and unless a better man can be found for the position it had better be dispensed with."[4]

Nevertheless, it was not the white instructor's degree of dedication that caused concern among officials in Washington, but rather the lack of results from the Indians. Few agents could write to their superiors in Washington that much progress had been made in converting the nomadic tribes into settled agriculturalists. Most agents found that enticing the relocated Plains tribes to settle on a reservation and adopt an agriculturally based existence proved next to impossible. One agent wrote: "My proposed innovation on their do-nothing every-day life is opposed by the extremely conservative class, who regard a change of any kind as synonymous with an attack to subvert their people, and they are unable to see anything but ruin and anarchy among the people in the following of the plow and living in houses, or, as they express it, getting on 'the white man's road.' " Many agents explained the failure of the agricultural experiment by concluding that Indians were inherently lazy. One agent com-

2. Columbus Delano, SI, in *RSI* 1872, 1:6; Henry M. Teller, SI, in *RSI* 1882, 1:v–vi.
3. Francis Walker, CIA, to Columbus Delano, SI, in *RSI* 1872, 1:399.
4. Report of Inspector Benedict on the Otoe Agency, R 38, Ponca, Pawnee, and Otoe Agency, 1885, RIIIA.

plained, "here, as among all Indian nations, there are many improvident persons, who, saving nothing, still expect to reap; whose minds are not prompted to industry until hunger and cold harass them." The agent asked for agricultural provisions to be sent to his agency, including plows, harrows, mowers, and hoes, for "it would increase the ability of farming, and, with the naturally lazy disposition of the Indians, anything that lessens labor is acceptable." Another agent complained that Native Americans were perpetually careless with the farming implements provided them. He claimed the Indian "seems to act upon the theory that when the crop is gathered he has no further use for his ploughs, hoes, rakes, etc., and next season he finds he has no means to put in his crop."[5]

One agent concluded that Indians did not lack the desire to succeed in farming, but that they were physically unsuited to undertake the demanding task of labor intensive agriculture. The agent claimed, "I think many of them want to work, but while the spirit is willing the flesh is weak. They are easily fatigued, and easily diverted from the business at hand. They will quit the most urgent job on the slightest provocation or simply to lie in the shade." Many Indian agents felt that the periodic intensity of the chase left nomadic Indians incapable of the constant labor needed to pursue a settled agricultural existence. The commissioner of Indian affairs noted in 1872:

> Unused to manual labor, and physically disqualified for it by the habits of the chase, unprovided with tools and implements, without forethought and without self-control, singularly susceptible to evil influences, with strong animal appetites and no intellectual tastes or aspirations to hold those appetites in check, it would be to assume more than would be taken for granted of any white race under the same conditions, to expect that the wild Indians will become industrious and frugal except through a severe course of industrial instruction and exercise, under restraint.

The supposed lazy disposition and physical weakness of Indians led some agents to conclude that the race was doomed to extinction. One Osage agent concluded, "They have become a nation of idle, worthless people, and have no idea or desire to work or do anything except eat and sleep, and the older men and women have become a burden to themselves." The agent also noticed "that the children of these old full bloods are of smaller stature than their parents, of very weak constitution, and following in the footsteps of their parents soon none of the tribe will be left."[6]

5. D. B. Dyer to CIA, Aug. 9, 1884, in *RSI* 1884, 2:117; J. W. Dunn to SIA, Oct. 1866, in *RSI* 1866, 1:318; George A. Reynolds to SIA, Sept. 25, 1866, in *RSI* 1866, 1:321.
6. John W. Scott to CIA, Aug. 15, 1884, in *RSI* 1884, 2:128; Francis Walker, CIA, to SI, in *RSI* 1872, 1:399; C. C. Duncan, R 34, Osage Agency, 1896, RIIIA.

Other Indian agents and many officials and reformers in Washington explained the failure of the agricultural experiment with the nomadic tribes not as a result of any shortcomings in the abilities of the Indians, but rather upon the practice of issuing rations to reservation Indians. Critics of the rationing practice argued that the guarantee of government rations destroyed any incentive among the reservation Indians to work for their own subsistence. The Kiowa agent concluded in 1879: "Though my stay on this Agency has been brief . . . I reach the conclusion that the so-called Quaker or peace policy has been a failure here. In a pronounced progressive sense a failure. It has been to grant everything and exact nothing in return, the result of which has been to create an army of dependants content to live on the beef and flour of the Government, without any purpose in life except nomadic vagabondism, and very certainly without any desire to work for any portion of the 'daily bread' which they have received." Many governmental officials came to argue that the Indians would never advance "if the government supplies all his wants and demands nothing from him." Reformers saw a direct correlation between idleness and vice. Most would have agreed with the assertion of the secretary of the interior that the Indian "must be taught to labor and care for himself, by persuasion if possible, by compulsion if necessary." One official in Washington wondered why the government should "support the able-bodied Indian who refuses to work, any more than it should the white man who refuses to exert himself for his support." Most officials felt that the cultivation of land or the care of stock should be made a condition precedent to receiving aid from the government. As the commissioner of Indian affairs noted: "It must be apparent to the most casual observer that the system of gathering the Indians in bands or tribes on reservations and carrying to them victuals and clothes, thus relieving them of the necessity of labor, never will and never can civilize them. Labor is an essential element in producing civilization. If white men were treated as we treat the Indians the result would certainly be a race of worthless vagabonds."[7]

Many officials and Indian reformers also criticized that rations were given to the tribes who had put up the fiercest resistance to U.S. authorities. Many wondered why the government should go out of its way to provide for those who were formerly their enemies when it made no such provisions for those tribes (in particular, the Five Civilized Tribes) who had begun to adopt Anglo-American ways. As commissioner of Indian affairs Hiram Price noted in 1881, "This course induces the Indians to believe that if they are to get favors from the government they must refuse to work, refuse to be orderly and peaceable, and must commit some depradations or murder, and then a commission will be appointed to treat with them, and pay them in goods, provisions, and money to

7. Arden B. Smith to CIA, R 384, Kiowa Agency, 1879, LR-RBIA; Henry M. Teller, SI, Nov. 1, 1883, in *RSI* 1883, 1:iv; Hiram Price, CIA, Oct. 24, 1881, in *RSI* 1881, 2:1.

behave themselves." The commissioner argued that this gave the Indians the impression that the federal government rewarded its enemies and punished its friends.[8]

Not all government officials, however, disagreed with the policy of concentrating hostile tribes on reservations and providing them with government provisions. Some officials argued that it was far less expensive for the federal government to provide rations of beef and flour to hostile tribes than to engage in constant warfare with them. Advocates of government rationing claimed that the policy saved not only millions of dollars but also thousands of lives. As Commissioner of Indian Affairs Francis Walker argued in 1872: "It is not a wit more unreasonable that the Government should do so much for hostile Indians and little for friendly Indians than it is that a private citizen should, to save his life, surrender all the contents of his purse to a highwayman; while on another occasion, to a distressed and deserving applicant for charity, he would measure his contribution by his means and disposition at the time."[9]

As more and more reformers came to see the issuance of rations as the primary cause of the failure of the former Plains tribes to adopt a settled agricultural existence, it is not surprising that many lobbied officials in Washington to bring the practice to an end. Gradually, through the course of the 1880s, the issuance of government rations of beef and flour was curtailed. The commissioner of Indian affairs notified the local Osage Indian agent in 1878 that, "Their vast extent of country is susceptible of easy and renumerative [*sic*] cultivation. . . . As long as they are fed and sustained by the bounty of the Government, and by a large annual depletion of their own resources, they will not see this necessity." The Indian inspector sent to the Ponca, Pawnee, and Otoe Agencies in 1885 recommended "that there is but one thing to impress on every agent in the Indian Territory; it is, to inform the Indians under their charge that rations will cease next year. They must get their farms in order at once." The inspector queried "why not have compulsory labor, as well as school attendance? I think both should be enforced."[10]

Not all officials and reformers blamed the failure of the Plains tribes to adopt agriculture successfully on the issuance of rations. Some in fact questioned the whole decision to put the tribes on reservations and force them to become farmers. One Indian Bureau official wrote to a United States senator, questioning the wisdom of the reservation policy. He noted that "savage tribes whose wants are supplied by the chase, never of their own accord suddenly abandon their nomadic habits and become cultivators of the soil." Rather, he argued, they uniformly pass through an intermediate condition—the pastoral state. The

8. Hiram Price, CIA, Oct. 24, 1881, in *RSI* 1881, 2:2.

9. Francis Walker, CIA, to SI, in *RSI* 1872, 1:392.

10. E. A. Hayt, CIA, R 638, Osage Agency, 1878, LR-RBIA; Frank Armstrong, R 38, Ponca, Pawnee, and Otoe Agency, 1885, RIIIA.

agent concluded, "Cease trying to make them farmers; make them shepherds or herdsmen. Make their first steps easy instead of difficult."[11]

Other officials and Indian reformers realized that the Indians resented having a foreign way of life thrust upon them against their will. Many interviews conducted with former Plains tribesmen revealed a profound resentment against the government's attempt to make them farmers or ranchers, "whether we wanted to or not." Even some contemporary observers recognized the resentment of the relocated Plains tribes. One white pioneer woman remembered arriving at the Indian agency at Anadarko, where more than two thousand Indians were encamped waiting for their annuity payment and issuance of beef, flour, beans, and rice. The woman recalled, "shortly after, soap, stoves, and white man's clothing were given. The soap and stoves were thrown out on the prairie; and the clothing was ripped up and tacked on the outside of the tepee, to show his [the Indian's] utter contempt for the white man and his ways."[12]

Many Indian agents complained that the Indians under their supervision felt themselves above agricultural work. This was particularly true of the full-blood Indians. An Indian inspector reported after visiting the Osage reservation, "The full blood Osage Indians are a very aristocratic people in their way, they say they do not have to work as they have enough to keep them without work." The Osage agent wrote in his annual report of 1885, "Farming with the full blood Osages is a failure, at least with the present generation, as they look upon work as degrading and to plow and hoe only fit occupations for poor white men who have to work for a living, and they are careful to impress this idea on the minds of their children." A division occurred in each tribe between "progressives" and "traditionalists." As historian Douglas Hale states: "Within each tribe there were 'modernizers'—mixed bloods or intermarried whites for the most part—who looked beyond the old, self-sufficient tribal society to the burgeoning wealth and power of late nineteenth-century American capitalism and wanted to become a part of it. They had faith in progress, education, private property, and individual effort. Their adversaries were the 'traditionalists' who clung to familial and tribal loyalties, favored the continuation of communal property, and followed a subsistence economy with little regard for the work ethic.[13]

11. Alfred H. Terry to Hon. William R. Allison, U.S. Senator, Jan. 26, 1877, R 122, Cheyenne and Arapaho Agency, 1877, LR-RBIA.

12. Sylvester Tinker Jr., interview, File 82.22, OHP; Anna R. Fait, "Reminiscences of Anna R. Fait," CCRP.

13. James Cisney, Indian Inspector, R 34, Osage Agency, 1892, RIIIA; quoted in Finney, "Progress in the Civilization of the Osage," 7; Douglas Hale, "The People of Oklahoma: Economics and Social Change," in *Oklahoma: New Views of the Forty-sixth State,* ed. Anne H. Morgan and H. Wayne Morgan (Norman: University of Oklahoma Press, 1982), 36.

In the relocated Plains tribes, the traditionalists reigned supreme. Most of the relocated Plains tribes clung to traditional ways, retaining, as historian Danney Goble states, "a tradition-bound way of life that corresponded more closely to peasant cultures than to the aggressive rising-capitalist attitudes of nineteenth-century America. . . . In a simple, nonmonetary economy, most Indians still lived by barter, trading goods and services within their villages or with immediately neighboring groups."[14]

Culturally, agricultural work was seen by the men of the relocated Plains tribes as degrading and unmanly in comparison with the excitement and danger of the buffalo chase. Hence, many Indian men objected to being forced to do what had traditionally been considered women's work. On the other hand, white officials considered the Native American tradition of women performing heavy labor as yet another sign of the barbarism of the relocated Plains tribes. The commissioner of Indian affairs noted in 1879 that "in the past all drudgery and much of the real work devolved upon the Indian women, while they laughed at and ridiculed any man who was disposed to labor." The Cheyenne and Arapaho agent stated in 1884 that "an Indian does not entertain the idea that girls exist merely to display fine drapery and look pretty; they have a decided notion that they were born to labor." The agent notified his superiors that it would be many years before the tribesmen treated their women as anything more than slaves. According to his perceptions, "Their women possess no will of their own, and would not be able to exercise it even if they did. They are sold at the age of twelve or fourteen years to the man who will give the most for them, and at once become his slave. They suffer beatings and general abuse, do nearly all the work, and enjoy (?) the affections of their liege lord frequently with several other wives."[15]

A very small minority of Indian reformers did not blame the supposed inherent laziness of Indians, or the issuance of government rations, or the stubborn pride of the nomadic tribes for the failure of the Plains Indians to adopt a settled agricultural life. One contemporary commentator argued that white officials had not given the relocated Plains tribes a fair chance at becoming successful agriculturalists because they had located them on reservations in the semi-arid regions of western Indian Territory, which doomed them to failure from the very start. George Bird Grinnell stated: "The Indian has every capacity for work—for he possesses strength, endurance and industry. If he can be convinced that his exertions will receive an adequate recompense, he is—at the present day—as willing to work as he was ready to toil at his hunting or to undergo the manifold hardships of the war-path. The old-time fashion of insisting that he should plow and sow in the midst of the waterless desert cast a blight,

14. Goble, *Progressive Oklahoma,* 45.

15. E. A. Hayt, CIA, to SI, Nov. 1, 1879, in *RSI* 1879, p. 75; D. B. Dyer to CIA, Aug. 9, 1884, in *RSI* 1884, 2:117.

on the Indian's industry, since it implanted firmly in his mind the conviction that for him work was useless, because work in the white man's ways brought him no return."[16]

While undoubtedly each of the factors mentioned so far played a part in the failure of the Plains tribes to adopt successfully a settled agricultural existence, yet another factor was probably the most important of all. White officials simply refused to recognize the differences between Native American tribes—to them, they were all just Indians. The Cheyenne and Arapaho agent perceptively noted in a letter to the headquarters of the Indian Bureau in Missouri in 1877:

> It appears to me, as it has seemed for many years, that the mistake made in the effort to interest the Indians in agricultural pursuits has arisen from the errone-ous idea that all Indian tribes are precisely alike, and that the Indian, wherever found, is precisely the same creature in habits, in ideas, and in modes of life. The Indians in different portions of this country are no more like each other in any of those respects than are the whites in various parts of Europe or this coun-try. They can no more be made to engage, as a whole, in agricultural pursuits than as a whole, the white people could be made to do so.
>
> . . . I think the failure to accomplish results at all commensurate with the labor and expense incurred in the attempt to make the Indian self-supporting, or more peaceable in his habits, is due largely to a want of due consideration of the diversities of character among the Indian tribes.[17]

It may at first seem perplexing to explain why in the face of such resistance and failure, the federal government did not abandon its effort to make the relo-cated Plains tribes into independent yeomen farmers. There are two important factors which must be kept in mind. First, the late nineteenth century saw "Darwinian"-based racial theories become pre-eminent. Racial theorists of the time posited that races developed along a continuum from primitive hunter-gatherers to settled agriculturalists and finally to urban industrialists. Each stage was considered necessary in the evolution of a race. Therefore, most govern-mental officials and Indian reformers felt it was crucial that the Plains Indians continue to advance along this racial continuum one step at a time, so that ulti-mately they could be assimilated into Anglo-American society. Second, and perhaps most important, to those who claimed that Indians were inherently unsuited to the constant physical demands of farm labor, defenders of the res-ervation policy had only to point to the success of the Five Civilized Tribes as agriculturalists.[18]

16. Undated newspaper clipping, Box 2, Indians, TAP.
17. Cheyenne and Arapaho Agent [to Headquarters of the Indian Bureau], R 122, Cheyenne and Arapaho Agency, 1877, LR-RBIA.
18. Thomas G. Dyer, *Theodore Roosevelt and the Idea of Race* (Baton Rouge: Louisiana State University Press, 1980).

Despite the pessimism of many government officials, agriculture thrived in the nations of the Five Civilized Tribes after the Civil War. In 1880, the Five Civilized Tribes in the Indian Territory had 314,398 acres under cultivation. They raised 2,346,042 bushels of corn, 336,424 bushels of wheat, 124,568 bushels of oats and barley, and 595,000 bushels of vegetables. In addition, they cut 124,000 tons of hay and harvested 16,800 bales of cotton. As early as 1872, Indian agents were encouraging members of the Five Civilized Tribes to cultivate cash crops such as cotton. The Cherokee agent wrote to his superior: "The culture of cotton has been commenced in the southern part of the nation with very encouraging success. There are a few large cotton-growers, but most of it is being grown by small farmers. This season there is a prospect of very fine cotton crops. This will bring money into the country, as no other crop will. I look at the continued culture of cotton as a source of permanent prosperity to the people." In the 1900 report of the Census Bureau regarding the Five Civilized Tribes, the official sent to the Chickasaw Nation noted that "Cotton is the staple of the Chickasaw Nation. For over a quarter of a century the Chickasaws had cultivated small cotton patches, demonstrating the value of their lands for the culture of that staple. Before the war their slaves toiled in the cotton fields and raised cotton, a bale and more to the acre, and of excellent quality." After the completion of the railroad through the nation and the influx of white settlers, the agent reported, "the production of cotton enormously increased. The nation now produces about 40,000 bales of cotton annually."[19]

The emphasis in the Indian nations of the Five Civilized Tribes upon cash crops tended to increase social stratification within the tribes, as some tribesmen gathered vast acreages of land. In the report of the Census Bureau on the Five Civilized Tribes, the official sent to the Cherokee Nation reported that "The intelligent, active, and thrifty have opened large farms on a southern-plantation style, the only thing 'in common' between them and others of the population being the title to the land, and of this the big farmer has had the sole benefit, often holding thousands of acres of the choicest lands." On the other hand, the official noted, "his co[-]tenants worked at moderate wages or existed in cabins on little patches of land in the hills too thriftless to contend in the race of life with more energetic neighbors." Many Indian Bureau officials complained that the ownership of lands in common in conjunction with the practice of plantation-style agriculture created "an aristocracy out of a few wealthy and powerful leaders, while the poor, although equal owners, are so impoverished as not to be able to assert their equal rights of property and manhood." By the mid-1890s, sixty-one Creeks held a third of

19. Carl Schurz, SI, Nov. 1, 1880, in *RSI* 1880, p. 5; John B. Jones to SI, Sept. 20, 1872, in *RSI* 1873, 1:573; Bureau of the Census, *The Five Civilized Tribes of Indian Territory* (Washington, D.C.: Government Printing Office, 1890), 54.

the territory of their nation, while twenty-three Cherokees controlled 174,000 acres. One wealthy Choctaw held 17,600 acres under fence. The commissioner of Indian affairs noted the discrepancy in wealth between Native American plantation owners and landless laborers, stating in 1886 that "In theory the lands are held in common under the tribal relation, and are equally owned by each member of the tribe, but in point of fact they are simply held in the grasping hand of moneyed monopolists and powerful and influential leaders and politicians, who pay no rental to the other members of the tribe, who, under their tribal ownership in common, have equal rights with the occupants." However, the labor of fellow tribesmen was not enough to support the huge demand that resulted from the significance of cash crops to the economies of the Five Indian Nations.[20]

Before the Civil War, large-scale cotton production in the Five Indian Nations had depended upon slave labor, just as it had done in the southern states. Thus after emancipation, Native Americans who owned large plantations faced the same predicament as plantation-owning white southerners. Not surprisingly, they came up with the same answer. Indians, like southern whites, sought to encourage the freedmen to remain on the lands of their former masters as free laborers. The federal government, as it did in the South, also supported the maintenance of black laborers tilling the fields of their former owners. When reports came to Washington that Native Americans were refusing to acknowledge that slavery had come to an end, a representative was sent from the Freedmen's Bureau. Brevet Major General John B. Sanborn impressed upon the Indians that slavery could no longer exist. He soon noticed the great demand for black labor among Indian plantation owners. On April 16, 1866, Sanborn concluded, "The rights of the freedmen are acknowledged by all; fair compensation for labor is paid; a fair proportion of crops to be raised on the old plantations is allowed; labor for freedmen to perform is abundant, and nearly all are self-supporting." Consequently, Sanborn's services were withdrawn from the Indian Territory.[21]

As in the South, the emancipation of African American slaves in the Indian Territory profoundly affected both slave and master. One Native American woman recalled the experience of freeing her slaves. She stated:

> In a few days, the Government notified us that our negroes were free. We did not know they were free until a government courier brought us word after the war was over. My husband called the negroes around him and told them they were free, that they were no more his. The negroes were surprised, said nothing

20. Perdue, *Slavery and Cherokee Society;* Bureau of the Census, *The Five Civilized Tribes,* 42–43; J. D. C. Atkins, CIA, to SI, Sept. 28, 1886, in *RSI* 1886, 1:86; Hale, "The People of Oklahoma," 36; J. D. C. Atkins, CIA, to SI, Sept. 28, 1886, in *RSI* 1886, 1:82–84.

21. Brevet Major General John B. Sanborn to CIA, April 13, 1866, in *RSI* 1866, p. 287.

but stood and looked at him in awe. At last, the old negro Soloman said: "Marster, what must we do?" My husband said: "you have got to think and do for yourselves now." Poor darkeys, they knew not what to do. . . . The Federals had possession of Ft. Smith and were sending out runners through the country making negroes believe that everything was paved with gold; so a lot of young negroes in our neighborhood banded together, anxious to get among the people that had freed them, thinking that they would have nothing to do but dress in fine linen and bask in glory. Two of my flock made a break. . . . I left them on the place; and when I left them, we had a big, big cry. People who have never owned negroes don't know how owners felt toward them."[22]

Like the ex-slaves in the southern states, many freedmen in the territory adopted different approaches in the immediate aftermath of slavery. Some, like those mentioned above, left their former masters to demonstrate their newfound freedom. Others however, like many southern blacks, elected to stay with their former masters to work on their lands as wage laborers. One Native American wrote to his absent father in January of 1866 that his former slaves had remained loyal to him despite a more financially lucrative offer from a nearby white landowner. The son wrote: "They have gone to work in good earnest, and we are looking daily for more hands. Soloman deserves praise and credit for his course since you left. He told the negroes in a public speech that he had more confidence in his old master in doing him justice than he had in all Yankee promises and other white men. They refused to have anything to do with Ballard. They said they were Indian negroes, freed by Indians, not Yankees and were a part of the Indian tribe and had nothing to do with white people."[23]

Many freedmen elected to stay with their former masters not out of loyalty but out of necessity. In the immediate aftermath of the Civil War, as mentioned previously, only the Seminole tribe immediately adopted their freedmen and gave them equal rights. The other tribes refused to adopt them as full members of the tribe, so therefore they were not entitled to any land held by the tribe. Lacking any land or the provisions necessary to remove elsewhere, most freedmen chose to stay the first few years and work for their former owners. As in the South, the system which came to predominate the agricultural sector of the Indian Territory economy immediately after the Civil War was share wages.[24]

As in the southern states, in the immediate aftermath of the Civil War, Indian governments passed a series of laws designed to regulate the conditions of labor. A standard scale of wages was fixed for eight classes of laborers, including children, with wages ranging from two dollars to ten dollars a month plus food

22. Sarah Harlan, interview, GFPHC, 28:75–80.
23. Son [name unknown] to Peter Pitchlynn, Jan. 9, 1866, Box 4, File 44, PPP.
24. [Unknown] to SI, R 177, Choctaw Agency, 1867–68, LR-RBIA.

and shelter. The laborers worked ten-hour days in summer and nine hours in winter, with Saturday afternoon and Sundays as holidays except during busy periods. The former masters were required to continue support of the aged, crippled, and infirm whom they had held as slaves. In some ways these laws were similar to the Black Codes passed in the southern states. The laws allowed freedmen to make labor contracts with their former owners (in which case the owners were considered the guardians of the freedmen in such contracts) or they could choose to make a contract with any other employer they so chose. The freedman was required to give the owner a specified portion of his crop. In return, the owner was required to clothe, provide medical care, and furnish dwellings for the freedmen. The laws set the dates for payment of wages, as well as the hours and days of labor. Like the southern Black Codes, the laws declared vagrancy to be a punishable crime.[25]

After a few years the system of share wages was replaced, as in the southern states, with share renting. Under the share renting arrangement, the freedman agreed to perform labor for the landholder and provide him with anywhere from one-quarter to one-half of his crop. In return, the landholder provided the tenant with a certain number of acres of land to cultivate and usually had to provide him with farm tools and occasionally with some mules or horses.

Not all Native Americans wished to exploit the labor of their former slaves after emancipation. Some wanted them immediately expelled from their nation. The Chickasaws attempted to have their freedmen removed from the territory and settled elsewhere. Many of the Chickasaws threatened freedmen who would not leave with violence. One Chickasaw freedman remembered:

Panola this county has a great many Freedmen in it before the war and after the war the said emancipated colored people were oblige to leave Panola county for Chickasaws who had farmly held them in slavely was about to kill their old negroes all the said Chickasaws that lived in that county were halfbreed Indians generally then the said freedmans emigrated from Panola County in to Pontotoc County just in order to save their own lives their old owners was so cruel to the said freedmans in fall of 1865 and early in the years of 1866 there was not one freedmans could be found in limit of Panola this is the reason the freedmans numbers like they do in the said Pontotoc county.

The Chickasaws were so harsh with their former slaves that many moved out of the nation into a more congenial atmosphere among the Choctaws or Creeks.[26]

25. M. Thomas Bailey, *Reconstruction in Indian Territory: A Story of Avarice, Discrimination, and Opportunism* (Port Washington: Kennikat Press, 1972), 150; Littlefield, *The Chickasaw Freedmen*, 31.

26. Littlefield, *The Chickasaw Freedmen*, 31; D. H. Grayson, Secretary of the Chickasaw Freedmen Convention, April 1886, Indian Territory, Special Files, Choctaw and Chickasaw and Cherokee Freedmen, 1898–1907, RG 48, Box 48, RDI.

The Choctaws, Cherokees, and Creeks eventually adopted their freedmen, which gave them entitlement to tribal lands of their own. Not surprisingly, the freedmen quickly withdrew their labor from Native American landholders to concentrate on cultivating their own fields. Hence, recognizing that the labor of their former slaves would no longer suffice to support the agricultural economy of the Indian nations, the Five Civilized Tribes came to argue that the savior of the economy would have to come from the labor of landless whites. Each of the Five Civilized Tribes passed laws which allowed white farmers to obtain permits to enter Indian Territory to work as sharecroppers on Indian land. The allure of free virgin land proved irresistible to many whites in the surrounding states, and each of the Five Civilized Tribes was flooded with applications for permits.

The federal government initially had some qualms about this policy, feeling that only the lowest order of whites would be willing to labor under Indian overlords and that these people would not be ideal agents of civilization. As the commissioner of Indian affairs noted in 1874:

> Since the emancipation of their slaves, these Indians have sought exemption from labor by inviting emigration of the lowest whites from the surrounding States, to whom they rent their lands for one-third of the crops raised. These whites, once in the country, are seldom known to leave, and thus their numbers are rapidly increasing; the result will be a mixing of the lowest white blood with the Indian, thus propagating instead of curing the indolence and unthrift with which they are already cursed, and from which they can be delivered only by the example and competition of industrious and enterprising white neighbors.[27]

To ease the concerns of federal officials as well as their own concerns, the Indian governments required each applicant for a permit to provide a recommendation of his good character. In 1880, the Quapaw agent received, in conjunction with a permit application from G. W. Bowman, a sworn affadavit, stating, "we the undersigned citizens of Seneca, Missouri, would respectfully represent that G. W. Bowman has lived among us, and we recommend him as an industrious, honest, hardworking man, and one who will make an effort to live strictly within the requirements of the terms of his contract, also strictly a sober man." In addition, in an effort to ensure that the applicants would not be destitute whites, the Five Tribes required that the white settlers buy permits that would allow them to settle among the Indians. The permit initially cost $25 for every male non-citizen over the age of eighteen, but was later reduced to $5. Those whites found living in the Indian nations without a permit were considered intruders and were subject to removal by federal authorities.[28]

27. Edward P. Smith, CIA, to SI, Nov. 1, 1874, in *RSI* 1874, p. 381.
28. National Records of the Quapaw Agency, Microfilm QA 16, OHS; Littlefield, *The Chickasaw Freedmen*, 44.

Permits, however, did little to discourage white settlers from entering the Indian nations as tenant farmers. One agent noted in 1879 that in the Indian Territory, "a system of renting has been carried on for some time, for several years, until most farming is done by white people, and the country presents very much the appearance of a white man's country." Another agent noted the presence of about 12,000 whites under permits from the Indian authorities as tenants or farm laborers for Indians; about 2,000 licensed traders, railroad employees, and employees of the government; and several thousand sojourners, comprising migrants, visitors, pleasure-seekers, and so forth. In addition to these, the agent reported, there were several thousand intruders, making in all a white population of about 90,000.[29]

It was not long before Indian tribes other than the Five Civilized Tribes petitioned the government to be allowed to hire white farm labor. One Osage man wrote the commissioner of Indian affairs:

> What we the Osages want is to alow us the same privliges that our neighbours the Cherokees Creeks Choctaws Chickasaws have, they can hire white men to help them work in there farmes and leas land and rent farmes by that means they are a prospers people if the genl government wants are wishes the Osages to do well the government must alow us a free privlege. The government has declard the United States with all its territorys free all we ask is for government to stand up to there constatution and alow us Osages some freedom as a people.

Another Osage man wrote the commissioner of Indian Affairs claiming he had a wife and seven children to support but he only had thirty acres under cultivation. The man wanted to break another sixty acres of prairie land into cultivation but could not do so, he argued, "unless I can get white labor." The man said, "I want to know whether I can lease or rent my land to a white man with a family or not, in other words I want to know whether I can get a permit from you or any one else to put a white family on my farm to help me and cultivate the same?"[30]

Whites seemed only too anxious to employ themselves under contract to Indian landholders. Many whites agreed to enter into contracts with Native American landholders in order to secure grazing lands for their cattle, although this practice was supposed to be illegal. The Quapaw agent described the effect of whites entering Indian lands on permits in a report to his superior in Washington. He stated, "They are allowed to bring heads of stock into and graze it upon the Indian lands, in some cases that is the prime object the cultivation of

29. J. M. Haworth, to CIA, Aug. 27, 1879, in *RSI* 1879, p. 184; Jonathan Tufts to CIA, Sept. 1, 1882, in *RSI* 1882, 2:147.

30. J. W. P. Mathes to CIA, R 639, Osage Agency, 1878, LR-RBIA; Frank Lessert to CIA, R 641, Osage Agency, 1880, LR-RBIA.

the soil being entirely secondary by such an arrangement they escape the heavy taxes of the new states paying to the Indian but a small consideration for the great privileges enjoyed with markets as handy as their tax paying neighbors of the adjoining states." Another Indian remembered how the Cherokees used to circumvent the laws against grazing. Stock grazing in the Cherokee Nation was operated on a fee basis. The owner of the cattle paid 50 cents per head per year for his pasturage concession. This fee went to the Cherokee citizen who supposedly maintained control of the range around this location. To circumvent the law against grazing leases, the Cherokee citizen ostensibly always "owned" the cattle he was merely grazing for another party. In many instances, however, and to make this practice appear more genuine, the Indian granting the pasture right was employed by the true owner of the cattle to assist in range riding and attending the cattle the agreement covered. This practice proved very lucrative for Cherokees who indulged in it.[31]

BY THE LATE 1870s and early 1880's, many governmental officials and concerned Indian reformers came to question the wisdom of allowing whites to reside among the Indian tribes, for it seemed to many that the presence of white laborers contributed to the "inherent laziness of the Indians." The Quapaw agent concluded that the presence of white farmers among the Indians, "instead of having been an advantage, it has encouraged idleness and dependence among the Indians." The federal government announced plans in 1879 to prohibit white renters from working Indian farmland. This policy evoked an outpouring of wrath from the local Indian tribes that had come to depend upon leasing their lands to white farmers. One Quapaw tribesman wondered, "why should the department curtail our liberties by an order which cuts us off from renting our surplus lands precisely in the same manner, and on the same terms, as whites have an undoubted right to do in the states? Why are we classed with the wild Indian, just as though we were incapable of managing our domestic affairs for our own profit and advantage? And why should the useful and law abiding white renter be prohibited from profitting [*sic*] by the advantages we offer him?" The chief of the Miami tribe wrote President Rutherford B. Hayes:

> For the past two years we have by yearly permits allowed white persons to aid us to cultivate our lands and to their experience, example, advice, honesty, and industry we owe all the knowledge which we possess of farming and other industrial pursuits and our advanced state of civilization. If our tribes by so doing would have become dependent and idle they would by this time have been demoralized beyond redemption. On the contrary the practice of granting yearly

31. J. M. Haworth to CIA, R 708, Quapaw Agency, 1879, LR-RBIA; W. L. Allen, interview, GFPHC, 12:283–85.

permits to honest, industrious white persons has increased the area of our arable and tillable land redoubled our energies increased our prosperity enhanced and improved our lands and has attained for us that degree of civilization which is the true policy of the government to have us achieve.

The mayor of the city of Fort Smith, Arkansas, also wrote President Hayes on behalf of the neighboring Miami and Peoria tribes. The mayor claimed he was "satisfied that if the class of white persons which they have permitted to occupy their lands to aid them in their cultivation are removed from their reservations that it will entail great suffering and hardship upon these tribes and will eventually end in their extermination." The mayor, therefore, recommended "that their request for a modification of the order of the Interior Department requiring the removal of all white persons from their reservations be granted and said order so modified as to said tribes as to permit white persons of good moral character under permission from the chiefs of said tribes to reside in said tribes."[32]

In the face of such opposition, government efforts to stem the tide of white immigration into the Indian lands under the permit system abated. Much to the delight of large Indian landholders, the government turned its concentration upon keeping illegal intruders from squatting on Indian lands. By 1900, most of the wealthy Native American landholders had estates worked by white farmers. Chief Porter of the Creek tribe, for example, had over 100 white men employed upon his 4,000-acre ranch. In fact, by 1900, the number of white tenant farmers actually quadrupled the Native American population of the Indian Territory.[33]

WHILE INDIAN landholders became increasingly involved with white tenant farmers, they became less involved with their former freedmen. Whereas in the immediate years after the Civil War, most large farms in the Indian Territory were worked by ex-slaves, by the 1880s and 1890s, most Indian landholders relied upon the labor of white tenants. The freedmen in the Indian Territory fought hard to escape the peonage blacks faced in the Deep South states. To a large extent they were successful. Part of their success can be accounted for by the decision of the Dawes Commission in 1894 to include the freedmen on its rolls in dividing up Indian lands. According to the provisions of the Curtis Act in 1898, each freedman received title to a parcel of land. As a result, many black farm tenants became farm owners. Also, many blacks who immigrated to Oklahoma Territory after it was opened to settlement were able to purchase their

32. J. M. Haworth to CIA, Aug. 27, 1879, in *RSI* 1879, p. 184; Moses Tooler to SI, R 710, Quapaw Agency, 1879, LR-RBIA; David Geboe to President Rutherford Hayes, R 707, Quapaw Agency, 1878, LR-RBIA; James Bonzzolara to President Rutherford Hayes, R 707, Quapaw Agency, 1878, LR-RBIA.

33. *El Reno News,* July 4, 1901; Baird, " 'Real' Indians in Oklahoma?" 9.

own land. By 1900, three-quarters of black farmers in the territories owned their own land. In fact, because of the inclusion of the freedmen in the division of tribal lands, by 1900, a greater proportion of African Americans owned their own farms than did whites residing in the two territories. Of the 13,225 African American farmers listed in the 1900 census, 9,944 owned their own farms (75.2 percent), while only 2,467 were share tenants working the farms of other landowners (18.7 percent). In contrast, of the 94,775 white farmers in the 1900 census, only 43,675 owned their own farms (46.1 percent). Of the rest, 30,880 were share tenants working the farms of other landowners (32.6 percent). In terms of access to landowning, Indian and Oklahoma Territories were indeed a promised land for blacks.[34]

But African Americans did not achieve their landholdings only through the charity of others. To a large extent blacks in Oklahoma Territory banded together and used their economic and political power to better their position. As elsewhere in America at this time, African Americans were dedicated to the principle of racial self-help. Black leaders in Oklahoma Territory appealed to African Americans to buy land and become independent farmers. One black newspaper wrote "The fundamental industry, especially for a race of primitive culture, such as the colored race is now, is agriculture. It contains the promise of complete independence. The thrifty colored man who owns forty acres and a mule is nobody's servant. He is infinitely freer than the white factory hand or clerk. He can bring up his children in the healthiest possible conditions. The only limit to his advancement is in himself." Black newspapers in Oklahoma Territory attempted to convince their readers that African Americans held power because they controlled a valuable resource—their labor, which was highly coveted in the territorial economy. The *Langston City Herald* proclaimed that "The Negro is the bone and sinew of this country and is succeeding as none others [*sic*] can. Were it not for his great brawny arm, earnest toil and fertile brain there would today be despondence and despair in the business air of even the capital city of the west—Guthrie. Yes, bankruptcy, failure, and a general dropping out of the bottom. But the negro is on the market with the product of his labor and the money begins to move, jingle and liven." African Americans were encouraged to use this power to their own advantage.[35]

While many territorial editors advocated the independence provided by farming, many African Americans also became involved in the industrialization of the territories. Mining became a relatively important sector in the economy of the Indian Territory on the eve of statehood. While most mines preferred to hire white immigrant workers, African Americans were often used as replacement workers during the numerous labor disputes of the late nineteenth century. As early as 1894, the Choctaw Coal and Railway Company paid off its

34. Bureau of the Census, *Negro Population of the United States, 1790–1915,* Table 56.
35. *Western World,* Feb. 4, 1905; *Langston City Herald,* Sept. 28, 1895.

striking miners and brought in three hundred African American miners to re-place the white workers. In 1899, the *Krebs Eagle* reported, "two carloads of colored miners were received at the Missouri, Kansas, & Texas Railway Company's mines at Coalgate last Saturday to take the place of striking miners. Sixteen Deputy Marshals accompanied the blacks to do guard duty." In reference to the same incident, the *Cleveland County Leader* stated, "Because these white men demand a small share of the enormous profits of the mining company, because the Negroes can and will live on the price of a drink and enough to enter a crap game at night, the Shylocks have turned the white men and their families down and live with black gamblers and wrecks." The superintendent of mines for the Five Civilized Tribes was concerned that the use of black "scab labor" might lead to violence. He wrote the local inspector of Indian affairs, stating:

> The strike situation at this place is arriving at the crucial stage when the strikers see that they are defeated and having expended their money and credit are liable to get hungry. They attribute their defeat to the negro miners and are extremely bitter, and at their meeting it was openly talked that the only thing left for them to do was to start a race war, and I know that there are some characters amongst the strikers who are sufficiently desperate men to carry out any program of that kind that may be laid out for them. It may come through a deliberately planed [*sic*] attack to make a raid through the darky quarters some night or what is much more liable, it may start from a personal altercation between a white and a negro.[36]

Not surprisingly, most white trade unions held African Americans in disdain because of the frequency with which they performed "scab labor." The feeling was mutual. Most of the leading black newspapers encouraged African Americans to avoid joining unions. One black editorialist noted:

> If there is any one thing that operates against the success of the Negro, it is that of trade union. We have been of the opinion that it is better for the Negro to keep out of unions. In the majority of instances where he is allowed to join at all, he is simply used as a tool to further the interest of the designing white men. I know of many cases where Negroes have been permitted to join the union and then are kept out of work by the union white men. The only excuse given is, that there is no vacant place; and the poor man who is a member, but whose skin is black, must tramp from town to town looking for work, but not daring to work if non-union men are working on the job. It would be far better in our

36. *Guthrie Daily Leader*, Apr. 22, 1894; *Krebs Eagle*, July 7, 1899; *Cleveland County Leader*, June 24, 1899; Edwin Ludlow to U.S. Indian Inspector, Apr. 12, 1899, in SFCTR, vol. II, pp. 163–64, OHS.

opinion for the Negro to join hands with the capitalist. He would receive fair treatment, good wages and never be without a job when there is anything to do.

The same paper argued a month later that "if the Negro is wise he will shun these unions as he would the deadly cobra. They are a menace to his progress and the goal of success. Keep out of all unions of the designing white man if you wish success." The paper noted that at the annual Labor Day parade, "there were only two colored men to be seen." The paper concluded this was appropriate because "organized labor is as a rule against the colored man."[37]

Organized labor unions were not the only problems for territorial African Americans in the labor market. Many black farm laborers found themselves physically threatened by whites who saw African Americans as cheap competitors for work on local farms. White laborers oftentimes saw themselves undercut by blacks who were willing to work for lower wages. In Greer County, Oklahoma Territory, after several carloads of African Americans were imported from Texas to pick cotton, a movement was started "to ostracize any farmer or other person in the county who hires negro help." Similarly, in Lincoln County, Oklahoma Territory, groups of masked whites entered the homes of African American farm laborers and whipped them in an effort to force them to leave the county. As the *Daily Oklahoman* proclaimed: "It is the object of these gangs, so it is alleged, to run the negroes out of the country so that they will not be rivals on the farm and in the workshops in Cleveland and Pottawatomie counties, where most of these outrages are going on. Cotton is the principle product, and negroes are experts in cotton fields, and get the best of white labor. The towns of Tecumseh and Norman, containing 2,000 inhabitants each, have not a colored inhabitant. All of them have been run out by secret hands."[38]

In response, African American leaders in Oklahoma Territory asked blacks to band together to protect their rights. They also encouraged blacks to unite and develop their own businesses. Many white businesses during the 1890s began to draw the color line, refusing to serve black customers. Some black newspaper editors, however, believed African Americans should forget protesting against hotels, saloons, and theaters that drew the color line, and instead build their own businesses, which would cater to an all-black clientele. The *Langston City Herald* criticized African Americans for complaining about segregated facilities rather than using segregation as an opportunity to develop all-black businesses. An editorial in 1893 said: "Our people are always growling, bringing suits and fighting about their being refused at the first class hotels, barbershops, restaurants, theaters, saloons, and riding in first class cars. Now if

37. *Muskogee Cimeter,* July 14, Aug. 8, Sept. 15, 1904.
38. *Beaver Journal,* Aug. 16, 1906; *Daily Oklahoman,* Jan. 6, 1897.

they want a free access to all these things, knowing that the white man will never make concession, why in the mischief don't they put their minds and their money together and build them?"[39]

Some African American leaders called upon blacks to boycott white businesses and to support black businesses out of deference to racial solidarity, in line with the self-help philosophy of Booker T. Washington. One editorial advised African American readers that "There is no excuse for the negro's failure to patronize his own race. The average Negro will walk a mile out of his way to buy an article from a white man at five cents less before he will take it from his race. . . . If the Negro would patronize his own race as the white does his, we could establish ample facilities to handle everything needed by the colored trade."[40]

To a certain extent blacks in both Indian and Oklahoma Territories, particularly in the all-black towns, did attempt to create their own infrastructure of businesses to serve the needs of their community. In some of the larger towns, such as Oklahoma City, Guthrie, and Tulsa, a group of black professionals arose to service the needs of the black community. The black sections of Oklahoma City had black dentists, doctors, preachers, and lawyers. In 1904, one African American editor produced figures that showed that the two territories had 332 black professionals, 806 blacks involved in trade and transportation, and 1,227 blacks employed in manufacturing enterprises. More and more, black workers were found in new places and capacities, as they moved into occupations normally thought to be "white jobs."[41]

Part of the success of black entrepreneurs in the territories relates to the availability of capital from African American banks. The all-black town of Boley, Indian Territory boasted a bank of its own, which loaned money to local businessmen. In many of the black towns, the local banker was considered the most prominent member of society. As early as the 1890s, many African American businessmen and professionals had savings of $200 to $1,000 in bank accounts. By 1891, one Guthrie bank held over $15,000 in black accounts.[42]

The black community in the territories even had some rags-to-riches stories of their own. One Cherokee freedman named Zack Foreman was illiterate but managed to amass a great personal fortune. In true Horatio Alger style, Foreman went to work as a small boy to support his widowed mother

39. Mellinger, "Discrimination and Statehood," 340–77; *Langston City Herald*, June 13, 1893.

40. Washington, "Boley," 28–31; *Langston Western Age*, May 24, 1907.

41. See Crockett, *The Black Towns*; Kenneth M. Hamilton, *Black Towns and Profit: Promotion and Development in the Trans-Appalachian West, 1877–1915* (Urbana: University of Illinois Press, 1991); Edna Slaughter, interview, File 397, OHP; Goble, *Progressive Oklahoma*, 138.

42. Goble, *Progressive Oklahoma*, 137.

after his father died. He worked as a laborer on farms and ranches, receiving between fifty cents and a dollar a day. On one of the farms he was working, a cow that had been sold broke its leg. The cow could not be transported to its new owner's ranch in No Man's Land, so the owner gave the injured cow to Foreman. The cow recovered and gave birth to a heifer. Foreman invested all the money he earned from his farm labor into purchasing more cattle. By the time he reached adulthood, he possessed an entire herd. Eventually, he became the wealthiest cattleman in the Cherokee Nation. When the railroad bypassed Foreman's ranch, he met with officials from the Kansas City Southern about letting him have a railroad offshoot. They agreed to lay the steel if Foreman would make the roadbed. He enlisted the support of local freedmen to whom he had loaned money. Those who owed him repaid their debts by working on the railroad. They graded it with teams and scrapers and laid the ties, and the railroad company put the rails down for him. One settler remembered that through hard work and determination, Foreman had become the "only Negro in the United States at that time who privately owned a railroad." It was this type of entrepreneurialism that black editors hoped to encourage in their readership. Many black editors promoted such success stories to encourage the idea that African Americans did not need the help of whites to prosper.[43]

HENCE, government officials in Washington faced the dilemma of reconstructing the economy of the Indian Territory in the wake of the dislocation of the Civil War and the emancipation of African American slaves. As in the former Confederate states, the federal government sought to maintain the economic and social status quo in the Indian Territory. Governmental officials were convinced that the future of both Native Americans and their former slaves lay in cultivating the land. Reformers hoped that by relocating the former nomadic Plains tribes onto reservations in the western regions of the Indian Territory, they would adopt the settled agricultural lifestyle of the white pioneer as the Five Civilized Tribes had done decades earlier. Isolated from white intrusion, the reservation was to serve as a laboratory wherein the Indians would learn to plant crops, till fields, and harvest nature's bounty. The ultimate goal of the federal government was to transform the former Plains tribes from nomadic hunters who followed the roam of the buffalo to independent, self-sufficient yeomen farmers. Reformers argued that once this transformation had occurred, the assimilation process could ensue. However, little progress was made in changing the former nomadic Plains tribes into independent yeomen farmers. Few of the relocated Plains tribes proved adept at farming. Many of the tribes became indigent, relying upon the issuance of government rations of beef and flour to survive. As a result, many government officials became disillu-

43. J. J. Cape, interview, GFPHC, 88:56–58.

sioned with the civilization effort aimed at assimilating Native Americans into Anglo-America. Some felt the lack of results forthcoming from the relocated Plains tribes justified the marginalization of those Indians.[44]

On the other hand, the Five Civilized Tribes experienced an economic boom after the Civil War. White observers took tremendous pride in the example set forth by the Cherokees, Chickasaws, Choctaws, Creeks, and Seminoles in establishing successful, agriculturally based economies. Relying upon first the labor of their former slaves, and later, the labor of white immigrants, the Five Tribes developed a sophisticated capitalist economy despite the maintenance of communal land tenure. To many governmental officials and concerned reformers, the economic success of the Five Civilized Tribes served as a glimmer of hope amidst a sea of darkness.

While federal officials and concerned humanitarians hoped to create a class of independent yeoman farmers among the Indians, they had a different view of the proper role to be ascribed to the freedmen in the territorial economy. The freedmen were expected to provide a pool of cheap labor which white and Indian landowners could draw upon. In the eyes of officials in Washington, the ex-slaves were to be farm laborers, not necessarily farm owners. In the aftermath of the Civil War, governmental officials sought to encourage former slaves of the Five Civilized Tribes to remain on the farms and plantations of their former owners as free laborers. They were encouraged to work the fields of their former masters providing the Indian landholder with a percentage of their crop, just as the ex-slaves in the southern states did. However, governmental officials were to be disappointed. The freedmen refused to accept such a circumscribed role in the economic realm of the Indian Territory. After years of petitioning Native American and white officials, the former slaves of the Five Civilized Tribes were finally given land grants under the provisions of the Curtis Act of 1898. By statehood, nearly three-fourths of the blacks engaged in farming owned their own land. Unlike the former slaves in the South, the freedmen of the Five Civilized Tribes finally received their "forty acres and a mule."[45]

Had white politicians and reformers been ideologically consistent, they would have applauded the Horatio Alger–like achievements of ex-slaves like Zack Foreman as the very embodiment of the American Dream. However, while white politicians and reformers hailed the pioneering spirit of white settlers who became independent farmers and politically active citizens, and sought to inculcate these civic responsibilities in Native Americans, they found themselves uncomfortable when blacks came to challenge whites within the economic, political, and social realms. As historian Danney Goble concludes,

44. Columbus Delano, SI, in *RSI* 1872, p. 6.
45. Goble, *Progressive Oklahoma*, 137.

"It was, in fact, because some Oklahoma Negroes were so 'progressive,' so forward-looking, prosperous, urban, and vigorous that they represented such a great threat." In the eyes of many white Americans, the lessons in the value of hard work, cooperation, and thrift they had hoped to instill in the minds of the relocated Plains tribes had been learned all too well by African Americans.[46]

46. *Ibid.*, 376–77.

A typical minstrel show advertisement

Reprinted from *Mangum Star,* August 23, 1906. Courtesy Newspaper Department, Archives Division, Oklahoma Historical Society

The Cherokee Outlet Land Run, ten seconds after the gun, September 16, 1893
Courtesy of the Archives Division, Oklahoma Historical Society

"A typical group of Oklahoma Indian girl students," read the caption for this photograph, which appeared in the *Indian School Journal.*

From the Fred Barde Collection. Courtesy of the Archives Division, Oklahoma Historical Society

Clara Peck (left), upon entering Chilocco Indian School
Courtesy of the Archives Division, Oklahoma Historical Society

Clara Peck (front row, middle) as she appeared after spending several years at Chilocco Indian School
Courtesy of the Archives Division, Oklahoma Historical Society

Pleasant Grove Freedman School with white teacher, Clarksville, Creek Nation, 1900
Courtesy of the Archives Division, Oklahoma Historical Society

Racially integrated school in the Seminole Nation, 1890
Courtesy of the Archives Division, Oklahoma Historical Society

Choctaw Indian justice in action. This freedman is being given one hundred lashes for stealing cattle.
Courtesy of the Archives Division, Oklahoma Historical Society

Seminole lighthorsemen
Courtesy of the Archives Division, Oklahoma Historical Society

Cheyenne and Arapaho scouts from Fort Reno, assigned to keep intruders out of Indian Territory, 1889
Courtesy of the Archives Division, Oklahoma Historical Society

Sandbar Saloon on the South Canadian River between Purcell,
Indian Territory, and Lexington, Oklahoma Territory

Democratic newspaper cartoon depicting the result of
political equality

Democratic newspaper cartoon depicting the consequences of Republican rule. The caption reads: "The democracy favors laws providing for separate schools, separate coaches and separate waiting rooms for the negro race. The democratic party will lift the Indian and white race to a plane above that to which it has fallen under republican rule."

From the *Mangum Star,* August 30, 1906. Courtesy Newspaper Department, Archives Division, Oklahoma Historical Society

SIX

The Imposition of Anglo-American Justice
The Search for Order

A S INDEPENDENT NATIONS, the Five Tribes before the Civil War held complete control over the administration of justice in their respective lands. Each of the nations, except the Seminoles, had a judicial system with local and supreme courts. In many ways the Native American justice system mirrored the law of the United States. For example, a written criminal code existed which specified illegal acts; the accused was entitled to a trial by jury; and property was protected from theft and damage by a code of civil law. However, in significant ways, the Indian justice system also reflected ancient tribal customs and beliefs. The Seminoles, in particular, placed an emphasis upon the town and clan as legal bodies with the power to enforce codes of conduct. In addition, Native American justice was retributive. Traditionally, if a man stole from another, he was expected to return or replace the goods taken. If a man killed another, the clan of the slain man avenged his death by killing either the murderer or one of the murderer's kinsmen. Indian courts punished offenders with fines, public whippings, or for serious offenses, death by shooting or hanging. There was no concept of rehabilitation, hence, there were few jails or prisons in the Indian nations. In many important ways, then, Native American justice differed from the legal system of Anglo-Americans.[1]

After the Civil War, the Native American justice system came under attack from former slaves of the Indians and from white settlers living in the Indian nations. The ex-slaves contended that they were not treated fairly by Indian courts. Freedmen complained that the prejudice of Native Americans towards them precluded them from getting a fair trial when charged with a criminal offense. One Chickasaw freedman commented that, "Now the collard people here stands a dredfull poor show of haveing any justice done them in or by the courts of the Chickasaws." J. J. Moore, a freedman preacher at the Fort Coffee

---

1. Debo, *And Still the Waters Run*, 10; Foreman, *The Five Civilized Tribes,* 213–14; Perdue, *Nations Remembered,* 19, 41; Debo, *And Still the Waters Run,* 10; Perdue, *Nations Remembered,* 41.

Church, claimed, "we do not want to live under Indian laws we live under that law before the rebeluen and we find no pertection in the Indian laws for the colard." One Cherokee freedman protested to the Principal Chief of the tribe that he had been convicted of murder but had not been allowed a lawyer to represent him or to present any witnesses in his defense. Dick Glass, a notorious black outlaw who had been in hiding for five years evading capture, wrote to the commissioner of Indian affairs and pleaded with him to intercede and guarantee him a fair trial, which he deemed would not be forthcoming from Cherokee authorities. Glass argued, "I know that I could not get a fair trial in the Cherokee Nation. The authorities would be powerless to protect me or to prevent violence or the intimidation of my witnesses. The trial would be a farce surely ending in my death." One settler remembered that most punishments imposed by Indian courts were a specified number of lashes at a public whipping post. The whipping of an Indian criminal raised little public attention, but if the criminal was a freedman, all the town would gather around close and "howl with glee as the negro twisted and screamed."[2]

The issue of Native American control over justice, however, did not gain prominence because of the concerns of the ex-slaves of the Five Civilized Tribes. It became a heated debate because white governmental officials and reformers believed that Indians had to be subjected to Anglo-American law in order to be civilized. Up until the 1880s, no crimes committed by Indians upon other Indians or their property were punishable by the federal government, regardless of where the crimes were committed. Indians could kill one another with complete immunity from any punishment from the federal courts. On the other hand, Indian courts had no jurisdictional power over white fugitives from the United States. Moreover, they held no jurisdiction over any Indian who committed a crime against, or in conjunction with, a white, for these crimes automatically fell under the jurisdiction of the United States court. As the commissioner of Indian affairs noted, "There is at this time no semblance of authority for the punishment of any crime which one Indian may commit against another. . . . so far as the law is concerned, complete anarchy exists in Indian affairs." Officials noted that whenever thirty thousand or more white men moved to and settled in any part of the West, the settlers could petition to be granted territorial status, and the United States extended over them its laws. In effect, American settlers who ventured west across the Plains took the American Constitution with them. Reformers therefore argued that "it can be neither a hardship nor an injustice to the tribes in the Indian Territory . . . to place

2. Thomas Randolph to SI, Indian Territory, Special Files, 1898–1907, Choctaw and Chickasaw and Cherokee Freedmen, RG 48, Box 48, RDI; J. J. Moore to SI, Indian Territory, Special Files, 1898–1907, Choctaw and Chickasaw and Cherokee Freedmen, RG 48, Box 48, RDI; "Colored citizen of the Cherokee Nation" to Samuel Checote, Microfilm CHN 81, NRCN; Burton, *Black, Red and Deadly*, 21; Hiram Impson, Box I, HIP.

them on a par with white men before the law." An eastern editor pointed out what he thought a strange dichotomy: "As the case stands now, the Indian has no legal protection whatever, and in this respect his case is peculiar and exceptional. A foreigner who comes here from Europe or Japan or China or the Isles of the Sea, no matter how ignorant or debased, can command the protection of the laws of the land for his safety and the security of his possessions; but the Indians, who are natives of the soil, cannot." The editor argued that the Indians should have the same justice as the white man, concluding "the law which is good enough for Massachusetts and Rhode Island is good enough for Ponca Land and Nebraska."[3]

As early as 1873, the commissioner of Indian affairs, Edward P. Smith, had recommended to the secretary of the interior that it might be practical to invest magisterial powers in Indian agents and superintendents of Indian affairs located on the western reservations. This was necessary, he argued, because the relocated tribes, unlike the Five Civilized Tribes, had no formalized constitutional system of justice of their own. By giving agents magisterial powers, they could summon a jury among the Indians or other local persons, before whom any serious offense against law and order would be tried. As well, he recommended that the local agents be given discretionary powers in dealing with offenses of a minor nature. The United States government did move to give local Indian agents on the western reservations discretionary powers over minor cases in the 1870s and 1880s. But as one of the local agents complained, "this is all right, but up to the present time there has never been any power here sufficiently strong to enforce it." This was a common complaint among Indian agents. The secretary of the interior stated that "there is no law enforcing obedience to the injunctions or compliance with the requirements of an agent, and hence he is to a great extent powerless unless aided by military authority." Agents argued that the only means of enforcing their disciplinary decisions was to have the force of the military at their disposal. Few found the government willing to commit troops to back up the agents.[4]

The question of jurisdiction over Indian crimes reached a crisis in 1883, when the Brulé Sioux chief, Crow Dog, was sentenced to death by the territorial court of Dakota for murdering a rival chief. In the case of *ex parte Crow Dog*, decided on December 17, 1883, the United States Supreme Court ordered the immediate release of Crow Dog on the grounds that the United States had no jurisdiction over crimes committed by one Indian against another. This decision caused great consternation among Indian reformers. As a

3. Finney, "Progress in the Civilization of the Osage," 3; Francis P. Prucha, *American Indian Policy in Crisis: Christian Reformers and the Indian, 1865–1900* (Norman: University of Oklahoma Press, 1976), 330; J. Q. Smith, CIA, to SI, Oct. 30, 1876, in *RSI* 1876, p. 390; *Boston Daily Advertiser*, July 29, 1879.

4. Edward P. Smith, CIA, to SI, Nov. 1, 1873, in *RSI* 1873, p. 373; Columbus Delano, SI, Oct. 31, 1874, in *RSI* 1874, p. viii.

result, after much debate, on March 3, 1885, Congress passed a law extending United States' jurisdiction over criminal offenses involving all Indians except members of the Five Civilized Tribes, who had their own judicial system (the law limited jurisdiction to seven major crimes—murder, manslaughter, rape, assault with intent to kill, arson, burglery, and larceny).[5]

After the passage of the Curtis Act in 1898, the United States Courts in the Indian Territory were granted exclusive jurisdiction over all criminal and civil cases, regardless of the race of the individuals involved. Hence members of the Five Civilized Tribes were now under the jurisdiction of United States courts.[6]

After 1898, Native Americans in Indian Territory had to make many adjustments to live under the Anglo-American justice system. One of the hardest was to accept a justice system which made no allowance for honor and integrity. Under Native American justice, offenders were given a trial and their sentence pronounced. The guilty party was then released and told to return on a certain day to receive his punishment. With the exception of the Cherokees, the Indian nations did not even maintain any jails or prisons to house suspects or convicted felons. Without exception Indians always appeared to suffer their punishment, even if the sentence pronounced was the death penalty. It was a show of honor to meet your punishment with dignity, and if a Native American had dared to break this tradition he and his family would have been disgraced in his tribe, and the tribe would have sought to punish him in the most degrading way possible. So when Anglo-American justice replaced Indian courts in 1898, the Anglo-American traditions of arrest and incarceration affronted Native Americans' sense of dignity and honor. They resented the refusal of whites to recognize the Indian honor code.[7]

White settlers also faced problems during the jurisdictional squabbles between United States authorities and Indian leaders. Throughout the territorial era, whites who resided in the Indian nations under permits were, of course, not citizens of those nations. Hence they did not fall under the protection of the Indian courts. Yet they could not be allowed to act with impunity, so in 1871, the United States determined that white citizens residing in the Indian nations were to fall within the jurisdiction of the United States Western Court District and that a new headquarters would be constructed as close to the border of Indian Territory as possible—Fort Smith, Arkansas, as it turned out. This created a serious impediment for white settlers to pursue civil suits and for law enforcement agents who had to transport prisoners. The secretary of the interior noted that the necessity of resorting to a court in an adjoining state "involves a burden of expense to litigants as well as to our Government which operates as almost a bar to justice," and "produces a condition of anarchy

---

5. Prucha, *Documents,* 162; Prucha, *American Indian Policy,* 334.
6. Burton, *Black, Red and Deadly,* 154.
7. Lee Mark, interview, GFPHC, 34:63–64; Robert Short, interview, File 726, OHP.

throughout the Territory under which life and property are in jeopardy." The long-distance travel involved was time consuming and expensive. As one agent declared:

> The chief defect in the administration of law at Fort Smith has been the great distances necessary for witnesses to travel who live in the remoter parts of this district. It is as much a punishment on the witness as it is on the accused, almost; for, owing to the pressure of business of the court, he has probably to make three or four trips, 150 miles each way, across the country, and thus go some 900 or 1,200 miles on horseback to tell what he knows about a horse-thief. This is very expensive, and people would rather let crimes go unreported than endure the loss incident to prosecution.

By 1890, a federal district court was established in Muskogee, Indian Territory, reducing the travel required to access a United States court.[8]

In addition, white settlers complained of racial difficulties of their own in the administration of justice in the territories. Territorial law specified that juries were to be open to members of all races. Few whites ever complained about having Indians sit in judgment of their actions, but many whites did object to having African American jurors control their fate after the federal government was given jurisdiction in 1898 over all judicial cases. In a case where a white man had repeatedly cursed a black man and was charged with disturbing the peace, the local constable created a furor by calling nine blacks as potential jurors. The white defense counselor objected, but when his legal number of challenges was exhausted, two black men were appointed to the jury. The white members of the jury objected vehemently to having to serve with blacks. So did the local community when word was received. They bemoaned that if juries are to be "padded with negroes, a white man will be unable to obtain justice in the courts." The white citizens also promised "reprisals will be made on the negro race as a consequence." Whites claimed it was humiliating enough that blacks should be allowed to serve as jurors, but they refused to accept that black jurors should be allowed in cases involving white defendants; this they claimed "was a menace to justice."[9]

THUS IT WAS THAT the transition from Native American justice to the Anglo-American legal system put a strain on whites, Native Americans, and African Americans alike. With Indian governments and federal authorities squabbling with each other over jurisdiction until 1898, and with judicial bodies often lacking the means to enforce their decisions, punishment of criminal be-

8. Burton, *Black, Red and Deadly*, 3; Columbus Delano, SI, Oct. 31, 1873, in *RSI* 1873, p. x; Robert L. Owen to CIA, Sept. 20, 1886, in *RSI* 1886, p. 375.
9. *Vinita Indian Chieftain*, Sept. 12, 1901.

havior was far from being a certainty. The task of bringing law and order to this untamed land fell upon a remarkably racially diverse set of law enforcement agents. Whites, Native Americans and African Americans all took part in enforcing frontier justice.

Officials in Washington and Indian reformers back east contended that for the Indians to accept the Anglo-American justice system they needed an active role in it. One of the earliest forms of law enforcement in the Indian nations was the "Lighthorse Police." The lighthorsemen were a Native American mounted police force dedicated to enforcing law and order in the Indian nations. They were paid and supervised by the independent Indian governments, and they acted as their law enforcement agents, bringing criminals before the Indian courts. But when U.S. courts gained exclusive jurisdiction over all civil and criminal cases after January 1, 1898, the lighthorsemen were disbanded. The Seminole lighthorsemen continued to serve for a few extra years, but by statehood the only law enforcement officers in the territories were the U.S. Marshals, their deputies, and municipal and county law officers.[10]

On the western reservations of the Indian Territory, Indian agents employed an Indian police force of their own, paid by the federal government and acting in conjunction with the local Indian agency. White officials felt that the Indian police force could be a great civilizing agent. The commissioner of Indian affairs foresaw numerous benefits from the western reservation Indian police force; he stated:

> But no less important than the police services rendered is the moral influence which this institution is apt to exercise upon the tribes among which it is active. It impresses the minds of the Indians with the authority of law; it discontinues and discourages their traditional practice of taking personal revenge for injuries received; it imbues them with a sense of duty and individual responsibility; it accustoms a considerable number of young men among them to a moral discipline formerly unknown to them; it inspires them with the pride of good conduct, as only men of exemplary habits are kept in the police force, it being the rule that every one of them who renders himself guilty of any transgression affecting his character is immediately discharged; it strengthens the authority of the government as against that of the chiefs by the active support of the Indians themselves, and thus prepares them for the dissolution of their tribal relations and their incorporation in the great body of the American people.

To ensure that they served as civilizing agents, the Indian policeman was allowed to have only one wife, and his appearance was to reflect "his commitment to the civilization program." Hence the policeman was asked to "give up

10. See William T. Hagan, *Indian Police and Judges: Experiments in Acculturation and Control* (New Haven: Yale University Press, 1966); Burton, *Black, Red and Deadly,* 154.

his long braids, cease painting his face, trade mocassins for boots, and eschew any other outward manifestations of the blanket Indian."[11]

The duties of the Indian reservation police were varied. Policemen acted as guards at annuity payments and rendered assistance in preserving order during the issuance of rations, protecting agency buildings and property; they acted as truant officers, returning recalcitrant pupils to school; they searched for and returned stolen property, whether belonging to Indians or whites; they aided in preventing depredations on timber and the introduction of whiskey on the reservations; they helped arrest and drive off whiskey-sellers and horse and cattle thieves; they made arrests for disorderly conduct, drunkenness, wife-beating, theft, and other offenses, turning over more serious criminals to civil authorities; they served as couriers and messengers; they acted as census takers, informing the local agent of births and deaths in the tribes; they notified the agent of the arrival of strangers on the reservation, be they Indian or white; and finally, they acted as protection for the parties sent to survey lots for white settlement. In minor cases, Indian police, due to the long distances involved in transporting criminals to courts, often acted as policemen, judges, and jurors.[12]

The popularity of the Indian police with white officials continued to grow throughout the territorial era. By 1880, two-thirds of the Indian agencies in Oklahoma Territory had Indian police, and by 1890 almost every agency had some Indian policemen—a total of 70 officers and 700 privates.[13]

While the Indian police of the western reservations in Oklahoma Territory got almost universal praise from white officials, they got decidedly negative reviews from their own people. Most of the old tribal leaders scorned the Indian police, seeing them as agents of the whites. Part of the problem arose from the fact that some of the official duties of the Indian police were to enforce agricultural work assignments and school attendance, oppose the influence of medicine men, and prohibit popular activities like dancing, gambling, and raiding horses. Not surprisingly, these actions aroused the ire of the old tribal leaders, who resented any accommodation with Anglo-American culture. In fact, sometimes the Indian police found it difficult to receive fair justice if the jury was composed of "conservatives." One Indian police lieutenant who had killed a suspect in a gun battle and had pleaded self-defense was convicted of manslaughter by a "conservative"-packed jury.[14]

Despite resentment from some of their fellow tribesmen many Native Americans were attracted to the lifestyle of the Indian policeman. The attraction was not financial, for the Indian police were very poorly paid (officers re-

11. Edward P. Smith, CIA, to SI, Nov. 1, 1874, in *RSI* 1874, p. 321; Hagan, *Indian Police and Judges,* 69–70.

12. Carl Schurz, SI, Nov. 1, 1880, in *RSI* 1880, 10–11.

13. Hagan, *Indian Police and Judges,* 42–43.

14. *Ibid.,* 70; Burton, *Black, Red and Deadly,* 153.

ceived eight dollars per month, privates five dollars). There were, however, opportunities to make money on the side. A policeman might receive extra rations for his family if he was stationed on a reservation where Indians drew rations. He might get some expense money from a private citizen or from the tribal council for a special effort on their behalf. And finally, many agents were provided duty schedules which allowed them to act as guards for coal-mining companies or as special agents for the railroads. But even given these fringe benefits, being an Indian policeman was not lucrative. Most of the Indians were attracted to Indian police service not for the money but because they saw this as a way in which they could help smooth the transition of Native American society into Anglo-America. What is striking when looking at the composition of the Indian police is that almost to a man, the policemen were dedicated "progressives" or those who sought ultimate integration into white society. They sought to use their power and prestige to encourage other Indians to adopt Anglo-American culture.[15]

By most accounts the "experiment" with Indian police was an unqualified success. They performed a valuable contribution in maintaining law and order in the frontier and they served as an important linkage between Indian society and the ever expanding white America.

Not only were Native Americans active in local police units, many served as scouts and auxiliaries for the United States Army. Indian scouts performed various functions in the army: they acted as messengers carrying messages from post to post, utilizing their knowledge of the terrain; they helped to guard the paymaster during ration and annuity distribution; they helped search for outlaws and deserters; and perhaps most importantly, helped to trail hostile Indian bands and arrest their leaders. Native American auxiliaries engaged in battle against tribes deemed hostile to the United States. Some of the most savage warfare in the territories was between Indian army auxiliaries and hostile tribes. Needless to say, this placed Indian army scouts and auxiliaries in a very awkward position. Among Native Americans they were universally despised even more than were Indian policemen for accepting Anglo-American culture.[16]

Many Indian scouts and auxiliaries joined the army because it was a way to maintain their traditional hostilities against certain enemy tribes. In fact, almost all the Indians who joined the U.S. Army did not do so for the pay, but for the chance to relive the life of the warrior. As historian Wilbur S. Nye surmises, "It furnished them a means of gaining prestige. . . . The Indians, like other nationalities, needed something to be proud of. The older Indians, the members of

15. Hagan, *Indian Police and Judges,* 43, 69–70.

16. See Thomas Dunlay, *Wolves for the Blue Soldiers: Indian Scouts and Auxiliaries with the United States Army, 1860–90* (Lincoln: University of Nebraska Press, 1982); Wilbur S. Nye, *Carbine and Lance: The Story of Old Fort Sill* (Norman: University of Oklahoma Press, 1942), 261–62.

the passing generation, had their war exploits to talk about. But the rising generation, being forced to become farmers, had little to look forward to, and no way in which to distinguish themselves. Agriculture is an honorable and ancient profession, and at times a profitable one. But not for the Indians." The army scouts and auxiliaries were able to capture a lifestyle lost to many of their generation: camping outdoors; riding horses; and trailing outlaws, bootleggers, or intruders for days or even weeks across the barren lands of the territories. For many Native American men the thrill of army life replaced the thrill of the hunt. At the same time, many of the Indians who volunteered to become scouts and auxiliaries for the United States Army were looking ahead, not backward. Like the Indian policemen, many Native Americans saw army life as a transitional phase in the assimilation process. As historian Thomas Dunlay notes, "The army gave many Indian men their first real introduction to the culture that would soon dominate their lives. By providing them with a mode of assimilation congenial to their inclinations, their talents, and their self-respect, scouting may have made that introduction a good deal less painful than any planned by either humanitarians or exterminationists."[17]

Many white army officers praised their Indian scouts and auxiliaries. They found the Indian troops had excellent marksmanship, were well disciplined, and were proud of the uniform. Many white officers marveled at the diligence and patience with which an Indian scout approached picking up the trail of an outlaw or intruder. Other officers, however, "regarded all Indians as cowards whose only skill was in running away." While the officer corps remained divided in sentiment over the value of Indian troops, the federal government remained dedicated to the experiment of using Indians in the army.[18]

However, some reformers and local Indian agents felt military service for Native Americans was harmful. They argued that military service tended to perpetuate the warrior psychology from which they sought to raise the Indians. The warrior continued to be glorified, and received material rewards for his efforts besides. This situation, reformers argued, worked against the desired reeducation toward agriculture, individual accumulation of property, and conversion to Christianity.[19]

Not only were Native Americans active in frontier duty for the U.S. Army, so too were a number of African Americans. Ever since the Civil War, black troops had been a controversial part of the military. Segregated into their own units under white officers, and paid less than their white counterparts, black troops suffered from discrimination in many forms. The frontier experience of black troops was no different. First, black troops were given the most undesirable jobs available. Most of the back-breaking manual labor tasks were assigned

17. Nye, *Carbine and Lance*, 261–62, 198.
18. *Ibid.*, 199.
19. Dunlay, *Wolves for the Blue Soldiers*, 217.

to the black troops. One black company left Fort Supply in 1881 and was assigned the task of constructing a telegraph line to Fort Dodge, Kansas. They were required to cut a thousand cedar poles by hand, then dig the holes for the poles, and finally string the telegraph wire. All this had to be done in the blazing heat of the Indian Territory. Many other troops were given escort duty for stages, trains, cattle herds, railroad crews, and surveying parties. Black troops patrolled roads and opened new ones, mapped vast areas of country, and pinpointed the location of water to sustain incoming settlers.[20]

Black troops were often placed in charge of the manual labor involved in constructing the forts. Fort Sill, for example, was constructed almost exclusively by the work of black troops in conjunction with white artisans. The black troops cut the limestone out of a local quarry and transported it to the fort site. Crude kilns were made where the lime was burned for cement and plaster. Other troops were assigned to transport sand from the bed of the Cache Creek to the fort. Both were heavy, tiresome jobs.[21]

Black troops carried out some of the most dangerous tasks in frontier service. For instance, they often had the task of responding to inter-tribal conflict, especially between the relocated Plains tribes and the Five Civilized Tribes. In fact, contact between Native Americans and African American soldiers was so common that the Indians gave the nickname "buffalo soldiers" to African American troops. Though the strict origin of the term is uncertain, the common interpretation is that the Indian saw a similarity between the hair of the buffalo and that of the black soldier. Since the buffalo was a sacred animal to Native Americans, the nickname was a sign of respect. African Americans recognized this and accepted the nickname with pride. In fact, a buffalo was the most prominent feature of the regimental crest of the all-black 10th Cavalry.[22]

The buffalo soldiers were often assigned to remove boomers—those white settlers who attempted to illegally enter the Indian lands and establish homesteads while the land was still supposed to be reserved exclusively for the use of the Native tribes—from the as yet unopened Indian land. This created tremendous resentment from the white squatters. Many times fistfights broke out between the white settlers and the black soldiers ordered to remove them. On several occasions boomers and black troops drew weapons upon each other.

20. See Arlen L. Fowler, *The Black Infantry in the West, 1869–1891* (Westport: Greenwood Press, 1971), and William H. Leckie, *The Buffalo Soldiers: A Narrative of the Negro Cavalry in the West* (Norman: University of Oklahoma Press, 1967); Fowler, *The Black Infantry*, 75; Leckie, *The Buffalo Soldiers*, 259.

21. Nye, *Carbine and Lance*, 105.

22. Jimmie Lewis Franklin, *Journey toward Hope: A History of Blacks in Oklahoma* (Norman: University of Oklahoma Press, 1982), 30; Leckie, *The Buffalo Soldiers*, 25–26. Charles A. Eastman in *From the Deep Woods to Civilization* argues that the Indians called the black soldiers by that name because of the buffalo robes and muskrat hats they wore in winter. Daniel F. Littlefield Jr., personal communication with author.

Typically the arrival of more troops (usually white) ended the standoff peacefully.[23]

Racial hostility and prejudice towards black soldiers did not abate when the government opened surplus Indian lands (Oklahoma Territory) to white settlement in 1889. When small towns began to proliferate, so too did racism. White civilians objected to seeing African Americans in a blue uniform. The local presses constantly criticized the capabilities of black soldiers. White newspapers claimed black soldiers were lazy, drunken, poorly disciplined, and often abusive to white townspeople, thinking they could not be punished because of their position. The reality was far different. In fact, black troops had unusually low rates of alcoholism and desertion, which were the two major problems of the army in the late nineteenth century. The 24th Infantry, a black regiment, had the lowest desertion rate of any regiment in the army during the years 1880–1886. Other regiments which shared the same posts had desertion rates twenty to fifty times those of the 24th.[24]

The black troops suffered racist treatment not only from the press and local white populace but from their own colleagues and superior officers, too. When temporary barracks had been completed at Fort Sill, the quarters were given to the cavalry troops, which included two black regiments. It was justified, superior officers said, because the cavalry troops had been in the field since the Civil War, whereas the infantry troops had lived mostly in barracks. Nevertheless, some of the infantry men objected on racial grounds, arguing that white troops should not be quartered outside while black troops enjoyed the comforts of the barracks. Another battle occurred between white officers and the black troops over a strange topic, the preservation of laundresses on base. Each troop of cavalry or company of infantry was allowed four laundresses, who received government rations and were paid for washing the men's clothing by fixed amounts deducted at the pay table. The current archivist at Fort Sill, Towana Spivey, maintains that the laundresses were poor white immigrant girls who acted as prostitutes. White officers petitioned to clean up the base and have these girls removed. Interestingly enough, the military courts decided not to remove the girls, rationalizing that the girls provided "care and service particularly necessary for the colored troops."[25]

In addition to the racism of their colleagues and superior officers, black troops had to contend with poor-quality equipment. The guns provided black troops were usually out of date and often malfunctioned when put to use in the line of duty. The horses provided the black troops were also of the poorest quality. As historian William Leckie concludes, the accomplished record of the

23. Rister, *Land Hunger*, 148–51.
24. Leckie, *The Buffalo Soldiers*, 259–60; Fowler, *The Black Infantry*, 137, 78–79.
25. Nye, *Carbine and Lance*, 120, 281; Towana Spivey (archivist for Fort Sill), interview by author, Fort Sill, Okla.

buffalo soldiers was all the more impressive because it was generally built on "second-rate equipment and the worst horse-flesh in the army."[26]

Part of the reason for the success of black troops and particularly their low rate of desertion related to the lack of opportunities for blacks elsewhere in frontier society. The thirteen dollars a month pay may have been meager for a white settler, but it was more than most African Americans could expect to earn as civilians, and when food, clothing, and shelter were added, many found a better life in the army than they could elsewhere.[27]

Up until recent times black troops received little recognition for their years of frontier service. Denied equality by their colleagues and superior officers, they were overlooked by generations of historians who wrote on the military in the West. But the truth is that several regiments of black troops served with dignity and honor in the frontier West.

The same could be said of the many African Americans who "wore the silver star" as deputy U.S. Marshals. For many generations it was assumed that the enforcers of law and order on the frontier were all white marshals. The truth is that quite a few African Americans served as federal law officers, and their contribution to the maintenance of law and order in the West was as significant as that of the buffalo soldiers. The black deputies performed all the usual duties required of federal law officers, and many did so with courage and distinction. Moreover, many of them were former slaves and thus lacked any formal education. One illiterate black deputy marshal used to ask witnesses or accused prisoners to read their subpoena, but if they were illiterate also, then he "read" it to them from memory. Taken as a whole the black deputy marshals were an exemplary group; none of them was ever discharged or reprimanded for their conduct on the job.[28]

The black deputy marshals ironically owed their position to Native American attitude towards whites. Some white marshals were known to abuse the fee system wherein marshals were paid by the number of prisoners they brought before the courts. Many Native Americans complained they were arrested on trumped-up charges for the remuneration fee secured for delivering the prisoner. As a result, Indians in the interior developed a deep distrust of white lawmen. Hence they preferred to have black law officers. As well, many of the black deputies were freedmen who had lived all their lives among the Indians and understood their culture. As historians Daniel F. Littlefield Jr. and Lonnie Underhill state, "In effect, then, these men were a part of the country in which

26. Leckie, *The Buffalo Soldiers*, 259.

27. *Ibid.*, 9.

28. Daniel F. Littlefield, Jr. and Lonnie E. Underhill, "Negro Marshals in the Indian Territory," *Journal of Negro History* 56, no. 2 (April 1971): 77–87; Nudie E. Williams, "Black Men Who Wore the Star," *Chronicles of Oklahoma* 59, no. 1 (1981): 83–89; Nudie E. Williams, "United States v. Bass Reeves: Black Lawman on Trial," *Chronicles of Oklahoma* 68, no. 2 (1990): 154–65; Burton, *Black, Red and Deadly*, 162, 204.

they worked, while to the white marshals, the Indian Territory was like a foreign country, whose people and customs they did not understand." Bass Reeves was one of the first, if not the first, African American to be commissioned a deputy U.S. Marshal west of the Mississippi, "because of his knowledge of the tribal languages, the territory, and its people. He also was recruited because he was black."[29]

Black deputy marshals in the West had the unusual authority to arrest or kill white suspects in the line of duty. Not surprisingly, this raised the ire of white settlers, who found such power in the hands of African Americans a travesty of justice. As the *Ardmore Appeal* stated in 1901:

> When Negroes are appointed as United States Deputy Marshals with full power to arrest white people it is indeed high time to call a halt. Even though there is no legal right to demand such a thing, yet the feelings of the people of this whole country demand it. The white citizens of the Southern District have no objections to Negro deputies appointed so long as they arrest only men of their color, but when swaggering Negroes armed with Winchesters and vested with authority to arrest, so far overstep the people's customs as to attempt to arrest a white man merely because he had made the remark to a friend that no "d—— negro deputy could arrest him," it is time for the installation of new public officials who have the interest of the people at heart.[30]

It would appear that the black deputy marshals recognized their unpopularity among white settlers, and some seemed to have accommodated their critics by giving greater attention to capturing black and Indian criminals. Bass Reeves, for example, reportedly asserted that Seminole Indians and freedmen were the hardest fugitives to catch, but he admitted it was "the Indians and Negroes" he went after. It was acknowledged that Reeves would rather go after desperate Indian or freedmen killers than do routine work dealing with whites. On one occasion Reeves tried to enlist the help of a fellow white marshal in tracking three white prisoners, the reward money for whom amounted to $1,000. The white deputy refused, claiming "he did not think a white man should work for a Negro." One white resident remembered, "Bass Reeves was a bad Negro and wasn't afraid to come out after the bad ones. He didn't bother much about the white outlaws but worried after the Creek and Cherokee Negroes and Indians." On one occasion Reeves did obviously go after a white criminal, for he killed Jim Webb, a notorious outlaw. But interestingly, in the initial reports describing the gun battle, Reeves was not mentioned by name. This was probably because territorial newspapers were reluctant to publicize

29. Littlefield and Underhill, "Negro Marshals," 79; Williams, "United States v. Bass Reeves," 154.
30. *Ardmore Appeal,* date unknown, 1901.

the killing of a white man by a black, even if committed in the line of duty. As historian Arthur T. Burton notes, "publicizing the fact that a black officer killed a white outlaw, even one with some Mexican blood, may not have set well with the local population. There were many residents with Southern sympathies, who at best tolerated the presence of black officers in the territory."[31]

Even though black deputy marshals attempted to placate their white critics, they were still victimized by white racism. Though many of the black deputy marshals had outstanding service records, none were ever promoted to the level of United States Marshal in the Indian Territory, nor were any appointed chief deputy marshal. And as a final insult, after years of meritorious service, with the advent of Oklahoma statehood in 1907, black deputy marshals were forced to resign their posts due to Jim Crow legislation. Most ended up like Bass Reeves, who after serving as a deputy marshal under Judge Parker for three decades, was reduced to being a beat cop for the municipal police force in a black district in Muskogee.[32]

Like the Indian police, and the Native American and African American soldiers in the army posts of the West, black deputy marshals played a valuable role in maintaining law and order in a frontier society. They all served as important linkages between their own cultures and Anglo-American justice, but at the same time they all faced discrimination in their efforts.

THE LAWMEN and Army officers of the West, whether white, Native American, or African American, all faced a precarious task in bringing law and order to the Indian Territory. For the West was indeed "wild." Contemporary observers marveled at the prevalence of crime and the proliferation of lawlessness. A famous contemporary saying was "There is no Sunday west of St. Louis—no God west of Fort Smith, [Arkansas]." It was rumored that there were "more bandits, horse thieves, counterfeiters, whiskey peddlers, and train robbers per square mile . . . than any other place in the United States at that time." The secretary of the interior referred to the territories as "a resort for lawless men and criminals, who take refuge thus in order to avoid the constraints incident to an efficient government, or to escape the penalties due for crimes elsewhere committed." Everyone seemingly carried a gun for protection. One Ardmore resident remembered attending church and watching the preacher lay down his gun on the pulpit every Sunday before beginning his service. Another resident wondered how the territories remained populated given all the killings. He concluded it was clearly a time "of the survival of the fittest or perhaps it would

31. Littlefield and Underhill, "Negro Marshals," 83; Burton, *Black, Red and Deadly,* 207, 191.
32. Burton, *Black, Red and Deadly,* 230, 215.

be best to say it was the survival of the one who could draw a gun the quickest."[33]

In many ways then, the actions of local white settlers undermined the efforts of federal authorities to impose law and order over the territories. Often as whites settled among the Indians they demonstrated Anglo-American vices rather than virtues. Government officials had hoped that white settlers would serve as a shining example of moral righteousness. Those who trangressed the law it was hoped would be swiftly and severely punished according to the traditions of Anglo-American justice. In reality, Indians found that whites were intent upon protecting their own property, but were unconcerned with protecting the property or the civil rights of Native Americans and African Americans. If Indians or blacks had their property stolen by whites, they found white jurors unsympathetic and most white thieves acquitted by a jury of their peers.[34]

Not surprisingly, one of the most significant problems to confront both Indian and federal authorities was theft. Many settlers seemed intent upon fleecing anyone they could of their worldly possessions. However, what is particularly noticeable is how often this occurred across racial lines. While settlers did not refuse to steal from their own racial group, certain inhabitants of Indian and Oklahoma Territories saw stealing from another racial group as less than criminal. Indians justified stealing from whites on the basis that whites had stolen their land, while whites justified stealing from Native Americans on the basis that the Native Americans were receiving undeserved handouts from the U.S. government. Black freedmen justified stealing from both whites and Indians on the basis of past treatment as slaves.[35]

The problem of theft confronted both Indian and federal authorities immediately after the Civil War. Many farms and homes in the Indian nations had been abandoned as their owners fled the ravages of war. Surrounded by poverty and despair, many of the ex-slaves of the Five Civilized Tribes were forced to sustain themselves by stealing corn, chickens, cattle, hogs, and horses from their former masters.[36]

Both the Choctaws and the Chickasaws formed vigilante committees who undertook mounted patrols to bring the depredations to an end. At times, Native American night riders raided black settlements and intimidated the inhabitants. Blacks were whipped, and if caught with a stolen hog, cow, or horse,

33. Hagan, *Indian Police and Judges,* 7; Burton, *Black, Red and Deadly,* 161; Columbus Delano, SI, Oct. 31, 1874, in *RSI* 1874, p. xiv; J. B. Kirk, interview, File 56.39, OHP; Victor Locke Jr., interview, GFPHC, 109:353.

34. Donald J. Berthrong, "White Neighbors Come among the Southern Cheyenne and Arapaho," *Kansas Quarterly* 3, no. 4 (1974): 105–15, 111.

35. *Ibid.,* 105–15.

36. Gibson, *Oklahoma,* 132.

were liable to be executed on the spot. The vigilante committees were so successful in curtailing the wave of crime that the Cherokees, Creeks, and Seminoles also adopted this method of vigilante justice.[37]

Native Americans themselves learned the harsh reality of racial prejudice when whites began to impinge upon Indian lands in massive numbers. Whites continually stole Indian farming tools and implements, as well as timber and livestock. The problem was that, as one Indian agent noticed, "to steal from Indians or the Government does not impress such unscrupulous persons as a serious offence." Short of cash and livestock of their own, white settlers looked with covetous eyes upon the possessions of the Indians.[38]

Part of the problem was the nature of the "fence law" in operation in the reservation lands of the Oklahoma Territory. Each landowner was required to fence in his own cattle, swine, and horses. But in practice both races often grazed their cattle on open range. This led to much friction. In the first instance, open ranging of livestock raised the possibility of trespassing and damaging farmers' crops. As one Indian inspector found:

> Most of all the allotments upon this reservation are surrounded by white settlers, and the law of Oklahoma which makes every section line a public highway prevents any very considerable portion of the land being used in one body for grazing purposes; and, in addition to this, there is very considerable friction between the Indians and white settlers growing out of their stock trespassing upon each other's land, and the stock of the Indians are frequently seized by the white settlers and held in payment for damages. Whereas, if the white settler's stock trespass upon the Indian's lands, the settlers retake their property and refuse to pay damages; and, from this cause, ill feeling is created between the two races, resulting—usually—to the detriment of the Indians.

Second, whites would claim the Indians' animals as strays, and then hold them until the Indian owner could redeem them. The white settler usually made the Indian owner pay to reclaim his property, and if the owner was unable, the white settler often claimed the stock for his own. The question of grazing rights became a bone of contention between whites and Indians which could often lead to violence. On the Cheyenne and Arapaho reservation, there was a threat of a race war arising from a dispute over the fence laws. The Indians claimed that they held sovereignty over all the land, and hence they allowed their cattle and horses to roam at will. Often the animals damaged neighboring white settlers' crops. The white settlers claimed the Indians were trespassing on their land and therefore they were justified in shooting any animals which entered their property. The Indians disagreed and began to retaliate by killing the

37. *Ibid.*
38. Berthrong, "White Neighbors," 111.

stock of white settlers. The dispute erupted into a gunfight between white settlers and Indians resulting in the death of two Indians and a white man.[39]

White settlers were often quite ingenious, if unscrupulous, in devising ways
to steal Indians' property. In one case, a Cheyenne Indian had to travel away
from the agency and left his wagon with a liveryman. The liveryman made use
of the wagon during the Indian's absence but upon his return demanded a fee
for looking after the wagon. The Cheyenne could not pay, so the liveryman demanded a chattel mortgage on the wagon and then proceeded to threaten fore-
closure. In another case, a Cheyenne Indian police officer, when ordered to
remove a flock of sheep that were illegally grazing upon some Indian allotments, accidentally killed one of the sheep. The officer took the carcass home
with him. The owner of the herd took the officer to court and demanded compensation for his loss. The white judge awarded him two of the Indian police
officer's horses.[40]

One opportunity for swindling the Indians occurred during the aftermath
of government annuity payments. The Indians living on the reservations of
Oklahoma Territory, who had not had much experience in dealing with white
"entrepreneurs," were particularly vulnerable. One agent complained of a
group of "white leaches [sic]" who "are laying around waiting from day to day
to sop a little blood from the government or the Indians." The distribution of
tribal funds always attracted a crowd of gamblers, bootleggers, highwaymen,
and sharpers. One missionary woman remembered the proliferation of gamblers who tried to cheat the Indians of their just due: "I have seen them drive
in after 'a payment' (Indian Government allotment), and stay until they had
won from the Indians every article [the] Government had issued them, over-
coats, suits, yards and yards of calico for shirts and dresses, shoes, dish pans,
coffee pots (all new, of course). If later the Indians wanted any of the things
back, they could buy them at good prices at nearby stores where these articles
were always deposited for sale. This was the regular system." At the payment
distributions, a carnival-like atmosphere prevailed, with all sorts of games of
chance designed to take money away from the Indians. The crowds proved a
haven for pickpockets, and many an Indian arrived back at camp only to find
his cash missing.[41]

White settlers had numerous opportunities to fleece Indians, and the repercussions they faced hardly served as a deterrent. On the western reservations,
where federal law prevailed even before 1898, even if the guilty parties were
brought to trial, one agent noted, "the penalties imposed have been extremely

39. C. C. Duncan, R 4, Cheyenne and Arapaho Agency, 1896, RSIAI; Berthrong,
"White Neighbors," 109; *Oklahoma State Capital,* July 28, 1894.

40. Berthrong, "White Neighbors," 111.

41. John Shorb, Microfilm SFSA 46, NRSFA; Crawford, *Joyful Journey,* 75; Burton,
Black, Red and Deadly, 42–43.

light, and in many instances, conviction before juries insensible to the rights of Indians has failed." The Indians learned they could not expect justice from all-white juries, for as one official found, "The local prejudice against Indians is such that nothing like fairness can be expected of juries in the State and Territorial courts." The testimony of a number of Indians rarely offset the statements of a single white man. Indians often appealed to the local United States attorney, but usually found him inundated with what he considered "more important matters." Officials simply did not have much sympathy for Indians who had fallen prey to unscrupulous whites, believing this demonstrated their primitiveness and lack of civilization.[42]

In some cases government officials engaged in frontier graft. Many officials abused the powers granted them by the government, preferring to pursue their own economic advancement rather than that of the Native Americans under their control. The opportunity for fraud and graft in the Indian service was great. The commissioner of Indian affairs noted: "The agent is too remote to be under the immediate and constant surveillance of the central office. He is in a great degree free from the espionage of an intelligent public, and those near him who are competent to detect frauds or criticise official conduct may be influenced by or be in collusion with him. The Indians to whom he distributes supplies are too ignorant to protect themselves from imposition, or, in case dishonesty is suspected, to bring the fact to the knowledge of this office." A few unscrupulous Indian officials took advantage of this state of affairs. One particular event which presented governmental officials with the opportunity to fleece the Indians was the distribution of annuity payments. One clerk at the Quapaw Agency accused the Indian agent of swindling the Indians by entering into an agreement with a local merchant who had the sole privilege of selling goods to the Indians. This meant that the trader could charge exorbitant prices to his customers. In return the trader gave the Indian agent a percentage of the profits collected from their arrangement.[43]

Numerous were the complaints from various tribes that their agents had not remunerated them to the extent promised them by treaty stipulations. Washington officials received many letters from tribesmen claiming the agents had withheld a portion of their funds for their own use. Indians petitioned Washington to have fraudulent agents removed. A petition from the Osage included a detailed description of official wrongdoings. They claimed that their agent "has shown favor and partiality in the distribution of the goods, provisions and funds of the Osages." They also complained that the agent had "failed to account to the Osages for their funds he has spent . . . and has never exhibited to us any statement of a settlement of his account with the Government at Wash-

42. Berthrong, "White Neighbors," 111; Merrill E. Gates, *RSI* 1885, 1:771.

43. J. Q. Smith, CIA, to SI, Oct. 30, 1876, *RSI* 1876, p. 381; H. A. Middleton to SI, R 713, Quapaw Agency, 1880, LR-RBIA.

ington." The petition concluded, "he has shown himself totally incompetent to his charges . . . he has been eccentric, passionate, prejudiced, biased, and has shown a degree of careless and reckless prodigality and want of economy and system . . . and has in this way abused the trust shown in him by the U.S. Government."[44]

Native Americans also complained over the fraudulent action of U.S. Marshals. Marshals, as has been mentioned, were not paid an annual salary, but rather received a fee for every prisoner they brought into court. Many times marshals falsely accused settlers of crimes to receive the remuneration involved in making arrests. Indians complained that they faced arrest disproportionate to their numbers, claiming the reason was that they were able to pay their court fees out of their annuity payments. One Indian inspector assigned to the Osage argued that "the half breeds and white men are generally worthless characters—not able to pay a lawyer for defending them, and as the Osages draw a large annuity from the government, so consequently are able to pay for their defense, it pays better to arrest them, and allow the real culprits to go free."[45]

The freedmen also complained about the behavior of the U.S. Marshals. In the Chickasaw Nation, freedmen fell under the "protection" of U.S. courts located in Fort Smith, Arkansas, since they were never adopted by the tribe as citizens and hence did not fall under the jurisdiction of Indian courts. Many found themselves arrested on trumped-up charges and relieved of their property as a means of paying their court costs. It was alleged that as soon as a freedman got a good horse, he found himself arrested and taken to Fort Smith only to return on foot. It was apparently common for African Americans to be blamed for crimes they did not commit. White settlers and Indian leaders were willing to accept that theft was the work of black settlers because as previously noted, they stereotyped blacks as untrustworthy and predisposed to a life of crime. This defense did not always work, however, as one mail carrier found out. One pioneer settler recalled:

I remember once when a fellow of the name of Aldrich was carrying the mail from Goodland to Doaksville and thence east to Clear Creek and Lukfata, Alikchi, and Eagletown. He was carrying it in a two horse hack. One day he had no passengers and he came in and announced that he had been robbed by two negroes at Salt Springs as he had gone east the day before, that they had held him up at the point of a gun and tied him up to a tree and had taken the mail pouches out in the woods and slit them open and rifled them, they returned the empty bags and went back to the hack and that he stayed tied up until he worked himself loose and went on to Doaksville. Father went to the scene of

44. Joseph Pawnenopashe to N. H. Van Vorhes, Aug. 17, 1876, R 636, Osage Nation, 1876, LR-RBIA.
45. J. L. Morphis to Attorney General, R 34, Osage Agency, 1892, RIIIA.

the robbery east of Salt Springs and investigated. The only tracks he could find were those of the mail carrier. Then he arrested him and went to his tent home to search for the money. The man's wife wanted to shoot father for searching her home but he found the money, about $120.00, in a sack of cornmeal.[46]

Many of the inhabitants of Indian Territory, whites, Native Americans, and their freedmen, complained of the practice of U.S. Marshals planting whiskey in the wagons of settlers coming into the Indian Territory. The marshals would stop a wagonload of settlers at the Indian Territory boundary and search for illegal liquor. One of the marshals would walk around the back of the wagon and pull from out of his jacket a few pints of liquor. He would then return to the front of the wagon and display his "find" to the dumbfounded settlers. The marshal would then "confiscate" the illegal liquor and arrest the settlers. Sometimes this led to serious violence. As one man remembered:

> One day they [three deputies] saw a man coming in with two covered wagons; he was driving the front wagon and his daughter the rear wagon. These three deputies slipped up and planted some bottles of whiskey in the rear wagon. They then rode up to the front wagon, stopped the man and told him that they were United States officers and would have to search his wagons for whiskey. "Well," says the man, "I don't use the stuff and don't have any about me or the wagons." They told them they would have to search the wagons. The man got down out of his wagon and with his rifle, too. He then told the three Deputy Marshals again that they didn't need to look, he didn't have any whiskey and that they had better not find any. They searched the first wagon and found nothing there, then went to the rear wagon and, of course, pulled out the bottles. The man opened fire on them, killing all three of them.

Another favorite ploy of unscrupulous U.S. Marshals was to arrest settlers falsely on the charge of cutting cedars from government land. Since the burden of proof lay with the defendant, the mere accusation that a settler's home was constructed of timber removed from government lands was often enough to ensure he would be forced to pay a fine. Not surprisingly, such actions committed by a very few U.S. Marshals led to a wholesale condemnation of the force as corrupt. The Indians and freedmen saw the marshals as usurpers, exercising an oppressive authority over them. The Cherokee agent wrote of the attitude of the tribesmen in his agency: "To all appearance the whole court, together with the deputy marshals and attorneys, co-operate to increase the business of the court—thus increasing their business and profits, and to oppress the Indians and take from them the little they possess." Many Indians, freedmen, and,

46. Littlefield, *The Chickasaw Freedmen,* 100; Paul Roebuck, interview, GFPHC, 81:446–47.

for that matter, white settlers did not see the U.S. Marshals as a force of law and order but rather a source of arbitrary justice and corruption bent on furthering their own pecuniary interest.[47]

WHILE NATIVE AMERICANS and African Americans complained of the actions of white settlers and governmental officials in trying to deprive them of their just possessions, white settlers and officials responded with complaints of their own. In their eyes the Indian Territory was a land filled with marauding Indians and their freedmen, who made a life out of plundering and terrorizing white settlers. Whites were quick to place the blame for depredations on the relocated Plains Indian tribes who resided on the western lands of the Indian Territory. According to their view, Indian and black outlaws preyed upon white settlements along the border and white settlers who dared travel through the reservation lands. Many of these gangs were racially integrated even up to the leadership level. Frequently the integration was between Indian outlaws and freedmen, but sometimes integrated gangs involved whites and Indians. Whatever their racial composition, after reaping sufficient rewards the outlaws would retreat to the interior of the reservations into the security of friends and relatives. As one white settler stated:

> the wild Indians seams to be running at large without restricshon thay seame to be privladge caractures for the want of compatent officers the general saying of the sitazens is that is we have got no officers and it is a true saying if thare was a man of sound sences in the country to witness the fact the whole country is infested with small bands of Indians prowling about and waylaying whoever thay may chance to lite on so that it is impossable for a man woman or child to travel the roads in this country with safety and the officers in comand dont seam to take any steps to put them down it onley seams that thay are in courage them to do more mischief so that thay may be more successfully if any man that is travling tryes to defend himself of the ascents off of the Indians he is arested and punished for it so there is no pertextion for travlers in the country[48]

Indeed the situation became so intense in the years after the Civil War, particularly among the relocated Plains Indians located on the western lands of Indian Territory, that an unofficial state of war existed between the roving bands and the U.S. military. The primary military function of the troops stationed at the various forts scattered throughout the Indian Territory was to prevent Indian raiding parties intent upon terrorizing white settlements. But despite the

47. William James, interview, GFPHC, 62:353–54; Arthur Black, interview, GFPHC, 90:332; John B. Jones to CIA, Sept. 1, 1872, in *RSI* 1872, p. 618.

48. Burton, *Black, Red and Deadly*, 10, 163–64; Hugh Quigley to Secretary of War, R 376, Kiowa Agency, 1869–70, LR-RBIA.

vigilance of the patrols, "small bands of warriors slipped by the troops on foot; they raided ranches and farms in Texas and Kansas for horses and arms, then slashed and burned the settlements." In 1874, the U.S. government was so concerned with making the border regions more safe for inhabitants that it placed General Nelson A. Miles in command of a large force of cavalry, infantry, and artillery whose sole purpose was to capture and arrest the ransacking bands of Indians. Some bands evaded capture with the help of their superior knowledge of the land. One settler remembered how the militia was detached to arrest a band of warriors, but their decision to camp for the night in a meadow nearby proved unwise. The Indians proceeded to light a prairie grass fire that night and "that put the militia out of here." Some bands opted to fight to the death. But gradually many of the bands voluntarily turned themselves over to authorities. The Cheyenne and Arapaho bands surrendered at the Darlington Agency, while the Kiowa and Comanche bands gave themselves up at Fort Sill. The longest holdouts were the Quahada Comanches led by the notorious Quanah Parker. They finally surrendered on June 1, 1875, at Fort Sill (where the famous Apache warrior Geronimo, after years of evading capture, would eventually be transferred to and incarcerated). As each band surrendered, the troops disarmed the warriors, confiscated their horses, and placed their leaders under arrest. By the end of the campaign, seventy-two chiefs had been arrested and removed to the military prison at Fort Marion in St. Augustine, Florida.[49]

While not evoking as much fear as marauding bands of Indian warriors, organized rings of Indian and freedmen horse thieves preyed upon settlers. Horse stealing was a very common crime in the territories, but one that brought severe punishments to those caught engaging in it. Numerous were the horse thieves found hanging from a tree. Most of the thefts were the work of professionally organized gangs who had an efficient system of distribution to buyers in the surrounding states, particularly Texas. Territorial newspapers are full of stories like this one from the *Norman Transcript* detailing the recent exploits of a horse gang: "several Creek Indians were jailed here yesterday on the charge of stealing horses. They are believed to belong to the gang that has been stealing horses and cattle by the wholesale for months and driving them to the Creek reservation."[50]

White settlers often argued they were powerless to stop the illegal traffic in stolen horses and cattle. One settler claimed that the Indians attempted to

49. Gibson, *The History of Oklahoma,* 94–95; Sam Sloan, interview, T282-BII, p. 6, DDOHI; Gibson, *The History of Oklahoma,* 94–95. For studies of General Nelson Miles's confrontations with the Indians of the West, see Ralph E. Bailey, *The Story of Nelson A. Miles: Indian Fighter* (New York: William Morrow, 1965), and Nelson A. Miles, *Serving the Republic: Memoirs of the Civil and Military Life of Nelson A. Miles* (Freeport: Books for Library Press, 1911).

50. Wilson Gunter, interview, GFPHC, 84:513; *Norman Transcript,* July 28, 1893.

fleece the white settlers by stealing their horses and then returning them to the owner for a reward. The settler described the system as follows:

> if you missed a horse you might as well kiss a $5.00 bill good-by [*sic*] if you suspected an Indian of the crime. The Indians had a method of their own and a person did not dare to refuse to pay them, though they knew the Indian had stolen the horse. If an Indian was connected with the crime he would usually drop by the owner's house a day or two after the horse had disappeared and ask if anyone had seen anything of a missing horse. The man of the house would of course reply that he had not but that he also had a horse that was gone and would offer to pay $5.00 for its return. The Indian would promise to keep a lookout for this man's horse and in another day or so would come in with the horse and collect his $5.00.

Other Indians sold white settlers thoroughbred horses painted with white wash to make them appear to be "Pintos," considered the best horses on the frontier. Unsuspecting whites found their mistake when the first rain came. White settlers claimed they had no monopoly on deception and graft in the Indian Territory.[51]

ANOTHER AREA of particular concern to law enforcers was the proliferation of whiskey peddlers in the Indian Territory. Since the inception of the Indian nations long before the Civil War, the Indian Territory had had temperance laws. It was unlawful for anyone to possess alcohol in the Indian Territory without a license from the Indian Bureau. Licenses were only granted to petitioners who could show a need for alcohol, such as physicians who needed it for medicinal purposes. Even these men had difficulty in procuring a license. One physician complained, "the season is rapidly approaching when Physicians need alcoholic stimuli for their patients. In this country Typhoid Fever and Pneumonia prevail to an alarming extent, and many deaths occur for want of proper means to support the patient." Physicians complained they were forced to undergo extensive bureaucratic procedures to qualify for a license, while whiskey peddlers sold liquor to the Indians with impunity. One Indian agent representing the physicians wrote to the commissioner of Indian affairs that "A miserable set of bad men are constantly smuggling bad whiskey into this Nation. Drunkards get it by stealth and do great harm, but physicians of the highest moral character cannot get the necessary stimulants to save the lives of their patients. If a remedy can be divised [*sic*] a great benefit will be conferred upon this country." But the government did have to be careful in assessing the validity of the request for a permit, because deceit could come from the most unlikely sources. For example, one priest requested a permit to purchase wine for

51. Wilson Gunter, interview, GFPHC, 84:513.

Communion. When his application was approved, he immediately requested two barrels.[52]

However, despite the government's concern, whiskey peddlers ran rampant in the Indian Territory. Though it was a federal violation to sell liquor to the Indians and their freedmen, many individuals found the illicit trade too profitable a business to ignore. The Indian police and U.S. Marshals did all they could to discourage the trade, but with profits as high as four dollars a gallon, it was a daunting task. There were simply not enough law enforcement officers to stop the flow of illegal liquor into the territory. Part of the problem was that while the introduction of intoxicating liquors was forbidden by local and federal law, Indian governments had no jurisdiction over white inhabitants who sold liquor to the Indians. If white authorities did not arrest a white whiskey peddler, Indian governments could only request that the settler's permit be rescinded and that he be forced to leave the country.[53]

In addition, numerous ways existed for unscrupulous settlers to circumvent the temperance laws. One of the most prevalent was the establishment of what came to be known as "sand-bar saloons." Liquor was prohibited in the Indian Territory, but that was not the case in Oklahoma Territory. Consequently, entrepreneurs set up saloons in Oklahoma Territory as close to the Indian Territory as possible. In many locations, these saloons were built on sand bars in the middle of the Canadian River, which separated Oklahoma Territory and the Chickasaw Nation. The *Langston City Herald* described one such establishment: "Purcell is a dry town, as are all towns in the Indian Territory, but just across the river, in Oklahoma, is a town, which is wet enough to please the most fastidious or thirsty individual, while in the river on a sand-bar is the 'Blue Goose,' a sort of floating saloon that flies and lights as near Purcell as the capricious channel will allow. The channel is the line and the 'Goose' lights as close as the law allows, and there disburses the liquor to all comers."[54]

Indian Territory was surrounded on all sides by areas where liquor could be sold legally. Hence saloons arose on the Oklahoma, Texas, and Arkansas borders. While Arkansas had a law that made it unlawful to sell alcohol to Indians, they found little difficulty in procuring all the liquor they wished, for as one settler remembered, "what could be easier on being refused whiskey by a saloon-keeper than for an Indian to place money in the hands of a white man or a negro and for the price of a drink have whiskey delivered to him in an alley or

52. Choctaw, Chickasaw 1875–1906 and Seminole 1845–1921 and Miscellaneous Papers 1874–1932, pp. 142–43, OHS; Frank J. Nash to Secretary of War, R 104, Cherokee Agency, 1871, LR-RBIA; John B. Jones to CIA, Aug. 26, 1871, R 104, Cherokee Agency, 1871, LR-RBIA; Fait, "Reminiscences of Anna R. Fait," CCRP.

53. Burton, *Black, Red and Deadly,* 145; Committee on Temperance to Union Agency, R 865, Union Agency, 1875–76, LR-RBIA.

54. A. N. Boatman, interview, GFPHC, 66:255–56; *Langston City Herald,* Nov. 16, 1895.

other out-of-the-way place." Indians often relied upon their former slaves to procure alcohol, for states such as Arkansas, which had laws against serving liquor to Indians, had no such restrictions upon blacks. As a result freedmen were very active in the bootlegging business, and territorial newspapers have numerous references to the arrest of "negro whiskey peddlers."[55]

Other settlers manipulated the laws by selling Indians liquor substitutes. Merchants stocked red ink, colognes, and flavoring extracts containing minute amounts of alcohol, and sold them to alcohol-addicted Indians. One settler remembered that this could have serious consequences. He told of a nearsighted clerk in his father's store who sold an illiterate Indian a bottle of Singer sewing machine oil instead of lemon extract, and the Indian proceeded to get very ill.[56]

Temperance laws remained a part of territorial history in the Indian Territory up to statehood. The government contended that officials in the field reported to Washington that there was a direct correlation between alcohol consumption and the prevalence of crime. The Cherokee agent reported that the number of disturbances, quarrels, fights, and murders was rising rapidly in his agency. Upon investigation he found, "whiskey had had much to do in aggravating the troubles and in some cases is the sole cause." A white woman recalled that the lawlessness of the local Indians "was due chiefly to Choctaw beer, a drink which made them both drunk and crazy."[57]

Alcohol consumption was blamed for some of the territories' more serious crimes of assault and murder. Newspaper editors were quick to blame alcohol for the proliferation of violent crime in the territories, particularly involving Native Americans and freedmen. Often disputes would begin between drunken parties but soon would escalate into a riot because of racial tensions. One settler reminisced that "the Iowa and Kickapoo Indians were very peaceable, but occasionally a few members of the Creek and Seminole tribes, usually bucks, would come to town and the bucks would proceed to get as drunk as possible," whereupon they would get quarrelsome and "want to start fights." The man remembered one occasion in the late fall of 1890, when several Indians came into town in an intoxicated state. They became enraged when ordered to leave town by local law enforcement agents. The group threatened to get more Indians and raid the town. On their way out of town they shot at a white newspaperman, wounding his horse. Anticipating a raid, the white townsfolk organized a night watch. However, the Indians never returned and further violence was avoided.[58]

55. Jordan Folsom, interview, GFPHC, 105:249; William Nail, interview, GFPHC, 81:179; *Cleveland County Leader*, Dec. 9, 1899.

56. James T. Lynch, interview, File 199, OHP.

57. J. W. Ingalls to CIA, 1875, Letters Received, Adjutant General's Office, R 224, M 619, National Archives, Washington, D.C.; Mrs. W. C. Jarboe, memoir, Box J-2, WCJP.

58. Frederick Pfaff, quoted in Anna R. Fait, "Reminiscences of Mrs. Anna R. Fait," CCRP.

Tensions also ran high between black and white settlers, and drunkenness was the cause of many violent racial encounters between these two groups. One settler remembered how groups of Cherokee freedmen would ride to Coffey-ville, Kansas, and get drunk. Upon their return, they would pull their guns on any white man they came across and make him get off his horse. They would then scare off the horse and make him walk, firing their guns at his feet. The settler recalled that one day his father became the target of their abuse, and a gunfight ensued in which his father wounded several of the drunken blacks. He claimed, "after that day my father was a marked man among the Negroes."[59]

Drunkenness also accounted for much of the violence among members of the same race. At an African American camp meeting at Melvin, one preacher was killed and three parishioners seriously wounded when an intoxicated parishioner raised a disturbance with the deacon. The two men engaged in a pistol duel, during which the preacher was killed, and two boys and a man standing near by were hit by stray bullets. According to the news report, however, "the meeting was not disturbed, and was not dismissed on account of the shooting."[60]

MUCH OF THE PETTY THEFT prevalent in the territories was a result of an individualistic pioneer spirit of economic advancement by whatever means possible, or simply the result of drunkenness. On the other hand, violent crime often had its origins in the profound racial tensions and antagonism which characterized relations between whites, Native Americans, and African Americans in the territories. This can be clearly seen in the number of race riots that were recorded in the territories in the late nineteenth century. Riots proliferated between whites and blacks, whites and Indians, and Indians and blacks.

Riots between Indians and blacks usually were localized affairs in response to a specific alleged wrong perpetrated by one of the parties. However, the fact that these alleged wrongs brought out violent responses demonstrated the underlying tensions between Native Americans and their former slaves. This was particularly true between freedmen of one tribe and Native Americans of another. One such occurrence happened in August of 1880. Cherokee residents complained that some black settlers from the Creek Nation were stealing horses and cattle from them. Two black suspects were taken from their homes and lynched in revenge, their bodies afterwards being shot up. The lynching led the local blacks to form a party intent upon exacting revenge. They came across two young Cherokee boys on horseback and ordered them to dismount. They commenced shooting, wounding one of the Cherokee boys nine times before the women of the family were able to pick him up and carry him inside. The Cherokee agent reported that a group of Cherokees were preparing to in-

59. L. C. Jenkins, interview, GFPHC, 5:440.
60. *Woodville Beacon*, Oct. 6, 1905.

vade the Creek Nation in search of the freedmen responsible, bent upon retaliation. In response, a group of 190 Creek freedmen took shelter at an old fort at Goose Neck Bend, armed with Winchester rifles and a brass cannon and preparing for the Cherokee invasion. They waited for an attack; it never came. Rather, the Cherokees enlisted the support of the authorities, who formed a posse which went to displace the freedmen. The *Norman Transcript* reported that "if the small force that the sheriff took with him should prove ineffectual against the negroes, there are plenty of volunteers here who will start at a moment's notice to reinforce him." There was no need, as the sheriff was able to arrest the leaders without further incident.[61]

Often racial tensions between Native Americans and their freedmen involved the actions of law enforcement agents. In one incident, a black man was killed by two members of the lighthorse police. He had sold an Indian a hog but had kept the head to eat himself. The Indian reported the black man for not fulfilling his end of the bargain, and two lighthorsemen were dispatched to arrest the suspect. The officers came across the man in the woods, but he did not take the charges seriously. When he turned to leave, the lighthorse police opened fire on him, killing him instantly. One freedman wrote President Grover Cleveland about the affair. He said that "These Choctaws are not giving us colored people equal footing. . . . these Indians dont think as much of us Colored people as they do a good old dog."[62]

Another incident arose out of the racial antipathy full-blood Cherokees held for freedmen who served as lighthorsemen members of the Indian police. In Muskogee, around Christmas time in 1878, serious trouble broke out when some African-Creek lighthorsemen attempted to disarm two young Cherokees from a prominent family. A white Texan passing through town took offense at the actions of the black officers. Enlisting the support of the enraged Cherokee youths, he began a gunfight with the officers, which resulted in the loss of one officer's life and the wounding of three other officers.[63]

Racial violence between whites and Indians was more common than between Native Americans and their freedmen. While the government had hoped that contact between white settlers and Native Americans would lead to a greater understanding between the two cultures and that white settlers would act as agents of civilization, the white settlers and the Native Americans themselves held a very different viewpoint. Indians saw whites as intruders in a land promised to them exclusively by the United States government, while white settlers saw Native Americans as savages who were an annoying obstacle to the opening of vast tracts of land to white settlement.

61. *Cherokee Advocate,* Aug. 4, Aug. 11, 1880; *Norman Transcript,* May 9, 1881.
62. J. J. Briarly to President Grover Cleveland, n.d., Indian Territory, Special Files, 1898–1907, Choctaw and Chickasaw and Cherokee Freedmen, RG 48, Box 48, RDI.
63. Burton, *Black, Red and Deadly,* 132.

These attitudes led to violent encounters over the question of who was trespassing upon whose land. Such was the case along the Kansas border. Indians habitually crossed the Kansas border from Indian Territory in pursuit of buffalo. The white settlers objected to the Indians' trespassing on their lands. Getting nowhere through official channels, they took the law into their own hands. When a group of Osage camped across the border in Kansas in 1874 the local "militia" ordered them to leave. The messengers sent out by the Osage were instructed to command the others to come forward and give up their weapons. Instead, the messengers instructed them to flee while attempting to make their own escape. The commanding officers ordered the militia to shoot, killing four Indians and wounding many others. All the men who testified later at a hearing on the incident admitted that the Indians were unarmed and had made no menacing gestures or threats. The Osage agent wrote to his superior calling the incident "a massacre." According to the agent the "massacre" had the full support of not only the local white inhabitants but also the governor of Kansas. In fact, the agent claimed that the men who shot the Indian party were ordinary citizens given militia status by the governor of Kansas after the incident, "to make them look less guilty of wrong-doing."[64]

Violence between white settlers and Indians took place because many white settlers saw Indians as something less than human. While the government had hoped that through its "civilization" campaign, the racial stereotypes of Indians as savages would recede, among many white settlers that was still the most prevalent characterization. As one settler recalled, "Well, in my way of seeing it, there's nothing to killing an Indian in them days. He didn't know very much, very little. All you had to do was shoot him and, as far as that was concerned, just like shooting a hog."[65]

Whites justified such an attitude because of Indian outrages upon white settlers. One settler remembered living in fear of Indian raids. She claimed Indians would leave a group of whites alone, but if they came across a white man by himself, they would "take his scalp." The settler recalled that a group of Indians had seized a woman and her child and killed them. She also claimed that the Indians stole horses, cattle, and children. She added, "If the child wasn't large enough to eat they killed it. They liked to capture these white children to rear as their own." Another woman wrote President Grant that her husband and son had been working as surveyors mapping out lots for white settlement, when the Cheyenne attempted to discourage white intrusion by killing all six surveyors. She remembered how she used to consider "the Red man my friend," and had always felt comfortable throwing her saddle upon the ground for a pillow and had slept unarmed in the midst of Indian lands. But now, she

64. I. T. Gibson, Osage Agent, R 56, RSIA.
65. Joe Harlow, interview, File T-376-1, DDOHI.

declared, "their treachery has robbed me of a loving husband, and a darling son, fourteen years of age."[66]

While conflicts over the issue of land rights and trespassing were more prevalent, the issue that aroused the greatest concern among white settlers was the protection of the chastity of white women from "savage" Indian men. No conflict aroused the ire of whites toward Indians more than accusations of Indian men raping white women. Native Americans had long been stereotyped by whites as asexual. However, by the middle of the nineteenth century, the stereotype of the Indian "savage" held by most white settlers included a fierce sexuality aimed at white women (though Indian men did not evoke as much fear in the minds of whites as black males). Hence, not surprisingly one of the cases which received the most press coverage in the territorial newspapers involved the alleged rape and murder of a white woman by two Seminole Indian boys on December 30, 1897.[67]

After the murder had taken place, the woman's husband returned home the next morning to find the body of his wife, "partly devoured by hogs." White settlers from Oklahoma Territory rallied to his support and began to organize a party to avenge the gruesome crime. They outfitted themselves with all the Winchester rifles and ammunition they could find. Within a short time several Indians were arrested, among them Lincoln McGeisey, the son of a prominent Seminole who owned the farm where the crime had been committed, and another Seminole, Palmer Sampson. After being tortured by his captors, Sampson reportedly confessed to the crime, saying he was drunk when the crime was committed. He alleged that McGeisey had aided him. Based on the boys' saying they had felt the woman's breasts, the newspapers reported that they had raped her. A few days after the arrests, a mob of about one hundred men, led by two preachers, took the prisoners across the border back into the Oklahoma Territory, where the two boys were burned at the stake. The mob thought there would be less danger from the officials in the Oklahoma Territory than the Indian courts in the Indian Territory. Newspapers reported that the victims were tortured while alive, and that after the burning of the Indians' bodies, the whites "took the charred bones and divided them up as relics." This apparent degradation greatly incensed the local Indians, who were appalled over the reported abuse of the human remains.[68]

The controversy did not end with the lynching, however. Immediately thereafter, the Indians proclaimed that the two boys were innocent and they demanded retribution. Thomas McGeisey, father of one of the victims, was in

66. Amanda Kimball, interview, GFPHC, 53:238.; Mrs. O. F. Short to President Ulysses Grant, Aug. 28, 1875, R 120, LR-RBIA.

67. For a detailed analysis of this event, see Daniel F. Littlefield, Jr., *Seminole Burning: A Story of Racial Vengeance* (Jackson: University of Mississippi Press, 1996).

68. *El Reno News,* Jan. 14, 1898.

Washington representing the tribe when the incident occurred. He immediately asked for a federal investigation and for the arrest of the lynching party. Congress agreed and provided $25,000 for the prosecution of the lynchers. A great number of arrests were made, and the lynchers were brought before a grand jury. All of the accused were able to give bond because all the white inhabitants offered their support to the prisoners. One white editor of a local paper defended the action of the lynchers:

> The burning of the two Seminole rapists near Wewoka a few days ago emphasizes the importance of the prompt prosecution of that class of criminals. The general public acts in such cases on the theory that it is infinitely safer to summarily execute such criminals than run the risk of seeing them turned loose upon the community for the want of prosecution. The people along the line of Oklahoma and the Seminole country are no exception to the generality of American manhood. If speedy justice is not had in the courts of the country, there is a surer and a swifter way, and there is no section on the American continent where the remedy will not be applied.

Support in Oklahoma Territory was so great for the lynchers that meetings were held and appeals were made through the newspapers in order to raise cash to pay for their legal defense. Within the white community the lynchers were regarded as heroes and martyrs, whose actions were a brave demonstration that white women would be protected at all cost.[69]

In all, sixty men were indicted in Oklahoma Territory for burning the two Indians, and forty more were charged in Indian Territory for kidnapping and thus acting as accessories to their murder. In the first case to be tried, that of Nelson M. Jones, the defendant was found guilty of kidnapping and sentenced to twenty years in prison. In addition to the criminal charges brought against the lynchers, the government initiated an investigation to determine the damages inflicted upon innocent Native Americans. Petitions included claims for physical harassment and for damages to property, including homes, barns, fences, and even outhouses burned or vandalized. After hearing months of testimony the U.S. investigation found that the two Seminole boys had been innocent of the crime, and thus the U.S. secretary of the interior awarded damages to the Indians. The parents of the two boys each received $5,000 in compensation for the burning of their property by the mob. So ended one of the most controversial cases in the territories, and one of the few instances in American history where the actions of a lynch mob were severely punished. This case is instructive in that it shows that white settlers were just as ready to lynch Native Americans as African Americans suspected of raping white

69. *Vinita Indian Chieftain*, Jan. 13, 1898; undated newspaper clipping, Indians File, Box 2, TAP.

women. At the same time, however, it demonstrates that the federal government did not condone the use of vigilante law upon Native Americans as it did with respect to African Americans. If the defendants had been African Americans in this case rather than Native Americans, the lynching probably would have occurred without repercussions.[70]

Rape was also a problem confronting Indian women. White men outnumbered white women in the early territorial days. This led to the frequency of intermarriage between white men and Native women earlier alluded to, but it also accounts for frequent reports of rapes against Indian women. White men abused Native American women almost with impunity because of the lack of U.S. Marshals to enforce the law, and because in the event of a white man committing a crime upon an Indian, the Indian government had no jurisdiction. The culprit had to be tried by a U.S. court. Thus whites had the security of knowing that even if they were arrested for their actions, they would be tried before a jury of men who held equally derogatory views of Indians. Judging from their actions, juries did not feel the rape of Native American women was a serious crime. Punishment was less than that for the rape of white women (though seldom did the offenders of white women ever make it to trial; most were lynched before legal action was undertaken). For example, a white man entered the home of an Indian and after asking to spend the night, reportedly raped the women present. The local Indian agent arrested the white rapist and sentenced him to fifteen days in jail.[71]

Native American women attempted to protect themselves in the absence of aid from the authorities. One Indian recalled how the women of the Ponca tribe used to carry knives tucked secretly inside their dresses so as to be able to protect themselves. Native American women felt particularly vulnerable to the whims of the white soldiers stationed in Indian Territory.[72]

While relations between white settlers and Indians were often marred by violence, by far the most serious outbreaks of racial violence occurred over disputes between white and black settlers in the territories. In terms of racial violence, territorial Oklahoma was as "southern" a state as Mississippi or Louisiana. Just as in the Deep South, white inhabitants in Oklahoma often placed ultimate power in the hands of "Judge Lynch." In a report originally published in the *Chicago Tribune,* a study showed that in 1896 Oklahoma Territory reported six lynchings and Indian Territory reported four (see Table 2). The combined total of ten reported lynchings for the year placed the territories be-

70. *Cherokee Advocate,* April 9, 1898; *Cleveland County Leader,* Feb. 25, 1899. Nelson M. Jones was a deputy U.S. Marshal who had one of the Seminole boys in custody but let the mob have him. Five other men indicted drew jail terms. Daniel F. Littlefield Jr., personal communication with author.

71. George Davenport to SI, R 744, Sac and Fox Agency, 1880, LR-RBIA.

72. William Collins Jr. and William Collins Sr., interview, File 87.179, OHP.

TABLE 2
Lynchings in 1896 as Reported by the *Chicago Tribune*

Alabama	15
Arkansas	4
Colorado	4
Florida	10
Georgia	9
Illinois	1
Indiana	1
Kentucky	9
Louisiana	25
Maryland	2
Minnesota	8
Mississippi	6
Missouri	5
New York	1
North Carolina	1
South Carolina	4
Tennessee	14
West Virginia	1
Texas	7
Indian Territory	4
Oklahoma Territory	6

Reprinted from *El Reno News,* March 5, 1897.

hind only Louisiana, Tennessee, Alabama, and Florida. Georgia, Mississippi, and nearby Texas, had fewer reported lynchings than did the two territories.[73]

A lynching was a communal experience and the means by which a community demonstrated what behavior it deemed unacceptable. It was at the same time, according to one recent study, "but one manifestation of the strenuous and bloody campaign by whites to elaborate and impose a racial hierarchy upon people of color throughout the globe." The only way lynching acted as a deterrent against deviant behavior, some reasoned, was through consistent application, thus making punishment for deviant behavior certain. The criteria involved in making the decision as to whether lynch law or the legal justice system should be invoked in Oklahoma and Indian Territories invariably was race. If the accused was black, settlers opted to invoke lynch law; if he was Indian the result depended on the nature of the crime; if he was white the accused usually would have his say in a court of law.[74]

73. See W. Fitzhugh Brundage, *Lynching in the New South: Georgia and Virginia, 1880–1930* (Urbana: University of Illinois Press, 1993); *El Reno News,* Mar. 5, 1897.
74. Brundage, *Lynching in the New South,* 2.

As soon as a violent crime was rumored to have been committed by a black person, white settlers banded together to form their own system of justice. One woman remembered being at a dance where "suddenly our partners disappeared" when word was spread that a black man had killed a white boy while attempting to attack the white boy's sister. Settlers took it upon themselves to be judge, jury, and executioner. Little time was wasted in gathering evidence. Accusation was usually enough to guarantee a man be condemned. Many newspaper editors in Oklahoma Territory were staunch defenders of the rule of lynch law for murder and rape, and often the papers themselves were used to notify settlers of the need to band together to find a suspect or to accuse a person of a particular crime. The *Woodville Beacon,* for example, contained a headline and story announcing:

LYNCHING EXPECTED
A NECKTIE PARTY CERTAIN WHEN NEGRO RAPIST IS CAUGHT

A dozen posses, composed of over 500 men, are scouring the country in this vicinity for Jack Smith, a negro who ravished Nellie Davis, a fourteen-year-old country girl near Crowder City. Two negroes came into the house while the girl was alone. Smith picked her up and carried her into a cornfield a short distance away and accomplished his purpose. His accomplice, who remained on guard, was caught by a posse and after a rope had been tied around his neck and thrown over a limb he confessed knowledge of the deed and gave up the name of the principal. When last seen the rapist was three miles from this city.

Newspapers made a habit of publishing all out-of-state lynchings on their front page, even though little other news from out of state received such extensive coverage.[75]

Any murder of a white man by a black in Oklahoma Territory usually brought about a ruling by "Judge Lynch." One pioneer woman remembered how her husband had often assisted the local sheriff when trouble developed in the black districts. The sheriff refused to go into a black area by himself, so when trouble occurred he came and deputized this woman's husband. On a Christmas Eve, the sheriff came and requested assistance. She watched with horror as in the distance she could see one of the blacks open the door with a gun in his hand and after a brief argument pull the trigger, killing her husband. Immediately a posse of white men was formed and they soon located the culprit. The men then came to the grieving widow's home and asked her what she wanted them to do with the murderer. She recalled, "I was beside myself and could think of nothing but that he had shot Albert. So I said I wanted them to hang him and shoot him full of holes." The mob went to the jail and broke the lock with a sledgehammer, tore down the door, and dragged the prisoner

75. Blanch Bennett, interview, GFPHC, 14:359–60; *Woodville Beacon,* Sept. 8, 1905.

across the street to a telephone pole. They then proceeded to lynch him and shoot his body full of holes as the widow had requested. The mob returned to the widow's home and asked her if she wanted to see her husband's murderer while he was hanging. She declined, but her mother went "for she was as blood-thirsty as the rest of town was." They let the body hang until sundown then took it down and cut the rope used into little pieces "for souvenirs." The widow claimed several years later that she still had her piece, which the mob had brought to her as a memento.[76]

The one crime which absolutely inflamed the wrath of white settlers was the rape of a white woman by a black man. There is reason to believe that white settlers in Oklahoma Territory were as paranoid about the danger black men posed to white women as their counterparts in the Deep South. White males were determined that they would protect their females from "black brutes" at all cost. One territorial editor concluded:

There is no punishment that can be meted out to the black brutes that prey upon defenseless women that is commensurate with their crime. Mental anguish is foreign to their brute natures, and any physical agony that may be inflicted upon them is infintesimal [*sic*] to the fearful agony endured by their victims. The slow process of the law in such cases is responsible for the prevalence of lynchings throughout the country, and until its defects are remedied, they will continue. The Pierce City (Mo.) lynching, Tuesday night, if confined to the guilty parties, would have received the endorsement of every community that contains a woman.

The editor of the *Stillwater Gazette* claimed it was "poppycock to call men cowards who put to death the murderers and outragers of defenceless women and girls."[77]

Lynchings of black rapists often brought out the most savage behavior in white mobs. A young white girl was allegedly raped by a black man who stopped at her home and asked her about a job chopping cotton. The young girl responded to the man, who then realizing there was no one else around, reportedly grabbed her and raped her. News spread rapidly over the vicinity, and men armed with rifles and led by bloodhounds began the search. The man was caught and brought back to the girl, who positively identified him as the culprit. The mob took him to a large oak tree and hanged him.[78]

Women who were able to fight off their attackers were considered territorial heroines for managing to protect the "integrity of the white womb." The *Kingston Messenger* carried a boldfaced headline proclaiming "BRAVE MRS.

76. Sarah McConnell, interview, GFPHC, 34:440–44.
77. *Vinita Indian Chieftain*, Aug. 22, 1901; *Stillwater Gazette*, Jan. 31, 1901.
78. *Woodville Beacon*, July 6, 1906.

COUDRAN WITH BABY IN HER ARMS PRESERVES HER HONOR AGAINST NEGRO."[79]

Whites refused to believe that any sexual liaisons between black men and white women could be anything but rape. Many a black man fell victim to lynch mobs despite the man's protestations that there had been no force involved in the sexual act, that the white woman had fully consented to the involvement. Indeed, there was so much paranoia over black men lusting after white women that a panic was created on one occasion when a black man was found hiding in some weeds. A lynch party was formed, for it was immediately suspected that the black man was intent upon raping some innocent white woman. However, three bottles of extract were found near the suspect, who, it turned out, was merely enjoying a few drinks by himself in the solitude of an empty field.[80]

Regardless of whether the lynch mob's target was accused of murder or rape, settlers often had to go to great lengths to ensure vigilante justice triumphed over the legal system. Often after an arrest was made, a battle ensued between the local law officers in charge of the prisoner and an angry, vengeful mob. Usually the power of the mob ruled supreme. After one black man had killed a local liveryman in a dispute over a wagon, the white townsfolk chased him and found him hiding in a nearby swamp. The sheriff arrested the murderer and placed him in the jailhouse. An angry mob formed outside the jail demanding the release of the prisoner to them for summary punishment. The sheriff refused, so the crowd dispersed only to return a few minutes later with two sledgehammers, which they used to knock down the jailhouse door. They grabbed the prisoner and tied a rope around his neck. The murderer was lynched from a telephone pole at an intersection near the jailhouse.[81]

Oklahoma Territory newspapers carried notices of occurrences in which law enforcement agents were powerless to prevent vigilante justice. One U.S. Marshal, however, was quite inventive in protecting his prisoner from a lynch mob. He was determined not to let the mob have his prisoner, "even if he was of no account." Traveling first by train, the marshal handcuffed one of the prisoner's hands to his seat and the other to the marshal's own hand, ensuring the mob would have to kill him first before they could get their hands on the prisoner. Then later, while traveling by covered wagon, he dressed the prisoner in women's clothing to avert suspicion. Another marshal was forced to run six miles with his prisoner in tow, hotly pursued by an angry mob intent upon lynching a black man accused of the attempted rape of a white woman.[82]

79. *Kingston Messenger,* Aug. 10, 1906.

80. Eugene Friegel, report, R 1, M 828, Territorial Papers, 1892, RDI; *Vinita Indian Chieftain,* June 28, 1888.

81. B. K. McElhannan, interview, GFPHC, 7:25–27.

82. George Mann, interview, GFPHC, 34:104; *Kingston Messenger,* Aug. 10, 1906.

More frequently the law enforcement officials had to cooperate with the mob for fear of their own safety. In one instance a crowd gathered outside a local prison awaiting the jury's decision on a black murderer's trial. Fearing that the jury might be lenient, they proposed to invoke their own punishment. The sheriff, fearing for his own life, was forced to awaken the judge, and have the jury decision read in the middle of the night. After hearing that the jury had returned a guilty decision and awarded the death penalty, "the crowd was satisfied, and disbanded after giving some cowboy whoops." One sheriff interrupted a lynching and warned the would-be lynchers that they were subject to arrest for their actions. When the mob angrily turned on him, he suggested that he could approach the murder suspect and endeavor to rile him to the point of exasperation and possible violent attack, giving the sheriff an excuse to kill him. The suspect undoubtedly disappointed all concerned by surrendering peacefully to the sheriff.[83]

While white settlers did all they could to ensure that lynch law would be invoked any time a black was suspected of raping a white woman or murdering a white, black settlers did all they could to condemn vigilante justice. Black newspaper editors in Oklahoma Territory were adamant in their denunciation of lynch law. They encouraged their patrons to fight back against white oppression even if it meant violent resistance. The *Langston City Herald* proclaimed that "Self-defence is the first law of nature, and he is a coward indeed who fails to take advantage of it. Lynch law must go!" An out-of-state newspaper article from Topeka, Kansas, published in 1906 in many of the black newspapers in the territory created quite a sensation among white settlers. It said:

> Notice! Take warning. We now notify you to get ready; buy shotguns and rifles, and put them in your houses and prepare to protect yourselves and your families. The Texans and Arkansas trash are preparing to take charge of the new state and thereupon falls upon you objectionable law. They will also continue their outrages in the new State, as they have carried them on in the old, lynching, burning and outraging negroes in every possible way. They will try to carry out their hellish designs, and place you under bondage. Sleep with one eye open from now on, organize yourselves together for your own protection.[84]

Black editors did not promote violence but did admit that as a last resort it was preferable to fight back than to blindly submit. The *Langston City Herald* argued that the African American should always be loyal and be a good citizen, but should also always be ready to defend himself against those "who seem to think that the Negro has no rights that they are bound to respect." "They must

83. Walter Pierce, interview, GFPHC, 93:317–18; Gomer Gower, interview, GFPHC, 26:213–14.
84. *Langston City Herald,* Nov. 17, 1892; *Kingston Messenger,* Nov. 16, 1906.

be made to know," the editor continued, "that they must treat the Negro as a man, as an American citizen or be made to bite the dust with him." In another editorial, the *Langston City Herald* warned African Americans that lynchers were still "on the warpath" with "Negro scalps hanging to their belts . . . trophy-like, displaying the grand and embellic weakness of our government to protect its citizens." It encouraged blacks to protect themselves and their families "with a six shooter, and a shotgun with forty bucks in it." Another black newspaper adopted an equally forceful approach. The *Langston Western Age* instructed its readers to "Shoot the life out of the white mob with the same precision and accuracy that you would shoot the life out of a colored one. Mobs as a rule are cowardly and will hardly ever go up against a shot gun or repeating rifle proposition when they happen to be in front of the muzzle and a cool calculating man is at the other end, with his finger on the trigger. Lynching will be permanently checked even without the intervention of the law when the intended victims make up their minds to check it." Black editors suggested violence only in retaliation to perceived wrongs, for black editors were quick to point out that the image blacks should be conveying was that of a law-abiding citizen. Editors consistently warned "bad niggers" to stay out of Oklahoma Territory—they were not wanted by white or black Oklahomans. The *Western Age* proclaimed that black settlers should shun criminals "be they black or white."[85]

Black editors were quick to point out that lynching was not only a brutal miscarriage of justice, but detrimental to the image of African Americans throughout the United States and the rest of the world. The fact that lynching was reserved almost exclusively for African Americans implied that blacks were different from other Americans, that somehow even in the eyes of justice, they were inferior. The *Langston City Herald* astutely recognized that

A Negro lynched and burned in Tennessee blazes the way for a more liberal display of hellishness in Texas. A Negro lynched creates "Jim Crow" cars and its concomitant evils. Sentiment against the root and branch of the iniquitous institution must be created at home, not in Europe nor Eutopia. Very often the victimized race decries the crusade against the institution. It is not in consonance with written or unwritten laws to hold a people in esteem that do not put the proper mark of appreciation on themselves; suffering themselves to be ruthlessly booted and spurred without turning over. God, it is said, only helps those who help themselves.

However, newspaper editors and other black leaders never advocated that blacks retaliate and adopt their own vigilante justice. Never was there sentiment

85. *Langston City Herald,* Oct. 20, 1894, April 20, 1895; *Langston Western Age,* May 25, 1906, Dec. 6, 1907.

that for every black victim lynched, there should be a white victim of black vigilante justice. When a white man assaulted a little black girl, the newspapers turned the tables, notifying readers that a "BIG BURLEY WHITE BRUTE" had made a "heinous assault on a little colored girl." The newspaper severely condemned the man's actions:

> Any man be he white or black who falls so low morally that he will commit such a horrible crime puts himself in the place of the lowest order of brutes, he is ten fold more dangerous to the human family than the most poison reptile is to an innocent child and deserves the same treatment one would give a rattle snake. (We should apologize here to the rattle snake because he always gives warning before striking but this d—— scoundrel like the midnight assassin gave his poor helpless defenseless victim no warning, he struck a blow that means a living death, and should the child recover an invalid for life.)

However, the paper reported it was "proud of the action taken by 100 Colored men who while wrought up to the highest pitch and boiling over indignation over this damnable and hellish crime . . . refrained from taking the law into their own hands and sending the scoundrel to hell by lightning express, but instead took the inhuman brute to the U.S. jail and like law-abiding citizens turned the leacherous [*sic*] devil over to the U.S. officials." The paper said the black citizens had "set a good example to follow."[86]

As the constitutional convention got under way, newspaper editors hoped that they could convince white legislators to adopt a similar attitude. Therefore they promoted the creation of anti-lynching bureaus to battle lynch law in the legal arena. In 1906, the "New State Anti–Lynch Law Bureau" was formed under legal charter. The corporation wanted to prevent lynchings, to suppress and prevent crimes leading to or causing lynchings, and to aid in legally prosecuting those who engaged in lynchings. As well the corporation was to furnish and publish the surrounding circumstances and facts connected with any lynchings occurring in Oklahoma, and to deliver lectures throughout the state to African Americans, informing them of the evils of lynch law. The corporation was headquartered in Guthrie, under the leadership of William H. Twine, journalist, prominent lawyer, and noted black-rights activist in Muskogee. The corporation raised money to aid in the prosecution costs of bringing lynchers to justice and offered rewards for information in identifying those responsible for particular lynchings. Unfortunately, the bureau was unsuccessful in its quest to get legislation passed prohibiting lynching and setting stiff penalties for violators under the new state constitution. Not surprisingly, it fell victim to the racism of the white legislators, who often were firm believers in the sanctity of "Judge Lynch." While certainly not every white citizen of the territories ap-

86. *Langston City Herald*, Dec. 21, 1895; *Muskogee Cimeter*, July 27, Aug. 3, 1905.

proved of lynch law, few whites were willing to speak out against its evils. Hence the silence of the majority allowed the virulent racism of the few to evoke the fear of the noose in every black soul in the territories.[87]

While African Americans had no legal protection against mob justice, they could rely upon racial solidarity. Many times black criminals sought refuge among their own people to avoid capture from a white mob intent upon vigilante justice. A black man accused of murdering a white sheriff successfully eluded a large posse. In his escape, he was supplied with guns, ammunition, food, and transportation by fellow African Americans. Another black man accused of raping a white woman was concealed by some local blacks and then hidden in a wagon and taken to Kansas, where he was eventually captured by authorities. In another instance, a black thief chased by a white police officer ran and took refuge in a store full of black customers. The customers jumped to the defense of the thief, and a prolonged gun battle occurred. At the end of the confrontation, three blacks and one white policeman had been wounded. In still another instance, prominent African Americans in Oklahoma City raised money and hired an attorney for a black man accused of murdering a white woman in Missouri. In all these ways, African Americans banded together in a demonstration of racial solidarity to combat the evils of vigilante justice.[88]

Whites were appalled. White editors claimed that such behavior made lynch law all the more necessary. Any threat to the existence of lynch law was seen as a move towards social equality. Both races understood that there was a hidden meaning behind the presence of lynch law, that it stood as perhaps the most obvious reminder of the ascendancy of whites over blacks.

Not surprisingly, Oklahoma and Indian Territories became a hotbed of racial tensions and violence as blacks fought to achieve equality and whites strove to legislate blacks to an inferior position. Not infrequently these tensions erupted into racial violence. The infamous Tulsa Race Riot of 1921 was not an isolated phenomenon but rather the culmination of years of racial tensions and violence between white and black Oklahomans. In 1903, for example, a riot broke out between black and white settlers in Braggs, Indian Territory. White settlers claimed to have been the victims of petty theft, which they blamed on local blacks. They banded together and grabbed a black suspected of stealing a hog and horsewhipped him. The local blacks were enraged by this and vowed revenge. Whites hearing this armed themselves and prepared for conflict. The two groups met on a stretch of land about two miles out of town and a bona fide battle erupted. When the smoke finally cleared, five blacks and one white man lay wounded. The two sides then retreated to their respective districts and stockpiled guns and ammunition awaiting further outbreaks of violence. A

87. *Woodville Beacon,* Nov. 9, 1906; Franklin, *Journey toward Hope,* 128.
88. *Lexington Leader,* June 12, 1908; *Daily Oklahoman,* Sept. 13, 1904; *Wilburton News,* Feb. 23, 1905; *Vinita Indian Chieftain,* Aug. 29, 1901.

force of deputy marshals was sent by the territorial government, and it secured peace, but not before settlers of both races spent many nights with patrols on guard. For weeks settlers, black and white, slept lightly with guns next to their beds.[89]

In Berwyn, Chickasaw Nation, a similar outbreak occurred. On Christmas Day, 1895, a black man came to the post office, allegedly drunk, and entered into an argument with the postmaster. The postmaster threw him out, and the drunken black went into the street trying to procure a gun and cursing the postmaster. The postmaster got his own weapon and began to pistol-whip the man. The next day three blacks came to town armed with hickory sticks and proceeded to beat the first white man they met. Whites rushed to aid the victim and several blacks came out of hiding, armed with clubs and guns. A full-scale riot erupted, and a number of blacks and whites were wounded. Again, for several days and nights, the local residents were unnerved, fearing reprisals. In Mangum, a riot started when a black boy struck a white boy with a serious blow to his head. A crowd of two hundred white men, armed with revolvers and clubs, attacked the black district in the southern part of town, and "for about thirty minutes there was a perfect fusilade of shots." Three blacks were wounded, one fatally, and one white policeman was severely beaten while attempting to disband the white mob.[90]

Racial violence also broke out when whites tried to run blacks out of town. After the reported murder of a white man by a black at Henryetta, whites drove all the African Americans out of town. The whites entered the black district and warned them to leave immediately. A few complied, but many more stayed. As one settler recalled, "The ones who wouldn't leave were beaten until they were glad to leave. There were three or four beaten with shinney clubs until they were almost dead, the others took that warning more seriously than the worded or vocal one and left." The African Americans left and volunteer guards kept blacks from returning. As the settler reminisced "if a man lived at the edge of town, he'd say 'No negro is going to get past my house, just let him try.' "[91]

Often whites intent upon running blacks out of town organized themselves into a fraternal society dedicated to maintaining white supremacy. Known as "whitecappers," the organization played a role similar to that of the Ku Klux Klan. Its members often wore hooded robes and attacked black districts at night. Hence they were also referred to as "night riders." In Waurika, whitecappers posted a notice in a number of public places which read: "Negroes: We

89. See Scott Ellsworth, *Death in a Promised Land: The Tulsa Race Riot of 1921* (Baton Rouge: Louisiana State University Press, 1982); *Cherokee Advocate*, May 17, 1902; *Vinita Indian Chieftain*, May 15, 1902.

90. Littlefield, *The Chickasaw Freedmen*, 98; *Mangum Star*, July 2, 1902.

91. Jim Simpson, interview, GFPHC, 101:385–86.

are white-cappers. We the sixty sons of Waurika, demand that the negroes leave here at once. We mean Go! Leave in 24 hours, for after that, your life is uncertain." In Lexington, Oklahoma Territory, whitecappers burned an African Methodist church to show their resentment of the black preacher's purchase of a new house in a fashionable part of town. The whitecappers left a large sign hanging in a courtyard tree, which read, "Last warning, negroes must leave this side of town; dynamite next time." In Guthrie, whitecappers broke into the printing room of the *Guthrie Guide,* a local black newspaper, and stole the printing press, dumping it into the Cottonwood River.[92]

Any whites who tried to import a number of African Americans into a local community as laborers often found themselves at odds with whitecappers. One Mangum citizen had an epidemic of typhoid fever in his family. He proposed to bring in a family of African Americans to help him while his family was incapacitated. Word soon spread and a delegation of whitecappers met the black family and warned them not to enter the town. However, the family continued to its destination. Immediately a mob formed outside, demanding the blacks take the first train east. The wife asked for the assistance of some fellow members of her husband's "Knights of Pythias." These gentlemen responded and discouraged the mob from attacking the house. When the men went home for the night, the mob followed them and assaulted them. The mob then returned to the house and renewed their demands for the black family to be given over to them. The wife persisted in protecting the black family, but the next day the African Americans "decided" to leave. Quiet was restored to the town, and as a result the local paper claimed, "white robed peace is brooding like a sucking dove over the scene of strife and riot and the day of much ado about nothing is gone." The Mangum paper proudly proclaimed, in its headline, "COON COON COON I WISH MY COLOR WOULD FADE AWAY AND IT DID FADE, FROM SIGHT."[93]

A white land developer near Blackwell, Oklahoma Territory, established title to several lots which he proposed to lease to African American settlers. But the whitecappers succeeded in scaring the settlers away through intimidation. In Bokoshe, Choctaw Nation, a white contractor brought in ten black families to work on the railroad. While they temporarily camped in one of the boxcars, a mob of angry whites surrounded the car and emptied their rifles into it in an attempt to frighten them off. The whites were successful in ordering the blacks out of town, but not before more violence erupted. In Geary, all the local black

92. *Daily Oklahoman,* Mar. 21, 1907; *Lexington Leader,* Aug. 27, 1909; *Lawton Constitution,* June 8, 1905. The "whitecappers" existed in many of the Deep South states and seemed intent upon driving African Americans off land they owned or rented. See William F. Holmes, "Whitecapping: Agrarian Violence in Mississippi, 1902–1906," *Journal of Southern History* 25 (May 1969): 165–85.
93. *Mangum Star,* Nov. 20, 1902.

residents were forced to leave town except the local black baker, who, one must assume, was regarded as indispensable.[94]

As with the case of lynching, African Americans did not take such an affront to their civil rights without fighting back. One whitecapper returned to his house on Christmas eve of 1894 to find it burned to the ground. On the property a note was left that said, "Davis Luis,—We will just give you our bill the first of January, 1895," (signed) "whitecaps." Under the signature was a sketch of a man in a coffin with a rope around his neck, and the other end tied around the limb of a tree. Two black suspects were arrested and charged with arson. In Muskogee, a bloody battle ensued when authorities tried to evict a black squatter from a house. The squatter was protected by members of an all-black organization called the United Socialists. Apparently this organization was formed in response to the whitecappers. The United Socialists argued that they did not recognize United States authority, so when the U.S. Marshals showed up to remove the squatter, they began shooting at them from the windows. By the end of the fracas, three African Americans and one white man were dead and several more were wounded.[95]

IN THE DECADES before the Civil War, the independent Indian nations of the Five Civilized Tribes had held exclusive jurisdiction over their own justice system, which resembled the American system while retaining tribal traditions. After the war, governmental officials and concerned humanitarians came to argue that to further the effort of assimilating the Indians into American society, Native Americans should be subjected to the American judicial system. The Board of Indian Commissioners stated in 1871: "A serious detriment to the progress of the partially civilized Indians is found in the fact that they are not brought under the domination of law, so far as regards crimes committed against each other. . . . we owe it to them, and to ourselves, to teach them the majesty of civilized law, and to extend to them its protection against the lawless among themselves."[96] Some Native Americans eagerly embraced the Anglo-American justice system, by becoming scouts or auxiliaries in the United States Army (which was often called upon for law enforcement) or by enlisting as Indian policemen. Many Native Americans, particularly the full bloods, however, vehemently objected to the loss of control over what they considered internal tribal affairs. Hence, those Indians who partook of Anglo-American justice system by becoming army scouts or Indian policemen were shunned by the "conservatives" in the tribe for selling out to whites. "Conservative" Indians, particularly those of the relocated Plains tribes who inhabited the reservations

94. *Beaver Herald,* Feb. 17, 1898; *Kingfisher Free Press,* Mar. 10, 1904; John Dean, interview, GFPHC, 22:134.

95. *Eufaula Indian Journal,* Feb. 1, 1895; *Carnegie Herald,* Apr. 5, 1907.

96. Prucha, *American Indian Policy,* 329.

on the western lands of the Indian Territory, denied that the whites who had taken their land and killed all their buffalo were cognizant of "justice."

At the same time, African Americans petitioned United States officials for protection from Indian courts, which they claimed denied them equal treatment. In addition, as white settlers poured into Oklahoma Territory, African Americans found themselves victimized by lynch law. They formed anti-lynching bureaus and pleaded to white officials to end this form of extra-legal action. However, while white governmental officials and concerned humanitarians argued to incorporate Native Americans into the American judicial system, whites proved unwilling to disturb the customs of arbitrary punishment imposed upon African Americans suspected of committing a crime. Many white legislators and newspaper editors in Oklahoma Territory condoned the practice of lynching African Americans accused of rape and murder. Ironically, while many Native Americans opposed being included in the American judicial system for fear of giving up yet another aspect of self-government, African Americans sought to be included so as to avoid the terror and unpredictability of Indian courts and vigilante justice.

SEVEN

The Politics of Race
Segregation, Disfranchisement, and Statehood

O NE POLITICAL DEBATE which affected Indian tribes was the question of United States citizenship for the Native American peoples of the Indian Territory. United States officials argued that the Indians were too attached to their traditions and separate nationality. They believed that while members of the Five Civilized Tribes deserved respect for their patriotic sentiments and noble principles, they should not be allowed to obstruct the westward expansion of Anglo-American progress and civilization. As the commissioner of Indian affairs noted in 1886:

> These Indians have no right to obstruct civilization and commerce and set up an exclusive claim to self-government, establishing a government within a government, and then expect and claim that the United States shall protect them from all harm, while insisting that it shall not be the ultimate judge as to what is best to be done for them in a political point of view. I repeat, to maintain any such view is to acknowledge a foreign sovereignty, with the right of eminent domain, upon American soil—a theory utterly repugnant to the spirit and genius of our laws, and wholly unwarranted by the Constitution of the United States.[1]

White officials also claimed that territorial status would help Indians from being subjected to the "jealousy, contention, and selfish greed of adventurous land-grabbers who now seem to regard the Indian a legitimate object of prey and plunder." They argued if the Indians would assume all the responsibilities of citizens of the United States, with American laws extended over them as a protecting aegis, "their fear and apprehension of marauding whites will forever be ended." Officials in Washington hoped that Native Americans would voluntarily submit to United States jurisdiction and accept territorial status, but most were ready to force acceptance upon the Indian tribes if needed. As one local

---

1. J. D. C. Atkins, CIA, to SI, Sept. 28, 1886, in *RSI* 1886, 1:86–87.

Indian agent asked, "Would a guardian be justified in allowing his ward to waste his money at the grogshop or gambling saloon simply because the ward prefers that course to a course of good education?" Some officials in Washington argued that if the United States had made millions of black freedmen in the South citizens overnight, there was no reason why the Indians could not be incorporated into United States citizenship as well. The *New York Tribune* declared, "The Indian, even the sun dancing brave, is just as ready for the polls as were the field-hands of Georgia or the Voodoo worshippers of Louisiana. Give him the ballot."[2]

The majority of Native Americans, however, were adamant that they did not want any change to their political right of self-government. They much preferred their independence to any supposed advantages to be gained from United States citizenship. Hence, Indian leaders universally opposed the idea of receiving territorial status. The Cherokee agent reported that "the great mass of the people of every class regard the organization of a territorial government with abhorrence." The Creeks also objected. Their agent declared that they were unanimously opposed to the measure, for they saw it as an attempt to deprive them of their last resting place and "a move that will fill their beautiful and fruitful country with white men who will be too numerous to be removed." The Seminoles likewise: "to force [on] them any form of government with which they are wholly unacquainted would be destructive," and that the result "would be equally injurious to their hopes if the territory were to be opened to white settlement." One Indian leader said in summary that the U.S. government had promised the Indian Territory to the Indians for their perpetual use. He noted, "We are sensible of the fact, that a Territorial form of Government will at this time in no wise benefit the Indians, but work for their certain ruin." The Indian leaders feared that bestowing territorial status upon the Indian nations was a prelude to opening the lands to white settlement. They astutely recognized that massive white settlement upon the Indian lands would most certainly bring about the end of Native American self-government. As noted earlier, Native Americans in the Indian Territory were successful in getting themselves exempted from the provisions of the Dawes Act. Hence the Indian nations remained independent until the Curtis Act was passed in 1898.[3]

With the passage of the Indian Citizenship Act in 1901, the peoples of the Indian nations were declared citizens of the United States with all the rights and responsibilities that attended such status. Much to their consternation, Native Americans were now under the "protection" of United States law and

2. *Ibid.*; A. Parsons to CIA, R 181, Choctaw Agency, 1874, LR-RBIA; Merrill E. Gates, in *RSI* 1885, 1:767; *Cherokee Advocate,* July 30, 1879 (reprinted from the *New York Tribune*).

3. John B. Jones to CIA, Sept. 20, 1873, in *RSI* 1873, p. 575; E. R. Roberts to CL., Sept. 30, 1873, in *RSI* 1873, p. 579; Henry Breiner to CIA, Sept. 1, 1873, in *RSI* 1873, p. 581; Samuel Checote, June 2, 1870, Box C-2, Part I, SCP.

were required to pay federal taxes. With the passage of the Curtis Act and the Indian Citizenship Act, self-government for Native peoples, centuries old in tradition, came to an end.

The Indian Citizenship Act, by granting all Native Americans who accepted their allotments citizenship in the United States, set the stage for the admission of the former Indian lands as a state. However, Native Americans initially opposed all efforts to incorporate their lands into a state. When it became obvious that Washington had every intention of going ahead, the leaders of the Five Civilized Tribes sought to ensure that their territory be admitted as a separate state, apart from Oklahoma Territory. The Indian leaders argued that if Indian Territory were to be combined with Oklahoma Territory to form one state, Native Americans would form an inconsequential "island" in a "sea" of white settlers.[4]

In March of 1903, the Principal Chief of the Choctaws, Green McCurtain, wrote to his fellow chiefs, "I am convinced that it is the duty of the Indians composing the Five Civilized Tribes, to make one supreme effort to erect a state out of the present boundaries of the Indian Territory." McCurtain called for a constitutional convention in which the Five Civilized Tribes would write a state constitution for the Indian Territory, a constitution that would then be submitted to Congress for ratification. McCurtain was convinced there was a powerful sentiment, both inside and outside of Congress, that was inclined to give the Indians a separate state of their own. McCurtain saw this as just retribution, for, as he claimed, "It seems to me, in the light of our history, it would be fitting and just to permit the Indian to have a voice in the erection of at least one state, on a continent to which he once lay claim."[5]

All the leaders of the Five Civilized Tribes eventually agreed to participate in a convention to discuss the possibility of single statehood for Indian Territory. As Pleasant Porter, the chief of the Creeks noted, "the meeting will be one of the most remarkable ever held on Indian soil. Five Indian governors formulating a plan to dissolve their governments and adopt the government of the white man." The fact that it took over a decade for the Indians to arrive at this decision after the issue of statehood for Indian Territory was first raised gives credence to the statement of ex–Cherokee chief, D. W. Bushyhead, who concluded in 1893 that "the inevitable is that we will be merged into [Anglo-American] civilization, that will be the ultimate solution. But it will not come at once. The sentiment of the Indians is against it." While recognizing the inevitability of statehood, Bushyhead argued it would not come fast to the Indian Territory. He cautioned that "while the white men carry things through at rail-

4. See Debo, *And Still the Waters Run*; Debo, *The Road to Disappearance*.
5. Green McCurtain to Governors of the Five Civilized Tribes, March 14, 1903, Choctaw Nation Papers, vol. I, 389–91, WHC.

road speed, the Indians are a little slow, and will be especially so in this case." In this case Bushyhead's statement proved prophetic.[6]

Hence the "last stand" of the Native American peoples of the Indian Territory to preserve their political power came with the Sequoyah Convention called in 1905 to provide for separate statehood for the Indian Territory apart from Oklahoma Territory. The election of delegates to the Sequoyah Convention divided the Indian nations along racial lines. Whites were greatly in favor of statehood and preferred joint statehood with Oklahoma Territory, mixed bloods generally supported statehood but preferred separate statehood apart from Oklahoma Territory, while full bloods were openly opposed to any form of statehood, preferring to maintain their independent status as separate nations.

Most of the tribal chiefs of the Five Civilized Tribes, recognizing the inevitability of statehood, argued in favor of separate statehood for the Indian Territory as opposed to joint statehood with Oklahoma Territory. Green McCurtain, for one, argued that while all Americans found self-government desirable, the Indian people, not wishing to see their ancient governments come to an abrupt end, would rather see them unite into "one fair commonwealth." This worried some white residents of Indian Territory, who felt that if the Indians were successful in getting separate statehood, whites would become outcasts. One white resident declared, "the Convention at Muskogee . . . looks to an Indian commonwealth, controlled and dominated by the red man, to the practical exclusion of his Anglo-Saxon brother." The white settler continued, "no graver error could be committed than in thus arraying the red man against the white and insisting that a small minority of Indians shall make a Constitution for the great majority—the whites."[7]

The mixed bloods proved resilient, and with the help of the intermarried white citizens of the Indian nations, they were able to write a proposed constitution for a separate Indian state to be known as "Sequoyah," out of respect to the inventor of the Cherokee syllabary. But Congress once again refused to accede to the wishes of Native Americans, and refused even to consider separate statehood for Indian Territory. Thus the worst fears of the full-blood Indians were realized, as Native American self-government was replaced by white rule when statehood united Oklahoma and Indian Territories in 1907.[8]

INDIAN LEADERS also warned of the potential danger of giving their ex-slaves full political participation, including the right to vote and hold office.

6. Pleasant Porter, editorial, *South McAlester Capital,* Sept. 18, 1902, in Creek Nation Papers, vol. I, 189–90, OHS; *Oklahoma State Capital,* Nov. 18, 1893.

7. Green McCurtain, "Addresses and Arguments by Prominent Men in Favor of Separate Statehood," Box 27, File 3, GMP; S. T. Bledsoe, "Addresses and Arguments by Prominent Men in Favor of Separate Statehood," Box 27, File 3, GMP.

8. Strickland, *The Indians in Oklahoma,* 50.

Many Native American politicians warned of a day in the not-so-distant future when the ex-slaves would seize control of tribal affairs. These leaders based their argument on the fact that the freedmen population was increasing while the full-blood Indian population was decreasing, the implication being that at some point the freedmen would outnumber the Indians and hence gain control of the reins of political power.

Thus, many Native American leaders in the Indian Territory appealed to voters on racial grounds in an effort to restrict the political rights of the freedmen. Candidates for tribal office were able to convince their constituents that their interest lay in protecting their racial purity and privilege from the invasion of "foreign influences" by putting into office those people who could be entrusted to resist such an invasion. Each of the Five Civilized Tribes differed in the extent to which it attempted to restrict the political rights of its freedmen.

The Seminoles allowed their ex-slaves full political participation and some freedmen held positions of prominence within the tribe. For example, J. Coody Johnson, the secretary to the Seminole chief, was reportedly "a negro as black as night." Johnson transacted almost all the chief's business, and represented the tribe in Washington, since the chief knew no English. Many other Seminole freedmen were able to use their knowledge of both Indian and the English languages to act as interpreters, while others were directly involved in tribal politics.[9]

Freedmen who were resident in the Creek Nation at the time of the 1866 treaty or who returned within the specified time limit enjoyed full political participation. The Creek freedmen had representatives in both houses of the Creek National Council, and a former slave, "Big Jeff," assumed the position of the highest judge in the Creek Nation. By 1876, the *Cherokee Advocate* could claim that there were "now more than 300 colored voters in the Creek Nation who were once slaves in the tribe."[10]

On the other hand, the Cherokees tried to deny their freedmen political participation. Ever since removal, the Cherokees had had a law which stated, "no person who is of negro or mulatto parentage, either by the father's or the mother's side, shall be eligible to hold any office of profit, honor, or trust, under this government." The freedmen who were Cherokee citizens according to the provisions of the 1866 treaty did, however, have the right to vote. But they soon found that Cherokee politicians were not willing to represent their interests because of the political unpopularity of black civil rights. One Indian agent noted that "it is unpopular in the Cherokee Nation to advocate a measure that provides for placing the colored man on an equality with the Cherokees." The agent argued that "the politicians are civilized enough to do

9. Choctaw, Chickasaw 1875–1906 and Seminole 1845–1921 and Miscellaneous Papers 1874–1932, p. 162, OHS.
10. *Cherokee Advocate*, May 6, 1876.

nothing that might lessen their chances for political success; hence until the sentiment shall undergo a revolution there will be no favorable action." The Cherokees remained steadfast in their desire to exclude the freedmen from a role in tribal politics even though they possessed the vote. The *Cherokee Advocate* noted its objection to allowing freedmen to serve in the Cherokee National Council, claiming that the freedmen lacked "the capacity to make laws for us." The paper noted that from past experience Cherokees realized that the freedmen cast votes "according to the dictation of others." The editor concluded, "We believe that we have Cherokees in sufficient number, and of ability, to legislate for us."[11]

The freedmen became very disillusioned with the Cherokee electoral process, feeling that their interests were not considered regardless of who won the election. One freedman warned his fellow ex-slaves:

> The leaders of both parties always told me next Council we will fix it, we almost got it through this time, just vote us in once more. Just so it is, next Council and next Council, like tomorrow, never comes, it is the delusive end of the rainbow, with its sack of gold always in sight, but never in reach, a receding tantalizing will-o'-wisp, leading you further into the morass of disappointment. However much they may honey you with sweet words and promises of citizenship, however much they may Mr. Smith and Mr. Jones you, they are only giving you a pill, sugar coated it may be, still only a pill to work through the election. I don't believe there is anything to hope for from these politicians.

Black freedmen in the Cherokee Nation also complained of intimidation during elections. They alleged that the old Confederate faction of the tribe used to get drunk and visit black settlements in squads to intimidate the ex-slaves into voting for their candidate. If the freedmen refused, the Indians would shoot at them.[12]

The Choctaws, like the Cherokees, did all they could to discourage their ex-slaves from voting. One freedman remembered how the Indians held their political meetings without notifying the ex-slaves of the time and place. He wrote: "Sir please your onor we wish to no if we have any right to voat at the Choctaw Lection they seems to be very anctious to get our voats it seems like a one sided peace of buisness we have no voice in nominate candidates there fore we want to no whither we have an rite to voat or not these indians holds there convention by night when the fredman are not notified to attend at none of these meetings." Even as late as 1898, when the Choctaws were to vote on the Dawes Commission recommendations, Governor McCurtain of the Choctaw

11. Microfilm CHN 10, NRCN; Jonathan Tufts to CIA, Jan. 26, 1882, in *RSI* 1882, 2:46; *Cherokee Advocate*, July 30, 1879.
12. Quoted in Littlefield, *The Cherokee Freedmen*, 63–64, 121.

Nation issued a proclamation denying the ex-slaves the right to vote. All county election officials were warned not to let any freedmen vote and to expect resistance and trouble. One local newspaper expected "desperate resistance on the part of the freedmen," and another paper said "there is liable to be trouble." Apparently the election passed without serious incident.[13]

Choctaw leaders justified denying their freedmen the vote to officials in Washington, arguing that the ex-slaves were not responsible with their voting privilege. They argued the ex-slaves were used as pawns by those interested in securing election. As one leader put it, "the negro as a people has lifted up his heels against his best friend, and in these political marches, hog like has followed the man who has the corn in his sack, and true to their nature have squealed all the louder when corn has passed their way and not been thrown to them." Green McCurtain, at this time a Choctaw senator, stated, "a negro is like a mule, put him up and feed him and he will turn around and kick you to death." Not surprisingly given such attitudes, the Dawes Commission in its report on the status of Choctaw freedmen painted a grim picture. The report criticized the treatment accorded Choctaw freedmen, claiming, "They are yet very far from the enjoyment of all the rights, privileges, and immunities to which they are entitled under the treaties. . . . but little participation in the management of the government of which he is a citizen is permitted him." The Choctaws responded that the freedmen were left unmolested and enjoyed "more rights than his brothers just across the line in adjoining states." This led them to conclude that all this talk from the commission of the poor condition of the Choctaw freedman was "the silliest traddle and they are either ignorant of his condition or knowingly misrepresent the facts." The Choctaws did admit that "unscrupulous men may have at some times and in some instances" trampled on the rights of the freedmen, but that was no worse than elsewhere in the United States, and these cases "were the exception to and not the general rule."[14]

As previously mentioned, the Chickasaws refused to adopt their freedmen and thereby denied them any role in tribal politics. They claimed that this was necessary because of concern for their political future. They argued that in the half-century which had elapsed since their own removal west, the percentage of the population that was black had greatly increased. This was the result of several factors: the natural rate of increase after the Civil War was greater in the freedmen population than in the Indian population; regiments of colored troops stationed in the Indian Territory after the war had decided to stay and

13. David Gardner to the President of the United States, Apr. 1, 1886, Indian Territory, Special Files, Choctaw and Chickasaw and Cherokee Freedmen, RG 48, Box 48, RDI; *Purcell Register,* Aug. 18, 1898; *El Reno News,* Aug. 26, 1898.

14. *Choctaw Papers,* vol. 1, 338–39, WCH; Sec. X, Freedmen File, Choctaw Records, OHS, *Atoka Indian Citizen,* Dec. 27, 1894.

intermarried with local freedmen; many freedmen sold or transported out of the Chickasaw Nation during the Civil War had returned and settled back in the nation. Hence, Chickasaws argued, they had to deny their freedmen citizenship rights or else they would lose control of their political affairs. The Chickasaws succinctly put forth their rationale for refusing the vote to their ex-slaves in a petition to the United States president, claiming, "the freedmen and colored immigrants constitute so large a part of the Chickasaw nation and increase in number so rapidly that they must soon outnumber the Chickasaws, and, if invested with the elective franchise, will be able to take possession of the government, and ultimately to deprive the Chickasaw people of their government and country." The Chickasaw governor, Douglas H. Johnston, contended that the African race was prolific, while the Indians were not. The Indians, he claimed, had been drastically reduced in numbers by destructive wars and diseases with the result that "it will be but a few generations until the full blood Indian will be no more, but as the Indian citizen vanishes, the Negro 'Chickasaw,' if such he is made by Congress, will multiply, and the time will not be far distant, if this iniquity is visited upon us, when the name of Chickasaw will carry with it approbrium [*sic*] and reproach instead of honor." The Chickasaws never did grant their freedmen political rights in the nation, and as historian Daniel F. Littlefield Jr. states, the Chickasaw freedmen were literally "a people without a country."[15]

WHILE FACTIONALISM was rampant in the Indian Territory, there were also major divisions between Oklahoma Territory residents. Up until statehood, it was the Republicans who dominated territorial politics in Oklahoma Territory. They were assisted by Republican dominance at the federal level. A Republican sat in the White House for thirteen of Oklahoma's seventeen years as a territory. Not surprisingly, during this time six of seven territorial governors were Republicans. The question which logically arises is, What led territorial Oklahoma voters to abandon the Republican Party by the advent of statehood? The answer to this question is found in the "politics of race" that came to dominate territorial Oklahoma.[16]

George W. Steele became the first governor of the territory of Oklahoma in 1890, beginning almost two decades of Republican rule. The Republicans were able to defeat the Democrats in part because of the consistent support from African American voters. While many blacks voted for the Republican Party out of gratitude for emancipation, they also received tangible benefits in terms of

15. Chickasaw Memorial to the President of the United States, Indian Territory, Special Files, Choctaw and Chickasaw and Cherokee Freedmen, RG 48, Box 48, RDI; quoted in Jeltz, "The Relations of Negroes," 37; Littlefield, *The Chickasaw Freedmen,* xi.

16. James R. Scales and Danney Goble, *Oklahoma Politics: A History* (Norman: University of Oklahoma Press, 1982), 5.

active involvement in political affairs. The Republicans ran several black candidates in local elections and doled out patronage appointments to staunch African American party members as well. Governor Steele set the precedent for active African American participation in Republican-controlled territorial government when in the summer of 1890 he appointed the most prominent African American, Edward P. McCabe, treasurer for Logan County. In the following year, he named another African American Logan County clerk. Hence, very early a connection was made between the Republican Party and African Americans. This alliance would serve as the basis from which the politics of race would evolve.[17]

By the 1890s, most of the Deep South states were in the process of disfranchising their African American population. In the end, the Republican Party went into eclipse there and the Democrats effectively established one-party rule. In contrast, Oklahoma Territory throughout the 1890s had fiercely competitive elections between Republicans and Democrats. In most instances the Republican Party emerged victorious, and hence African Americans were able to maintain an active role in political affairs that was denied them in the states of the Deep South. Their aspirations prompted them to reject mere political tokenism and strive for true political participation.[18]

African Americans soon learned that they could use their voting strength to their advantage in gaining concessions from Republican officials. They were not above using pressure tactics to ensure that the party met their demands. In 1896, African American voters in the Fifteenth Legislative District reminded their fellow Republicans that they "are not only expecting one of their race to be nominated for the legislature, but they say he must come from the country, not from the city, otherwise they declare they will take little interest in the coming election." Similarly, the African American voters in Enid in 1907 asked that if the Republican ticket was elected, they be given a black policeman to protect the heavily African American area known as "the flats," and a black deputy street commissioner.[19]

When the Republican Party nominated a white candidate to run in the Twenty-eighth Legislative District, African American supporters decided to run their own black Republican candidate. As the *Daily Oklahoman* proclaimed: "The negroes apparently understand thoroughly the art of politics. They are aware that if they threaten political violence upon party nominees, the leaders will promptly quail before their numbers and accede to their demands. And then the objectionable planks, adopted in convention, will be quickly con-

17. Tolson, *The Black Oklahomans*, 107.

18. See J. Morgan Kousser, *The Shaping of Southern Politics: Suffrage Restriction and the Establishment of the One-Party South 1880–1910* (New Haven: Yale University Press, 1974); Williams, "The Black Press in Oklahoma," 313.

19. *Kingfisher Free Press*, Sept. 24, 1896; *Beaver Journal*, April 4, 1907.

signed to the limbo on innocuous desuetude." Hence African Americans did all they could to maintain a high profile and an active voice in the political affairs of the territory while it was under Republican rule. Unlike in the Deep South, where Democratic Redeemers during the 1890s were replacing Republican rule and excluding African Americans from the political sphere through intimidation, violence, poll taxes, and literacy tests, African Americans found they held significant influence in territorial politics in Oklahoma.[20]

Needless to say, the prominence afforded African Americans in the Republican Party agitated whites regardless of party affiliation. Many felt that African Americans were given political appointments simply because of their skin color, and many adamantly believed that blacks should not be allowed to hold public office under any circumstance. The Democrat-controlled *Guthrie Daily Leader* warned that all that enticed blacks to political participation was their ability to secure political appointment from Republican administrations.[21]

Democrats in Guthrie remained determined not to allow African Americans to hold office and dominate local political affairs. At a Democratic convention the delegates pledged to eliminate black officeholding. They declared, "our unalterable opposition to the selection and election of negroes to office, as a social commercial and political blemish on the good name of our city and an immeasurable barrier to good government."[22]

Democrats also complained of improprieties in elections. They claimed the Republicans would often import a number of African Americans from Kansas and other surrounding states to pose as residents of Oklahoma Territory and vote in the elections. In 1892, a local newspaper proclaimed, "the Republicans are up to their old tricks of importing destitute negroes into Oklahoma for their votes at the November election." The paper reported that "the streets of Guthrie are said to be swarming with strange negroes who are a charge upon charity." In 1894 the Democratic organ, the *Guthrie Daily Leader,* warned:

This city is the Mecca of a lot of Kansas negroes. They were brought up in the different Kansas cities on the Santa Fe road. They came in car lots during the week, and now the city is full of them. On every street corner, strange negro faces are seen. They are housed with the prominent negro politicians and are to be palmed off as old residents of Guthrie. These negroes are the dependence of the Republicans to carry the election. Democrats watch the polls, and convince yourselves that every voter is a legal one. Don't allow your rights to be voted away by negroes and imported thugs. Challenge every voter and know who he is. Drive all imported negroes out of the city.

20. *Daily Oklahoman,* Oct. 19, 1906, Oct. 13, 1906.
21. *Guthrie Daily Leader,* July 24, 1894, Feb. 9, 1894.
22. E. J. Giddings, "New State Negro Address," Sept. 22, 1906, File 82.97, FBP.

The same paper reported during that same election year that black delegates to the Republican convention had openly sold their votes to the highest bidder. The paper alleged that a whole delegation of African Americans was bought out on the floor of the convention for five dollars each, and supposedly in two instances, "the money was openly counted out" to each of the delegates. Democrats also criticized Republicans for holding political meetings under the guise of picnics in wards with high concentrations of black voters. This was reportedly done "to throw the public off the trail and lure on the ignorant colored voter with ice cream and cake and watermelons."[23]

With every passing election in territorial Oklahoma, "the Negro question" began to assume ever greater importance. The Democrats were able to exploit the race issue, charging the Republicans were "nigger lovers" and in favor of "Negro domination." Republicans found themselves on the defensive, arguing that the race issue was a smokescreen behind which the Democrats tried to hide.

As early as 1894, the Democratic Party urged Oklahomans to vote for the party which represented the interests of the white race as opposed to the black race. One Democratic paper contended, "the Republicans of this county have renewed their allegiance to the negro voter and embrace him with a fervor and warmth which is a caution to see. . . . they fall on his neck with brisk thuds of adulation, take him to their homes, sit him at the family table, and wine and dine him with peculiar ardor." According to the Democrats, the Republicans gave more sympathy to the African American than to the white American. One Democratic newspaper queried: "Who does not know that the strength of the republican party is the negro? Who will deny that the negro makes it possible for republicans to hold office in Oklahoma, and is the hope of the aspirant for office in the new state? Can a party that owes its success to the negro do those things the negro says must not be done, and still hope to win?"[24]

The Democrats, however, claimed they were satisfied that the Republicans were so anxious to look after the interests of the black race; they wanted nothing to do with African Americans. As the editor of the *Guthrie Daily Leader* claimed: "Well, we are glad the negro has some one to care for him, kindly and so tenderly. The Democrats don't want him—not in this county. We want no variegated office holders. The white man is good enough for us. . . . We want no negroes in our county conventions, unless they have left their slave state, and bathe occasionally. Democrats are not overly particular, but they know where to draw the line. Democracy is not boosting the negro. He is no better than the white man." Democrats continually asserted in political rallies and in

23. *Lexington Leader,* Oct. 8, 1892; *Guthrie Daily Leader,* Apr. 1, 1894, Aug. 23, 1894, July 25, 1894.
24. *Guthrie Daily Leader,* Aug. 23, 1894; *Purcell Register,* Oct. 18, 1906.

their newspapers that the Republicans favored blacks over whites but that their own party stood firmly behind the interests of white supremacy.[25]

The Republicans entered the politics of race on the defensive, arguing that they gave no preference to blacks over whites but merely favored equal treatment for both races. Some territorial Republicans professed that they desired to see equal opportunities for white, black, and "red" Americans. One territorial Republican newspaper described the principles of Republicanism by stating: "This paper is for Americanism in its true sense—for but one kind of American citizenship for every man, regardless of color, nationality, or financial condition—and this means that every man shall have equal rights under the law, equal opportunity; that he be given an even start and a fair field, untrammeled in his energies and chances, unhindered in the enjoyment of all he earns; that every man shall be gauged according to his merits. Any man who attempts to travel on any other platform ought to, and will, fail."[26]

Such statements provided fuel for the fire that burned in the politics of race. Democrats seized upon such comments and wrote long diatribes in response, emphasizing the horrors to come from Republican "nigger equality." In response to the above comment from a Republican paper, the Democratic *Purcell Register* raised the infamous bugaboo of racial intermixing:

Has the editor of the Free Press a daughter? Or, as he was, we believe, but recently married, suppose we say a sister? Would he be willing that sister should welcome at her home a negro suitor, accepting from him the gallantries and courtesies usually accorded between persons who mutually esteem each other? Would he, without protest strong and vigorous, see that sister attended to church, to social festivities and to the various scenes in which young people mingle, by a negro? Would he like to see this intimacy continue until it has its usual culmination in marriage of that sister to an African? Continuing even beyond this point, would he be proud to have the mulatto children of his sister calling him uncle?

. . . Candidly, Bro. Admire, how would you like such a practical illustration of your social equality theories?[27]

However, more important than racial slurs, Democrats did their best to convince the electorate that the Republican Party actively encouraged "negro domination." Democrats tried to instill a fear in white Oklahomans that the country would soon be overrun with ex-slaves from the Deep South. One commentator noted in 1906 after Booker T. Washington had visited the all-black town of Boley, that Washington and other emigration agents had been going

25. *Guthrie Daily Leader,* Aug. 23, 1894.
26. *Oklahoma State Capital,* Aug. 4, 1894.
27. *Ibid.*

throughout the South telling African Americans that the best place for them was the new state of Oklahoma. He then queried, "Can it be said that with these plans and these efforts at colonization, there is nothing in the negro question?"[28]

One Democrat responded that the threat of "negro domination" was very real. He warned settlers, "it is, indeed, but a poor character of statesmanship that merely looks at the present conditions! The state going Republican when the negro question is an issue, opens up the gates to a great horde of negro emigration." Democrats tried to convince the white electorate that if they did not support the Democratic Party and its staunch defense of white supremacy, Oklahoma would be flooded with ex-slaves seeking to escape the oppression of the Deep South states. The threat seemed real enough. After all, territorial African Americans, as we have seen, possessed the vote, held public offices, often owned their own land, and sent their children to schools. To African Americans trapped in the oppression of the American South, Oklahoma Territory in the 1890s must have indeed appeared a "promised land" of unparalleled opportunity. The Democratic *Purcell Register* in 1906, warned that

> It must be remembered that Oklahoma lies in close proximity to the black belt of the south. In those states where the negro population exceeds the population of the whites the negro necessarily is held down by the whites who own the property. Just as sure as the republicans gain control of Oklahoma and begin to preach the equality of the races, just that sure will the hoards [sic] of the black belt pour in upon us. Whenever the negro population feels that any section will be liberal toward him, he immediately turns his eyes in that direction, and looks for fields in which he can aspire to political and social equality.[29]

Many Native American politicians also feared the threat of "negro domination." It may at first seem surprising that Native Americans tended to support the Democratic Party in the years just prior to statehood. The Indians would seem to have had every reason not to vote Democratic. After all it had been the Democrat Andrew Jackson who had been responsible for the Trail of Tears. But anti-black racism drove them into the arms of their traditional enemies. Many Indian leaders espoused the Democratic Party line to their tribesmen, claiming the Republican Party was the party "of the Negro." One Choctaw, D. C. McCurtain, proclaimed to his fellow tribesmen that he could not understand how any Indian could bring himself to vote for the Republican Party, which he claimed was "so closely connected with the negro and so strongly committed to his interests." McCurtain concluded, "I am for the Indian as against the negro, and am, therefore, not a Republican." McCurtain reminded his tribes-

28. Giddings, "New State Negro Address."
29. *Ibid.*; *Purcell Register,* Sept. 13, 1906.

men that it was the Republicans who had forced them to make new treaties with the United States government, treaties in which they were compelled to give citizenship rights to their black freedmen. McCurtain queried:

> The Republican party, the boasted friend of the Indian people, would and did take the Indian's property without compensation and give it to the negroes; and all this they did in the name of the United States government. Did the United States government, under the control of the Republican party, ever do so much for the white people, as it has for the negro? Did the United States government ever provide homes for the white people in Indian Territory, as it has for the negro? Not only that, did the United States government, under Republican rule, exact of the other slave owners the same requirements it exacted of the Indians? Were the people of Arkansas, Texas, Mississippi and the other slave owning states required to provide for their negro slaves as were the Indians?[30]

Contemporary observers, both white and Native American, agreed on the importance of the race question in territorial elections in Oklahoma. Many felt that Oklahoma was a battleground where the "race question" would be settled once and for all, and either the "southern" or "northern" treatment of blacks would predominate. One writer declared, "All eyes are turned on Oklahoma in this campaign. The issues here are not only understood by the citizens of the new state but of all other states in the great American Union." Another writer summarized the situation by stating, "the negro question was paramount. Shall we have the negro giving people a Kansas dose of his ideas, or will we let him know that he is to be cared for as he is in Texas, was an idea that took form rather than expression."[31]

A look at the town of Muskogee illustrates how this question took form in territorial Oklahoma. White residents of Muskogee saw themselves involved in a battle with African Americans for political control of the town. They contended that the presence of so many blacks in their town hurt business and kept potential capital investments away. They argued visitors were not attracted to their town because they found "too many Negroes here." In the election campaign for delegates to the Constitutional Convention of 1906, Democrats, focusing on the race issue, won a decisive majority. As the *Daily Oklahoman* proclaimed:

> The election of delegates has settled the negro question. This is a white man's country. At the polls the negro was given to understand his situation. Every-

30. D. C. McCurtain, Box 27, File 10, GMP.
31. Giddings, "New State Negro Address"; *Sturms Oklahoma Magazine* 3, no. 4 (Dec. 1906): 5.

where negro ambition asserted itself politically it was administered a crushing and indisputable rebuke. The enormous democratic majority in the state shows that the southern methods of handling the negro will be used here. This has given the white people great relief and it has had its immediate effect industrially and commercially. Foreign capital that hesitated before is eager to get in now. There are more people in Muskogee now looking for investments than there has [*sic*] been for a year before and there is a healthier feeling among Muskogee businessmen. They know that the negro question has been settled.[32]

As was common in southern politics, racial slurs were a prominent feature of territorial election campaigns. Democrats used racial propaganda, labeling Republicans "nigger lovers" in an attempt to defeat their political foes and as a means to instill a fear that the country would soon be overrun with ex-slaves from the South. In a 1904 election campaign a Republican candidate found he had given his Democratic opponent an opportunity to employ the politics of race by allowing a black deputy land commissioner to stay over at his house and serving him breakfast. One territorial newspaper described the event in "colorful" language, stating:

It was not so very long ago that the nigger,—who is deputy land commissioner at Guthrie, was entertained by Dr. Elliott. We have it from good authority that the coon was set down at his table and the fatted calf was killed. You remember that when Roosevelt entertained the kinkie [*sic*] haired Booker T., he saw to it that his own daughter, Miss Alice, was next the guest of honor. We are not informed whether the republican candidate for commissioner in the southern district had the grace to go the Rooseveltian limit or not.

The Democratic paper reminded its readers that "the Democracy stands for all white Anglo-Saxon supremacy. It takes no stock in Roosevelt's idea of nigger equality. If the President wants to dine with a coon that is his privilege, and so too with Dr. Elliott." And no one could mistake the racism in the statement of a noted Oklahoma politician who once remarked that "Wagoner . . . is tired of Orangutang government." White voters were reminded by such virulent racist statements that their territory was unusual in still allowing African Americans active political participation.[33]

White Democrats in Oklahoma Territory, like their counterparts in the Deep South states, were not averse to using every form of chicanery to try and remove African Americans as an active force in political affairs. One Oklahoma resident remembered how at a political debate between a Republican and a

32. *Daily Oklahoman,* Nov. 20, 1906.
33. Dr. Elliott to Walter Scott Ferguson, Oct. 10, 1904, Box 36, File 4, WSFP; quoted in Franklin, *Journey toward Hope,* 109.

Democratic candidate, the Democrats had hired a black lady to sit in the front row and say loud "amens" at every pause in the Republican candidates' speech. Another Oklahoman remembered how in Webber's Falls the local polling place for African American voters was segregated from that of the whites and placed in the back room of the local funeral home. The voters actually had to place their completed ballots in an open casket laid out in the back room. The woman recalled that many African American residents of the town were either too frightened or too superstitious to undergo such torment and therefore lost their voting privilege. The Democrats also challenged the ability of African Americans to vote by using the "affidavit system." According to a Republican newspaper in 1907, hundreds of African American men in Muskogee had their voting eligibility challenged by Democratic supporters. The men then had to obtain a sworn affadavit and pay a notary public for the acknowledgment, setting forth their qualifications as voters. The paper reported that in many instances the black voters did not have the money to pay the notary public and therefore lost their vote. The paper warned, "This system will, no doubt, be attempted again in September and provisions must be made by republicans to counteract its effect to the end that every legal voter may cast his ballot and have it counted. This is Oklahoma, not Mississippi nor Alabama."[34]

In addition to such tactics, white Democrats also resorted to their tried-and-true method of physical intimidation and violence. When tactics such as those outlined above did not dissuade enough black voters from staying away from the polls, Democrats formed "Democratic clubs," which went in groups into black areas and beat or whipped black Republican candidates and supporters. Violence at the actual polling stations was not an uncommon occurrence either. In 1902, Governor Thomas B. Ferguson had to call in the militia to protect African American voters from the efforts of white residents of Lawton to prevent them from exercising their right to the franchise. In all these extra-legal ways white Democrats sought to eliminate the voting privileges of African Americans long before disfranchisement actually came to the new state of Oklahoma in 1910.[35]

African Americans did not take such affront to their voting rights lying down. In numerous ways, blacks fought to maintain their precious hold on the franchise in Oklahoma Territory while watching with horror as each of the Deep South states effectively eliminated African Americans from active political participation. One of the most important means of combating Democrats intent upon eliminating blacks as political participants was the creation of Negro Voters Protection Leagues. Many of these protective leagues appeared at the local level to protect black voters in exercising their voting privilege. In McAl-

---

34. Chester Spitler, interview, File 298, OHP; Eliza Wilson, interview, File 665, OHP; *Oklahoma Weekly Times Journal,* Aug. 23, 1907.
35. Allan Williams, interview, File 851, OHP; *Alva Review,* Apr. 10, 1902.

ester, the black residents formed a political club with the stated purpose to ensure "the colored men of the territory will be so organized as to secure full representation in territorial conventions." The political clubs were not only a line of defense against Democratic attempts to restrict the voting rights of African Americans, but also a means by which African Americans could make known their demands to Republican policy-makers.[36]

By the mid-1890s it was becoming clear that the Democrats were gaining support with their racist views and political tactics. Increasing resistance appeared to the elevation of African Americans into even minor roles of power in the political structure, for fear that this would entice hordes of African Americans to leave the oppression of the Deep South states for the opportunities and freedom offered in Oklahoma. The candidacy of G. N. Perkins, an African American from Guthrie, for police judge raised a storm of protest in 1896 and demonstrated how the politics of race had come to dominate territorial politics. One territorial paper reported that Perkins received 444 votes; the majority of his support came from black Republicans but about 100 white Republicans supported his candidacy. More important, the paper noted, was that about 200 white Republicans refused to cross the color line and vote for Perkins. The paper wrote, "It is useless to expect other results. Most white men will not overlook race distinctions in favor of a negro. Guthrie is the only locality in the territory to try the experiment, and yet under the most favoring influence it was a failure." While Perkins was victorious, his narrow margin of victory due to the refusal of many Republicans to cross the color line was an ominous sign that blacks could expect a challenge to their participation in political affairs not only from white Democrats but also from white Republicans.[37]

The electoral successes of the Democrats indicated to many white Republicans that the connection between African Americans and the Republican Party was more a hindrance to success than a benefit. Consequently, there arose within the Republican Party a faction known as "lily-whites," who sought to remove African Americans from participation in the affairs of the party and the territory at large. One group of lily-white Republicans from Alderson met and expressed their dissatisfaction with "perpetual colored rule." They complained that there had been black deputies in their district throughout the Republican-dominated territorial era. They argued, "We have had a long and uninterrupted experience with their [black deputies] beneficient [*sic*] efficiency. We fear that a further continuation of this great blessing among us would surfeit our capacity for enjoying anything republican in character." They also charged that African Americans held too much power at the local level and whites disliked serving under "negro domination." The delegates professed no hostility towards blacks, but concluded, "we do not accept as true that the superior race

36. *El Reno News,* Jan. 25, 1899.
37. *Edmond Sun Democrat,* Apr. 17, 1896.

shall be subjected to the care of the inferior race, no matter what words or what their number that may be used as qualifiers." As early as 1894, the connection between Republicans and their black voters was beginning to tie an albatross about the Republican Party's neck. One Democratic newspaper recognized this: "The Republicans are in a queer fix. They are compelled to nominate a negro for a county office this fall or go up against certain defeat. This they will do; and with a 580 majority polled against their last experiment in this line, the chances of the colored brother are a trifle apparent." With each passing defeat for the Republicans, the lily-whites were able to argue that the connection with African Americans was a hindrance which needed eliminating. The party spent the next decade in a bitter internal struggle over the role of African Americans, all the while watching the Democrats' popularity grow. By 1904, Democrats had won local elections in Purcell, Lawton, Shawnee, and Muskogee.[38]

By the eve of statehood the Republican Party was divided. One wing supported black civil rights and officeholding, while the other was firmly against any participation by African Americans in the party structure. A group of Muskogee lily-whites during the election of delegates to the constitutional convention in 1906 noted that the Republican Party had discharged its obligation to black civil rights. They noted their opposition to "negro domination" and were steadfast in their defense of separate schools, coaches, and waiting rooms. They then pledged their commitment to prevent the nomination of any African American candidates.[39]

Democrats could not help but notice the recent conversion of the Republican Party to the cause of white supremacy. In response, the *Lawton Constitution* claimed that it was ridiculous to insinuate that the Republican Party "possesses no love for a coon." The paper ended its editorial with a familiar warning to white voters, "do not be deceived; the negro question is a burning issue in this campaign. Do not extend them a standing invitation to come to Lawton by electing republican officials."[40]

Not surprisingly, African Americans became alarmed. It did not take them long to recognize that they were becoming a thorn in the Republican Party's side. But like their fellow white Republicans, blacks were divided over how best to combat the move to restrict their political participation. Most chose to remain loyal to the Republicans and fight vigorously any attempts to restrict their participation in party affairs. Lily-white Republicans tried to convince African American supporters that they should not expect to hold public offices. Most African Americans refused to accept this, and they were encouraged by black newspaper editors to "fix bayonet, and stand ready to charge the fortress of Republican political prejudice and assist in annihilating the enemy forever."[41]

38. *Purcell Register,* Feb. 20, 1904; *Guthrie Daily Leader,* July 25, 1894.
39. *Muskogee Cimeter,* Sept. 27, 1906.
40. *Lawton Constitution,* date unknown, 1905.
41. *Guthrie Daily Leader,* Aug. 14, 1894.

Some African Americans, realizing the strength of the lily-white faction within the party, argued that they should cooperate with the lily-whites by agreeing not to seek political office. Proponents of this argument reasoned that the only hope for African Americans lay within the Republican Party and therefore they should cooperate and reap whatever benefits they could from their traditional white Republican allies. Those willing to cooperate accepted the lily-white philosophy outlined in a territorial paper, which instructed black voters: "Let the good of the people impel you in selecting candidates at Saturday's convention. Republicanism means good government. It takes good men to make good officers. Look to principles and honest men to ballast them, rather than to personal candidates." In 1906, in Muskogee, a local black lawyer and journalist, William H. Twine, asked his fellow African Americans to adhere to the lily-white doctrine that no black candidates appear on the Republican ticket so as to avoid splitting the vote and thereby allowing the Democrats to win the election. Twine was able to convince his fellow black Republicans and the Muskogee GOP won a resounding victory.[42]

However, some African Americans were defiant. While most remained loyal to the Republican Party, a few chose to end their affiliation and to do the unthinkable—seek political opportunities in the Democratic Party. As early as 1894, black Republicans were denouncing in the press and at political rallies the rise of lily-whitism in their party ranks. At a rally in Guthrie, one African American complained of how blacks had been treated by lily-whites, stating: "We are villified and abused by Guthrie lily-whites until election time draws near and then the crack of the whip is heard. I have talked to all my brethren and they are mad. We won't stand it any longer. We are as much men of principles as white people. We revolt. Republicans won't vote for a colored man but they want his vote, and they don't think of the dark skin when they come to levying taxes." The speaker then invited his audience to renounce their attachment to the Republican Party and support the Democratic ticket. Following that speech, another speaker chastised the Republican Party and claimed that African Americans "were as much in need of pie as the lily white Republicans." The theme of all the speeches that night was for the black voters to desert the Republican ranks, since the party had reportedly "never gave the negro anything."[43]

A very few Democrats did try to entice disgruntled African Americans into the Democratic fold. As early as 1894, a Republican paper reported that a Colonel Corbett was "the author of a new democratic school, in which the negro is embraced." The paper retorted, "how lonely Col. Corbett must be! And what powerful ingredient has taken possession of his southern soul?" The *Oklahoma State Capital* wondered about the supposed transformation of the

42. *Ibid.*; Mellinger, "Discrimination and Statehood," 363.
43. *Guthrie Daily Leader,* Feb. 9, 1894; *Oklahoma State Capital,* Feb. 9, 1894.

Democratic attitude, stating: "Two years ago the 'd——n nigger,' the democrats howled, would kill Guthrie. Then they issued circulars boycotting all negroes and calling upon the people to drive the negroes from the town. Now they call them 'my deah colored brothar'—and all because some democratic hypocrites think the negro is ignorant and hope to gull him into voting for his old and everlasting enemy." One Republican editor questioned Democratic sincerity when he considered that "one squib appeals to the negro to vote the democratic ticket, and another squib calls them coons."[44]

Black Republicans looked upon those of their race who abandoned the Republican Party in favor of the Democrats as the most shameful of traitors. One diatribe against such "turn-coats" warned African Americans that "a black Democrat is the lowest order of God's creation . . . the missing link between the Jackass and the braying ham-sandwich fool. . . . they are without money, property or principle, father or mother." But Republicans had little to worry about, as few African Americans were convinced that the Democratic Party would look after their interests, and the Democratic Party's relaxation of its strict support of white supremacy was isolated to a few candidates well outside the powerful inner circle of Democratic leaders.[45]

AS THE nineteenth century drew to a close and as Oklahoma moved closer to statehood, one issue came to dominate territorial politics—segregation. Oklahoma, however, was not unique in this regard. The race issue became an important aspect of the agenda of so-called progressives. Every southern state passed segregation laws in the 1890s, and the movement was given legal sanction in the 1896 Supreme Court decision of *Plessy* v. *Ferguson,* which found that separate facilities for blacks and whites were legal provided they were "equal." What was unique about the segregation debate in Oklahoma is that it took place much later than in the southern states. By the late 1890s the southern states had strict segregation laws in place, whereas segregation did not become part of Oklahoma's laws until 1907. What accounts for this delay? Part of the explanation lies in the fact that unlike the southern states, Oklahoma still gave blacks the vote at the time when the call for Jim Crow laws was first heard.[46]

African Americans fought vehemently to prevent segregation laws from being passed during the territorial period. They were assisted by the fact that Republican administrations dominated not only the territorial legislature but also in Washington. The Negro Voters Protective Leagues were active in passing resolutions that condemned segregation of African Americans. Through

44. *Oklahoma State Capital,* Feb. 2, 1894, Mar. 25, 1894, Mar. 24, 1894.

45. "[W]arning to Creek freedmen voters," File 82.97, FBP.

46. See Dewey W. Grantham, *Southern Progressivism: The Reconciliation of Progress and Tradition* (Knoxville: University of Tennessee Press, 1983).

the leagues, blacks were able to put pressure upon the white leaders of the Republican Party by threatening to stay away from the polls if the party did not oppose bills to establish strict segregation. The black press also played a significant role in denouncing segregation. Editors wrote diatribes on the evils of segregation, denying that separate facilities could ever be equal. As one editor wrote, "Every man realizes that separate institutions mean inferior institutions. The Negro cannot hold his own with the white man, and once he is discriminated against, his institutions from lack of adequate resources, age and the standing which belongs to long and established ideas fail to come up to the mark." There was universal feeling in the African American community that blacks should fight any proposed segregation laws in the courts, and that African Americans should contest all efforts by white society to ostracize them socially. For African Americans realized that Oklahoma Territory represented their last stand against legalized segregation. All of the southern states had adopted strict segregation laws, and territorial blacks resolved that they would not lose the rights and privileges they still enjoyed in territorial Oklahoma. The *Oklahoma Guide* advised its readers in 1902: "The Fatty Matter saloon has told several colored gentlemen that his rot gut whisky was for white men. Every Negro should see to it that no man prosper by drawing the color line, see your merchant and all your white friends and ask them to not patronize these peace disturbers, and show them that they can not build up a trade on race prejudice." Similarly in 1904, the *Muskogee Cimeter* warned: "Every Negro should stay away from the steam merry-go-round and avoid trouble, they have drawn the color line to start with and that means friction. Preachers and teachers advise those under you to shun this trouble breeding amusement resort. Treat the owners as our people in the states treated the separate street car, and the cuss who runs the business will lose many a dollar." Thus African Americans were adamant that they should not be shut off and separated from the rest of society, and therefore they fought for their right to enjoy all the privileges of citizenship.[47]

Some African Americans violently resisted efforts to enforce de facto segregation. The *Muskogee Cimeter* reported that an African American preacher who attempted to occupy a seat next to a white man on a northbound Katy train "got smashed in the mouth by the white man and is minus a few teeth and some hide." The black man was the Reverend Mr. Walker, who "everybody knows . . . will defend himself." The paper reported "the preacher fought like Hades." A law enforcement officer broke up the melee and levied a ten-dollar fine on each of the participants. The African American paper, approving of the fierce resistance demonstrated by Walker, proclaimed, "separate coach don't go here, yet, brother, if you need one we advise you to migrate to the twin hell,

47. Williams, "The Black Press in Oklahoma," 317–18; Tolson, *The Black Oklahomans*, 129; *Oklahoma Guide*, Oct. 9, 1902; *Muskogee Cimeter*, Sept. 1, 1904.

Arkansas or Texas." To many African Americans, however, Oklahoma Territory in the 1890s still represented a promised land where their civil rights were protected.[48]

White residents of Oklahoma Territory also recognized that Oklahoma Territory represented a potential haven for the oppressed blacks of the South. In their minds, this was what made segregation laws necessary. Democratic politicians took the lead of the segregation campaign in the late 1890s. Democrats wanted to pass legislative acts which would enforce the segregation of African Americans to separate facilities, for they argued that if Oklahoma did not follow the Deep South states in restricting the civil rights of African Americans, the territory would be flooded with ex-slaves seeking a more racially tolerant society.[49]

The Democratic Party in Oklahoma became the staunchest advocate of Jim Crow legislation, one prominent Democrat declaring, "every platform so far adopted by the Democrats, either in the formation of a Democratic club, in a Democratic convention, or otherwise has declared specifically for three things—separate schools, separate coaches on the railroad, and separate depot accomodations." As seen earlier, Democrats were successful in getting a separate-school law passed in 1901. Fresh from this victory, Democrats then turned their attention to enforcing segregation of the races on railway coaches. Later in 1901 a Democratic member introduced a bill providing for separate coaches for whites, Indians, and African Americans. The bill was sent to the railroad committee, where it was amended by striking out the provision that Indians had to be separated from whites. The bill died in the Senate, reportedly because of the amendment. In 1903, another separate-coach bill was introduced in the House, imposing heavy fines for violators. The proposal called for any railroad company which refused to provide separate coaches for African Americans to pay a fine of $500 to $1,000 for each offense. Conductors who allowed passengers to ride in the wrong coach were to be fined from $25 to $100. The rider was also subject to the same penalty. Interestingly, Native Americans, by the terms of the bill, were given the option of choosing a car. This particular bill was also defeated; legalized segregation would not come to Oklahoma railway lines until after statehood.[50]

48. *Muskogee Cimeter,* June 2, 1904.

49. African Americans entered Oklahoma Territory as free immigrants seeking a fresh start in a land which promised greater opportunity than the place they left. Unlike the Deep South, where race relations had to undergo the transition from a slave society to a free labor society, Oklahoma Territory (unlike the Indian Territory) had no such burden. As well, racial exclusion was limited to urban centers, and Oklahoma was an overwhelmingly rural society. Hence the argument made by Howard Rabinowitz, that segregation represented a violently achieved compromise between white desires for exclusion, and African American desires for integration, is not applicable to the rise of segregation in Oklahoma Territory. See Howard Rabinowitz, *Race Relations in the Urban South, 1865–1890* (New York: Oxford University Press, 1978), 331–32.

50. Giddings, "New State Negro Address"; Tolson, *The Black Oklahomans,* 128.

Democratic newspapers hailed the *Plessy* v. *Ferguson* decision and drew on its reasoning. The *Shawnee Daily Herald,* for example, justified separation of the races on rail coaches in the following way:

> If the passenger coach set aside for negroes, say on the Rock Island, is just as good in all respects as the one next to it for white passengers on the same identical train; if the seats, saloons, water supply and all other conveniences accorded the white passengers are furnished the colored passengers, and they arrive at their destination simultaneously with the whites, where is the inequality in the law? Of what constitutional right had the negro traveler been deprived? Has he not in every respect fared equally in all the transportation facilities furnished for any individual of the traveling public?

Hence even though the Democrats were unsuccessful in getting a Jim Crow law passed by the territorial legislature, the fear that if Oklahoma failed to adopt the segregationist stance of its southern neighbors it would become a promised land attracting thousands of African Americans from the Deep South states led to de facto segregation. Railway coaches, for example, came to enforce compliance with Jim Crowism sentiment. By the early 1900s, the *El Reno News* could report that while segregation was not legally binding, de facto segregation had taken root. The paper claimed, "the Frisco now runs separate coaches into Oklahoma for white and negro passengers. Each car carries a sign showing which race it is provided for." One Oklahoma resident remembered, "You know they used to have Jim Crow car. When they hit the Indian Territory, well, by God, them niggers had to get back in their own car. Up in Kansas they allowed them to ride together." After 1896 and the *Plessy* v. *Ferguson* decision, segregation of the races became the predominant practice in Oklahoma Territory, leading the *Oklahoma Guide* to report that Jim Crowism had become an epidemic. Oklahomans established separate public toilets, separate drinking fountains, separate amusement rides, separate barber shops, separate theaters, separate hotels, and separate eating places. Thus by the advent of statehood, in an effort to discourage African American immigration to Oklahoma, racial separation was firmly established if not legally entrenched.[51]

It is testimony to the power of the politics of race that the "negro question," and in particular the issue of segregation, came to dominate the constitutional convention. Faced with the knowledge that Indian Territory would be joined with Oklahoma Territory in any future statehood plans, Democrats looked for an issue to solidify their voters and to attract Republicans. The constitutional convention campaign run by the Democrats was dominated by the issues of progressivism (i.e., the need to avoid monopolization, the desire for

51. Tolson, *The Black Oklahomans,* 140; *El Reno News,* July 4, 1900; Sam Sloan, interview, File T-2954, DDOHI; Tolson, *The Black Oklahomans,* 130.

increased participatory democracy, and the necessity of regulating business), but the central issue was also a familiar aspect of the progressive agenda—the need to segregate African Americans. Democrats believed that the time had come to show that Oklahoma had no intention of being a promised land of opportunity for African Americans. One Democrat asked voters, "Would it not be better to fight it out in the first election and settle it for all time, rather than have it [the race question] hang over our heads for future settlement? Is there anything wrong in the Democratic position that it should be settled now and forever, rather than it should be passed up for the future to pass judgment upon?"[52]

Democrats argued that the eyes of the nation were on Oklahoma as its voters prepared to elect delegates to draft a constitution for the proposed new state. They claimed that the election in Oklahoma would determine the future of race relations in America. It was imperative, they said, that African American aspirations for active political involvement and social equality be soundly rejected. As one Democrat stated:

> Mark it, the people of the Union know that the negro question is being fought out in the new state of Oklahoma. The new state being partly northern and partly southern in its population furnishes upon this question an interesting situation for the student of economics. Newspapers thoughout the entire Union, in issue after issue, are heralding the fact that negroism is the main issue in the state of Oklahoma; that the Democrats are taking a stand against it, and the Republican politicians are combatting the Democratic theory. Will it then be a good advertisement for the new state of Oklahoma to let it go Republican under such conditions?

The Democratic commentator answered his own question by claiming that "Republican success, means that the new state of Oklahoma will be advertised as a haven for the negroes," and therefore, he warned, "such an advertisement means a great negro emigration."[53]

The Republican Party entered the campaign to elect constitutional delegates in utter disarray. The politics of race had completely fragmented the party into bitterly opposing factions. The Republicans were not able to confront the Democrats on the most important issue of the campaign, African American civil rights, because their own party was so divided in sentiment. In fact, the Republicans ran three different campaign strategies at once. The lily-white faction of the party ran a campaign much like that of the Democrats, stressing

52. Suzanne J. Crawford and Lynn R. Musslewhite, "Progressive Reform and Oklahoma Democrats: Kate Barnard versus Bill Murray," *Historian* 33 (spring 1991): 473–80; Giddings, "New State Negro Address."
53. Giddings, "New State Negro Address."

white supremacy—the need for segregation laws and the disfranchisement of African American voters. In many ways the lily-white Republicans and the Democrats in their racist way tried to "outnigger" each other, turning the election campaign into a contest of racial slurs designed to prove which party hated the African American more. The lily-whites, however, found it hard to beat the Democrats at their own game. Therefore in the interest of maintaining white supremacy, lily-white Republicans were sometimes willing to cooperate with their Democratic opponents to ensure that any delegates sent to the convention would be white. In Muskogee, which had a large African American population, the two forces joined together to nominate one Democrat and one lily-white Republican for the two districts to represent Muskogee at the constitutional convention. This was done to stave off the possibility of sending an African American candidate from the Republican Party.[54]

Another faction of white Republicans objected to the virulent racism of the lily-whites but was also cognizant that the connection of African Americans to the party was a burden. To the best of their ability, these candidates tried to sidestep the "negro question." When Democrats asked them for their position on Jim Crow legislation and the disfranchisement of African American voters, they remained silent. Instead, they pointed at the Republican dominance of territorial government and argued that the key issue in the election was not race, but the huge economic growth of Oklahoma under Republican tutelage.

Finally, a few white racially liberal Republicans and the few African American candidates nominated to run as constitutional delegates attacked the Democrats for their white supremacist views. They demanded that any constitution written for the future state of Oklahoma have a guarantee of African American civil rights. They vehemently opposed all efforts towards segregation and disfranchisement.

The Democratic appeal to white supremacy in conjunction with the disarray in the Republican ranks over the issue of race led the Democrats to their first sweeping victory in the history of the territories. Of the 112 delegates elected, 99 of them identified themselves as Democrats. Democrats believed that it was their firm stance on the race issue, and in particular on the question of segregation, which attracted formerly loyal Republican voters to vote for the Democratic Party. The constitution of the new state of Oklahoma was to be written by a group of men dedicated to white supremacy and elected on the platform of segregation and disfranchisement.[55]

One of the first actions of the convention was to elect a president. "Alfalfa Bill" Murray of Tishomingo, known as a staunch supporter of white supremacy, was chosen. In his acceptance speech to the convention, Murray argued that African Americans were generally failures as doctors, lawyers, and in

54. *Shawnee Daily Herald*, Oct. 7, 1906.
55. Goble, *Progressive Oklahoma*, 201.

other professions. Blacks, he argued, were only suited to be barbers, shoeshine boys, and porters. Murray also suggested training in agriculture, horticulture, and mechanics, but noted "it is an entirely false notion that the negro can rise to the equal of a white man in the professions or become an equal citizen to grapple with public questions."[56]

Immediately the convention came to concentrate on the issue of segregation. The Democrats had been elected on a platform of Jim Crow, so it was assumed that the delegates would write segregation laws into the constitution. African Americans hoped that moral condemnation from other states would bring enough pressure to deter them. As early as 1905, African Americans had vowed never to accept a constitution which abridged their civil rights in any way. At the Western Negro Press Association meetings held in Muskogee in September of 1905, the delegates resolved that "It being the settled policy of the white people of the Southern states to abridge the political rights of the colored people, and thereby nullify the fifteenth amendment, a memorial will be presented to the president and to congress, opposing statehood for the two territories, Indian Territory and Oklahoma, unless an absolute guarantee can be given that no 'Jim Crow' coach laws and others discriminating between the races in public places [will be passed]." African Americans reacted quickly to the threat posed by the Democrats controlling the constitutional convention. They passed resolutions condemning segregation and petitioned through the press and through the Republican Party in Washington for a constitution which would recognize the rights of all men. When separate galleries were constructed at the convention hall at a cost of $30,000, blacks refused to sit in them and boycotted the sessions.[57]

African Americans did, however, seemingly have one important ally. At the time of the constitutional convention, a Republican, Theodore Roosevelt, sat in the White House. They hoped that they could convince him not to sign a constitution that undermined their civil rights. Democratic strategists were worried, since all the recently admitted states had clauses in their constitutions denying discrimination on the basis of color. Oklahoma's own Enabling Act contained a similar clause. Democrats feared, therefore, that a Republican president might conceivably reject a constitution containing an article permitting segregation, thereby postponing statehood, and leaving the Democrats impotent to fulfill their campaign promises to their electorate. Roosevelt remained silent on his position, but this did nothing to allay the fears of territorial Democrats. Democratic strategists were able to convince most of the party leaders that Roosevelt had lost a good deal of black support over his recent actions in the Brownsville incident, and that he might attempt to placate his critics by re-

56. Murray, quoted in Shepard, "Oklahoma Black Migration," 4.
57. Unidentified newspaper clipping, Sept. 22, 1905, Indians File, Box 2, TAP; Tolson, *The Black Oklahomans,* 139.

jecting a Jim Crow Oklahoma constitution. As Democratic delegate Charles N. Haskell related, "There is no necessity of antagonizing the president on this subject and giving him an opportunity to make a grandstand play, which he surely would do, for the sole purpose of rehabilitating himself with the negroes at the expense of the democrats." The dilemma of the Democrats was put into the form of a poem by an anonymous contributor to the *Muskogee Daily Phoenix*:

> Old Jim Crow! Old Jim Crow!
> Lawd a massy man we love you so.
> The Constitooshin's weak without you Jim
> But dar's Teddy Roosevelt we are scared of him.
> He squints, and he grins, but won't let us know
> Just what to do with old Jim Crow.[58]

Party strategists were successful in convincing most of the Democratic leaders that they should avoid putting a clause relating to segregation into the constitution and wait for the first state legislature to be called, at which time they could then make a bill relating to segregation the first order of business. Some die-hard Democratic defenders of segregation fought against this strategy, arguing for a clause in the constitution now, rather than awaiting the election results determining the first state legislature. Delegate Graham of Marietta warned his fellow Democrats: " 'Jim Crow' today for Oklahoma or 'Jim Crow' never, gentlemen; that is the question. You break faith with your people and there will be more political graves in Oklahoma than in the national cemetery and they will not contain republicans, either." Graham reminded his fellow Democrats that fully 90 percent of the delegates elected to the convention had been elected on their pledge to put a Jim Crow section in the constitution. The powerful leaders of the Democratic Party, however, overruled such objections, and the Democrats pledged to pass a state constitution without any offending clause imposing segregation.[59]

This did not placate African Americans, however. They astutely realized that

58. Shepard, "Oklahoma Black Migration," 5; *Kingston Messenger*, Nov. 30, 1906; *Muskogee New-State Tribune*, Dec. 13, 1906; *Muskogee Daily Phoenix*, Feb. 10, 1907. The Brownsville incident involved President Roosevelt's decision to court-martial a group of black troops stationed in Brownsville, Texas, for a disturbance with local whites. African Americans denounced the president's actions. White inhabitants of Oklahoma used the incident to enunciate their disapproval of black troops in general. As one particularly vitriolic editorial claimed: "Uniform makes a fool of a negro and they think 'Uncle Sam' will protect them it matters not what they do. We indeed glory in the spunk of the President who handles the big stick. Every last mothers' son of the black devils should have been hung to some convenient tree and their carcass left for the buzzard to pick." *Kingston Messenger*, Nov. 30, 1906.

59. *Kingfisher Free Press*, Feb. 28, 1907.

what the Democrats were really doing was delaying the day of reckoning until after statehood. They knew that this strategy could have dire repercussions for them, for they recognized that the federal government would be reluctant to involve itself in any legislation the new state might pass. They therefore vowed to fight against the ratification of the constitution. They sought to arouse support for their cause across the nation, but particularly among the Republicans in power in Washington.

The Negro Voters Protection Leagues immediately became involved in the campaign to defeat the ratification of the constitution. African Americans made it clear that they asked for no special legislation in their favor; they merely demanded that no laws be enacted against them on account of their color. As they stated: "We certainly protest against any law for keeping a nigger in a nigger's place, as some of our so-called white enemies would say. We pledge ourselves to resist to the bitter end the efforts of our deadly enemies in attempting to mould a sentiment here against us after the southern methods." Across Oklahoma Territory, African Americans held meetings denouncing the proposed constitution. The *Oklahoma State Capital* described one such meeting, which had 300 delegates representing the interests of the 50,000 African American residents of the territory. The delegates condemned the constitution as prepared by the conventional delegates, and "recommended that the colored voters of the new state use every honorable means to defeat the constitution when the special election is held in August."[60]

African Americans, in a final bid to protect their civil rights from certain infringement at the hands of the Democrats, appealed to federal Republicans to turn down the proposed constitution for Oklahoma. They appealed to the "negroes of Illinois, Indiana, Ohio, West Virginia, New York, Massachusetts, Connecticut, and Rhode Island, to lend us their assistance in defeating a constitution that is not republican in form and one that is contrary to the Enabling Act." The petition continued, "Help us to defeat a constitution that lays the foundation for the disfranchising of our people in the new state and for giving us Jim Crow Cars and other class legislation and measures calculated to humiliate and degrade the whole race." In an effort to gain support from federal Republicans, a party of eleven African Americans from Oklahoma and Indian Territories was sent to Washington to protest the proposed Constitution. President Roosevelt agreed to see them, but he offered them little support. He told them to file their protest with the Justice Department. When one of the delegates began to discuss the defects in the proposed constitution, the president rebuked him, saying "please do not ask me not to sign it." The cries of African Americans were also unheeded by Republicans in other areas of the United States. Without outside support, and living in a land where they were outnum-

60. *Kingfisher Free Press*, Feb. 25, 1904; *Oklahoma State Capital*, Apr. 27, 1907.

bered by whites by more than ten to one, African Americans had to prepare to accept the inevitable.[61]

African Americans could not even count on the support of Native Americans, as most of them supported the Democrats out of fear of "negro domination." One Creek politician clearly stated his view of the "race question" by arguing: "The negro is a negro and belongs in Africa, he was not found here when the Indian was discovered by the white men. The Indian did not bring him here, he was brought here as a slave. The Indian recognizes him as a separate, distinct and inferior race and does not want to be associated with him in any manner. The Indian stands for separate schools, separate coaches, and separate waiting rooms." Democrats were able to convince many Indian leaders that their best interest lay in supporting their party while the Republican Party represented the interest of their freedmen, with whom many of the tribes were at odds. In return for the electoral support of Native Americans, the Democrats provided that Native Americans be classified as "white" for the purposes of enforcing the segregation law. In effect, in return for supporting the Democratic Party, Native Americans were granted honorary membership in the dominant race in a society which increasingly only recognized whites and blacks. Article 23, Section 11, of the constitution, entitled "Definition of Races," noted: "wherever in this Constitution and laws of this state, the word or words, 'colored,' or 'colored race,' 'negro,' or 'negro race,' are used, the same shall be construed to mean or apply to all persons of African descent. The term 'white race' shall include all other persons.[62]

The people of Indian and Oklahoma Territories voted overwhelmingly in favor of ratifying the constitution—it passed 180,333 to 73,059. The returns showed that 71.17 percent of the inhabitants of the territory supported the constitution, while only 28.83 percent of inhabitants opposed it.[63]

THE ELECTION CAMPAIGN for the first state legislature was likewise centered upon the fear of African American immigration. Charles N. Haskell, the Democratic candidate for governor, appealed to voters on the familiar basis of racial fear of "negro domination." Haskell warned the white voters of the new state: "If you by a majority vote, put your stamp of approval upon the men who are on the Republican state ticket and upon the state and local platforms . . . you thereby extend an open and cordial welcome to the negro race of other states, and it is not overestimating to say that Mississippi, Louisiana, Texas, and Arkansas will practically become depopulated of the negro race by their grand rush to the new state."[64]

61. *Muskogee Cimeter,* Sept. 27, 1907; *Shawnee Herald,* Oct. 29, 1907.

62. James Sapulpa, "Prominent Indians' Views of the Political Parties of the Day," Box 27, File 10, GMP; Oklahoma Constitution (1907), art. 23, sec. 11, R 5, M 828 Territorial Papers, 1907, RDI.

63. Goble, *Progressive Oklahoma,* 258, n42.

64. *Daily Oklahoman,* Aug. 11, 1907.

THE POLITICS OF RACE • 197

The election results demonstrated African Americans' greatest fear—that the white voters of Oklahoma had come to embrace the Democratic doctrine centered upon white supremacy. In the House, there were 93 Democrats as opposed to 16 Republicans. In the Senate, there were 39 Democrats as opposed to 5 Republicans. Haskell won the governorship by a count of 137,579 to 110,293. The state legislature election results cleared the way for the Democrats to legislate their white supremacist views into law.[65]

When the legislature convened on Dec. 2, 1907, the new governor immediately pressed for the passage of Jim Crow legislation. Haskell recommended emergency legislation be passed providing for separate railroad coaches and waiting rooms for persons of African American descent. Thus Jim Crow statutes became the first order of business for the new state. Three days after Governor Haskell's speech, the Railroad Commission issued an order compelling all railroads to provide separate coaches for whites and blacks, with the order to come into effect in four weeks' time. On December 6 each house of the new state of Oklahoma passed a bill requiring separate coaches and waiting rooms for persons of African descent. On December 18 Governor Haskell signed Senate Bill Number 1 into law, and hence Jim Crow became the first act passed by the new state.[66]

Immediately African Americans protested against this violation of their civil liberties. Black editors admitted they "were not surprised at the early passage of the separate car bill by the legislature." But they did admit they were surprised at the "unkindest cut of them all, five of the republican members voted for the separate car bill."[67]

African Americans raised a storm of protest against the Jim Crow law, but they received scant sympathy from the legislators. They decided their best opportunity to overturn the act lay in the courts. Therefore, African Americans began to raise funds to begin a court fight, hoping to have the new law declared unconstitutional. Soon after the law was passed, several hundred Kansas and Oklahoma African Americans held a large gathering in Coffeyville, Kansas, to raise funds to begin the court challenge. Early in 1908, two prominent African American leaders, Edward P. McCabe and William H. Twine, entered separate injunctions to prevent railroad companies from carrying the separate coach law into effect. In April of 1908 Judge J. H. Cotteral denied the injunction, claiming the courts did not have the power to "limit the power of the state to legislate on the subject of the separation of passengers by means of separate coaches or compartments."[68]

While battling against the segregation law in the courts, African Americans

65. Goble, *Progressive Oklahoma*, 258, n42.
66. *Langston Western Age*, Dec. 13, 1907; Tolson, *The Black Oklahomans*, 147.
67. Tolson, *The Black Oklahomans*, 147.
68. *Ibid.*, 149; Box 293, File 4, Western District of Oklahoma, Guthrie, USDCR.

198 • *Contested Territory*

also engaged in civil disobedience and acts of violence in a last-ditch effort to overturn this affront to their civil rights. On February 1, 1908, it was reported that the lieutenant governor had been the victim of an attempted assault "by a burly Negro," who objected to having to sit in a separate coach. The secretary of the lieutenant governor pulled out his revolver, and the disgruntled black man returned to his seat. The train's conductor noted, "it looks like all the negroes are carrying revolvers and there seems to be an organized effort to resist the enforcement of the separate coach law." In Taft, Oklahoma, a black mob burned the Midland Valley depot as a protest against the construction of a separate waiting room. At Red Bird, Oklahoma, a train carrying state officials and delegates to the Democratic convention being held at Muskogee was attacked by a group of African Americans, who "hurled stones and great chunks of coal through the windows." Governor Haskell and Sheriff Bud Ledbetter both received death threats in addition to being warned that some African Americans were allegedly intent on blowing up Guthrie, the state capital, if the Jim Crow law was enforced. However, all efforts at having the offensive legislation removed failed. Segregation was to remain an integral part of Oklahoma race relations for more than half a century.[69]

However, African Americans in the new state of Oklahoma, unlike those who resided in the Deep South states, were still able to enjoy political participation and influence. Democrats were forced to recognize this when Albert C. Hamlin, a black Republican from Guthrie, was elected to the House of Representatives from a district that was overwhelmingly African American.[70]

The Democrats reacted to this affront to white supremacy with force. Relying on methods perfected during territorial days, they used every possible means to eliminate African American participation in the political affairs of the new state. With the Democratic Party in control of the state election apparatus, they had it within their power to influence the outcome of elections. The example of one county will suffice to illustrate the length to which Democrats were willing to go to eliminate African American voting and thereby help perpetuate their own rule. The Okfuskee Election Board gerrymandered the precinct lines to incorporate small precincts with large numbers of African Americans into larger precincts where they would be a small minority compared to white voters. This was necessary, according to the Democratic *Waleetka American*, using by now a familiar argument, because otherwise "negroes would run things with a high hand." The paper continued: "Crush the insolence of the negro now. Rebuke the white men who have encouraged and abetted them in their efforts to make themselves the peer of the white race, and you will have checked the influx of negro populations, guarded the purity of your homes, and provided safety and honor to your wives and daughters."[71]

69. *Eufaula Indian Journal,* Feb. 7, 1908; Tolson, *The Black Oklahomans,* 149, 151.
70. Franklin, *Journey toward Hope,* 108–109.
71. Bittle and Geis, "Racial Self-Fulfillment," 257.

The election board forced the residents of the all-black town of Boley to vote at Van Zandt precinct, twelve miles away, even though their town had more residents than many white towns allowed polling stations. The African Americans were not to be discouraged, however, and when the election officer arrived at the Van Zandt precinct, he "found a handful of white men there and some 100–150 Negroes." Many of the African Americans had camped at the voting place the night before to ensure they would not miss the chance to exercise their franchise. They demanded that an African American be placed on the local election board to ensure that their votes would be honored. A debate ensued and the election officer fled, fearing for his life. The African Americans had taken possession of the ballot box before the officer had left, so they formed a line and marked their ballots in favor of the Republican candidates. The final election results showed a clear majority for the Republicans, but the Okfuskee Election Board refused to recognize the returns, claiming the Van Zandt returns were illegal. Not satisfied, the Okfuskee Election Board continued to redraw precinct lines in an attempt to destroy areas of Republican Party support. One Republican paper could at least maintain a sense of humor, claiming:

> The precinct lines of this county have been changed so often that it is becoming monotonous. The voter cannot keep up with these changes without neglecting his ordinary business. He can't tell "where he is at." The map maker would work himself into a premature grave to keep up with the changes. A citizen may go to sleep in one precinct and wake up in a precinct in which he is a perfect stranger. When the citizen goes to bed his precinct may be no bigger than a good-sized farm, and wake up in the morning to find that his precinct has spread over half the county. . . . he may have to swear out a search warrant and finally locate his voting place. . . . So far as is at present known no voting places have been moved entirely outside the county, but it would be well for surrounding counties to guard their boundaries, as an invasion by the Okfuskee county election board is liable to occur if further changes are contemplated.[72]

Democrats did not content themselves for long with such ad hoc measures. By 1910, they proposed that as in the states of the Deep South, an amendment be made to the state constitution requiring voters to be literate. They defended the measure as part of their "progressive" agenda, claiming it would take the franchise away only from those people who were not qualified to use it wisely and independently. In reality, the proposed measure was a means to bring about the end of African American voting. The proposed amendment stated:

> No person shall be registered as an elector of this State, or be allowed to vote in any election held therein, unless he be able to read and write any section of

72. Bittle and Geis, *The Longest Way Home,* 37–39, 52.

the Constitution of the State of Oklahoma; but no person who was, on January 1st, 1866, or at any time prior thereto, entitled to vote under any form of government, or who at that time resided in some foreign nation, and no lineal descendant of such person, shall be denied the right to register and vote because of his ability to so read and write sections of such Constitution.

The "grandfather clause" could be of no assistance to African Americans, since the date at which the lineal descendant must have possessed the right to vote was before the passage of the Reconstruction Acts, which gave the vote to blacks in the South. Interestingly, a court ruling determined that since the Indians of the Five Civilized Tribes had an electoral form of government prior to 1866, descendants of these tribes would be exempted from the literacy qualification; however, their adopted black freedmen would have to fulfill the literacy requirement. Members of the relocated Plains tribes removed to Indian Territory in the 1870s and 1880s did not have representative forms of government before 1866, and therefore they fell into the same category as African Americans—they too had to submit to a literacy test before being permitted to vote.[73]

Needless to say, having recently been subjected to discriminatory Jim Crow legislation, African Americans raised a storm of protest. They held mass meetings denouncing the proposed amendment and appealed to Republicans in Washington to intervene. The Republicans, however, proved reluctant to involve themselves in the politics of the new state. In fact, the only sympathetic response came from Oklahoma Socialists, who denounced the disfranchisement of African Americans. Though their popularity was on the rise, the Socialists were still a fringe party in 1910 and their cries of injustice went unheeded. Hence, given little more than moral support from federal Republicans, African Americans resolved themselves to the inevitable and began to raise funds to challenge the future law in the courts.[74]

White Democrats and lily-white Republicans defended the proposed amendment, relying upon the tried-and-true arguments that they had perfected during the era of the politics of race. Again white candidates raised the specter of Oklahoma becoming a haven for all the dissatisfied African Americans of the southern states. Lee Cruce, later governor of Oklahoma, cautioned white voters:

> There are communities in this State where the negro population is in such numbers as to be a menace to good government. The fact has been published abroad that in Oklahoma, the negro is permitted to run for and hold office and

73. Edward L. Ayers, *The Promise of the New South: Life after Reconstruction* (New York: Oxford University Press, 1992); Box W-38, File 3, JRWP; James R. Green, *Grass Roots Socialism: Radical Movements in the Southwest, 1895–1943* (Baton Rouge: Louisiana State University Press, 1978), 53–54.

74. Green, *Grass-Roots Socialism*, 94.

nothing, my friends, appeals more to the negroes than the idea that he is the equal of the white man in political affairs.

The result of this advertising of our State abroad has been to make this a dumping ground of all the dissatisfied negroes of the South, and they are coming into Oklahoma now in multiplied numbers. I have no ill feeling toward the negro race, but I don't want to see this State hindered in its growth and development by the menace of negro domination.[75]

Democrats realized that support for the amendment, while strong, was not so large as to guarantee its passage. In an effort to further their own cause, the Democrat-controlled election boards designed a ballot which contained the wording of the proposed amendment followed in small type by the words "For the Amendment." Anyone wishing to vote against the proposition had to cross out these words with a pencil. If he did not do so, and marked the ballot in any other way, it was automatically counted as a vote in favor. African American papers took great pains to explain the exact process required to vote against the amendment, and reminded voters "be sure to have your lead pencil with you."[76]

The final tally of votes revealed that the amendment had passed by a relatively narrow margin—135,443 in favor, 106,222 against. In fact there was some question as to whether it was fraud which provided the amendment's margin of victory. There were 20,364 more votes cast in the amendment election than in that year's gubernatorial election. In one precinct voters were intimidated by an armed election guard, while in another an inspector stepped into the polling booth and marked the ballots for voters himself. Regardless of whether the vote was fraudulent, though, the passage of the suffrage amendment overnight took away the right to vote from an estimated 20,000 to 30,000 African American citizens of the state of Oklahoma.[77]

Before the election campaign, Governor Haskell made it abundantly clear that in order to vote a black man "would have to read like a professor." As African Americans began to discover in the months after the passage of the suffrage amendment, this was no idle threat. As historian R. Bruce Shepard relates, "one black man who could read and write not only English, but Greek and Latin as well, was turned away. Black professional men presented themselves at the polling station armed with affidavits testifying to their voting competency, but were turned down. Several of them began reading sections of the State Constitution aloud, only to be denied again." A deputy sheriff in Wagoner caught a Democratic election judge who stuffed the ballots of African American voters into his boots rather than into the ballot box. While African Ameri-

75. Lee Cruce, speech on grandfather clause, May 20, 1910, Box W-38, File 4, JRWP.
76. Quoted in Bittle and Geis, *The Longest Way Home*, 51.
77. Thompson, *Closing the Frontier*, 133.

cans filed lawsuit after lawsuit in an effort to have the suffrage law ruled unconstitutional, they were effectively shut out of active political participation in the new state of Oklahoma.[78]

HENCE, THE ERA from the end of the Civil War to the birth of the state of Oklahoma in 1907, was marked by the politics of race. In both Indian and Oklahoma Territories, political leaders placed primary importance upon the fear of "outside influences" gaining control of the reins of political power.

In Indian Territory, Indian leaders argued that Native American self-government was crucial to their survival as a distinct cultural group. Hence, Indian leaders fought all attempts to bring the independent Indian nations under the aegis of Anglo-America, first by resisting efforts to impose territorial status upon the Indian lands, and later, by opposing joint statehood of Indian and Oklahoma Territories. Native American leaders quite astutely recognized that after the Indian lands received territorial status, it would be impossible to stop the flood of white immigrants. Indian leaders could foresee that the political consequence of massive white settlement would be the death knell of Native American self-government. At the same time, many Indian leaders also came to warn of the potential danger to be derived from giving their ex-slaves full political participation, including the right to vote and hold office in tribal politics. Many Native American politicians warned of a day when the ex-slaves would seize control of tribal affairs. These leaders based their argument on the fact that their freedmen population was increasing while the full-blood Indian population was decreasing, the implication being that at some point the freedmen would outnumber the Indians and hence gain political control. Thus, many Native American leaders in the Indian Territory appealed to voters along racial grounds. Candidates for tribal office were able to convince their constituents that their interest lay in protecting their racial purity and privilege from the invasion of "foreign influences" by putting into office those people who could be entrusted to resist such an attempt. When Native Americans lost the right of self-government and sovereignty over their lands, they had to reconcile themselves with the consolation that they would be categorized as "white" in a society which increasingly only recognized whites and blacks.

When surplus Indian lands were opened to white settlement and territorial status was bestowed upon Oklahoma in 1890, the politics of race soon came to the forefront there too. Political parties quickly became acutely aware of the importance voters attached to racial matters. Consequently, in their selection of candidates, and in the formation of their electoral platform, both Democrats and Republicans sought to place a firm emphasis on "the race question."[79] Af-

78. Shepard, "Oklahoma Black Migration," 21.
79. Campaigns often centered upon the "race question" because it consistently brought traditional party voters out to the polls and because it didn't alienate either the Republicans' or the Democrats' traditional supporters. Scales and Goble contend that "The electoral suc-

rican Americans predominantly remained true to the Republican Party which had freed them, while the Democratic Party was vehemently Negrophobic. By the turn of the century, as Oklahoma moved toward statehood, Democrats united around white supremacy and began to campaign for strict segregation laws affecting African Americans, and for the restriction of black voting rights. Republicans were divided, with those who argued in favor of maintaining their traditional support for black civil rights in conflict with a growing group of Republicans known as "lily-whites," who wished to entice white voters away from the Democratic Party by disassociating the Republican Party from African Americans. When the call came for Oklahoma to conduct a convention to discuss preparations for statehood, the political agenda was as much tied to the issue of race as it was in any state in the heart of Dixie.

In the Indian Territory, the politics of race came to be centered on the question of "outside influences" gaining political power. In Oklahoma Territory, the overwhelming issue was "Negro domination." Above all else, Democrats based their political platform on the need to discourage African American immigration from the surrounding southern states. Democratic politicians conjured up images of a massive intrusion by African Americans seeking a place where their civil rights would be respected. Eventually, candidates claimed, African Americans by their superior numbers would come to dominate society and take control of the political realm. Democrats emphasized the aspiration of Edward P. McCabe to have Oklahoma declared an all-black state under his leadership as governor.

The bombastic Democratic charge of impending Negro domination was not entirely campaign rhetoric. The potential for massive African American immigration was quite real. Domination, however, was another matter. In fact, the black population of Oklahoma in the years between 1900 and 1910 increased 147 percent whereas the white population only increased by 115 percent. By 1910, 137,612 African Americans resided in Oklahoma, making it the sixteenth most populated state in terms of its black population. This is not surprising, for in its early years, Oklahoma afforded blacks opportunities denied them elsewhere. African Americans possessed the vote, held political office, were integrated into the education system, and in large measure owned their own land. As the southern states turned to segregation and disfranchisement to restrict the rights of their black population, blacks came to see Oklahoma as a

cess of either party depended upon its securing a larger turnout than its rival on election day. Both, therefore, had to present united fronts and base their campaigns on long-perfected appeals to the electorate's established allegiances, which usually dated from the Civil War. To the Republicans, this meant 'waving the bloody shirt,' emphasizing their party's identification with the Union. To the Democrats, it meant summoning up the real or imagined horrors of Reconstruction. For both, it meant that issues of more recent controversy were understated or sacrificed, for to take either side of any currently divisive issue would guarantee a party's defeat." Scales and Goble, *Oklahoma Politics*, 7–8.

potential promised land. The trend was clear. African Americans were leaving the oppression of the Deep South states for the opportunities afforded by the more racially tolerant Oklahoma. Massive black migration to Oklahoma, hence, seemed not only possible but even probable. Therefore, by the advent of statehood, Democrats were able to convince the majority of Oklahoma voters that segregation laws and ultimately the disfranchisement of African Americans were necessary to prevent Oklahoma from becoming a haven for the oppressed ex-slaves of the South. According to Democratic politicians, these laws were necessary to ensure the new state would be "a white man's country."[80]

80. Bureau of the Census, *Negro Population in the United States, 1790–1915*, Table 8, Table 6.

CONCLUSION

I N THE AFTERMATH of the Civil War and Emancipation, American society underwent a profound transformation in race relations. Though the focus has always been on the adjustment of southern whites and blacks, race relations had to be redefined in the West as well. The Five Civilized Tribes had held slaves just as southern whites had done. Therefore, they too found themselves having to adjust to a free-wage economy. Hence the Five Civilized Tribes experienced their own Reconstruction. The 1866 treaties re-establishing relations between the Five Civilized Tribes and the United States required the tribes to protect the rights of their freedmen and give them full citizenship in their respective Indian nations. Each of the Five Civilized Tribes, with the exception of the Chickasaws, eventually adopted their ex-slaves as citizens. Since land in the Indian nations was held communally, granting the freedmen tribal citizenship, consequently, gave them equal rights in ownership of tribal land. When Indian lands were alloted by the terms of the Curtis Act in 1898, the ex-slaves received the "forty acres and a mule" so desperately sought by their fellow freedmen in the South.

However, as more and more white settlers came to settle in the Indian lands, Native Americans, particularly the mixed bloods, came to espouse a prejudice towards their former slaves equally virulent to that of their new white neighbors. In return for their support of "white" supremacy, Native Americans were granted honorary membership as "whites" in a society that increasingly only recognized whites and blacks.

The former slaves of the Five Civilized Tribes demonstrated mixed attitudes towards Native Americans. Some freedmen were part Indian themselves and were proud of their tribal heritage. Some ex-slaves who did not have Indian blood in them could still relate to Native Americans as a fellow oppressed people who suffered discrimination at the hands of white society. But other ex-slaves resented what they perceived as the relative higher social status afforded Native Americans by white society. Most infuriating to many freedmen was the fact that blacks were being segregated while white society invited Native Americans to assimilate.

After the Civil War, many white politicians, philanthropists, and humanitarians turned their attention to the interests of Native Americans and African Americans. With respect to Native Americans, humanitarians began to look to the West as a battleground between the forces of progress and civilization on the one hand and the forces of traditionalism and savagery on the other. Indian reformers clearly believed that peaceful co-existence would not take place so long as Native Americans clung to their traditional ways and culture.

As the nineteenth century drew to a close, most politicians and humanitarian reformers felt this was the last stand for Native Americans. Influenced by the theories of racial Darwinism, they argued that if the Indians did not embrace Anglo-American civilization now and adopt its traditions and culture as their own, they were doomed to extinction. Surrounded by white settlement, the Indian population could no longer rely upon isolation from white society. The secretary of the interior concluded in 1885 that the Indians had reached a crisis in their history. They could no longer live in a semi-civilized state; the practice of moving the Indians to more distant reservations was no longer possible.[1]

Governmental officials in Washington, and concerned white humanitarians, most of them well-educated Easterners, began a movement to ensure the assimilation of Native peoples into white society. The multi-pronged policy embraced economic, educational, judicial, political, and social reform. Boarding schools were set up under the auspices of missionaries and humanitarians, where Indian children were taken away from their families and tribes, with the avowed purpose of re-educating Indian youth in Anglo-American skills and values. The government attempted to instill a respect for Anglo-American styles of justice by replacing the Native American tradition of retribution, which included restitution, fines, corporal punishment, and reliance on honor, with the Anglo-American practice of incarceration for criminal acts. To further this aim they sought the active involvement of Native Americans as law enforcement officers. Government agents encouraged Native Americans to embrace agriculture, and those who did not do so soon found their government rations withdrawn, as the government tried to starve them into submission. Despite these policies aimed at assimilating Native Americans into Anglo-American culture, by the late nineteenth century Native American culture still flourished. Government officials and reformers then came to argue that the greatest boon to the civilization of the Indians would occur through the allotment of Indian lands in severalty. By becoming landowners and farmers, surrounded by white settlement, Native Americans, it was argued, would abandon their traditional culture and become part of Anglo-American civilization. In essence, late-nineteenth-century politicians and humanitarians proposed to eliminate the "Indian problem" by eliminating the Indians as a culturally distinct entity.

1. L. Q. C. Lamar, SI, Nov. 1, 1885, in *RSI* 1885, 1:23.

Whites proved willing to accept Indians only when they in fact ceased to be Indians.

The Native American response to the policy of assimilation differed from tribe to tribe and according to the degree of Indian blood. Many mixed-blood members of the Five Civilized Tribes eagerly embraced Anglo-American culture. Accepting their individual allotments according to the dictates of the Curtis Act, they dressed in Anglo-American clothing, sent their children to white schools, and organized local businesses to serve the towns. They became the small yeoman farming class the government had hoped to create. On the other hand, many of the full bloods of the Five Civilized Tribes and almost all of the relocated Plains tribes refused to accept Anglo-American culture. Many of these Indians questioned the sincerity of the supposed benevolent motives of Eastern "humanitarians." One Creek Indian concluded: "The philanthropist in Boston shrieks with horror at the selfishness of man, but the Bostonian has done the same thing time-out-of-mind and his chief desire to save the red men is prompted by curiosity. His ancestors made them scarce and he loves the red-man as a curio-collector loves an old stamp or coin. . . . The descendants of those who trample these people under foot will mourn over them, even as many of us sorrow now at the cruelty of the thing; but that is all." Hence, ironically the assimilation policy of the federal government served to unify many formerly hostile Native tribes creating a pan-Indian identity that had not existed previously. Native American leaders argued that whites should accept the differences between the cultures rather than trying to impose their culture over reluctant Indians.[2]

Many of the "conservative" Native American leaders could see no "humanitarianism" in the policies of eastern governmental officials and Indian reformers. When the former secretary of the interior Carl Schurz claimed in 1881 that "I am a warm friend of the Indians; our aim is to absorb them in the body of the Nation, for they have no alternative but civilization or extermination," a Native American editor responded that this appeared to Indians like a spider's invitation, "Come into my parlor, thou pretty little fly, for I love thee, and will treat thee as my own." The editor argued that the assimilation of Native Americans meant they must "forfeit all which they hold sacred and dear from their ancestors for the creeds and customs of those who have for generations debased and destroyed them." Faced with intransigence and lacking the funds and the will to undergo a more encompassing assimilation campaign, by the early twentieth century, governmental officials and reformers abandoned the policy of assimilation in favor of the marginalization of Indians in American society.[3]

In complete contrast, there was never a concerted effort to assimilate African

2. *Creek Papers,* vol. I, 133–36, WHC.
3. *Eufaula Indian Journal,* June 2, 1881.

Americans into Anglo-American culture. Most white officials argued that African Americans would never be accepted into white society as equals, hence, the marginalization of blacks was the best that could be achieved. White officials proved to be more concerned with keeping the races segregated than in bridging any gaps between the cultures.

In the immediate aftermath of the Civil War, American race relations between its white and newly enfranchised black citizens underwent a profound transformation. Social lines between the two races, which in the past had been unmistakable, became blurred. As historian Danney Goble has stated, "For longer than men could remember, most blacks and whites had found themselves enmeshed in a social order that guaranteed white supremacy by an invisible but powerful social line that permanently divided the races. The most obvious example was slavery. . . . One was free. The other was bound. One owned property. The other was property." In the early years of emancipation in the territories, as elsewhere in the nation at the time, there was a battle to redefine the essential elements of white-black relations. As elsewhere, African Americans played a decisive role in the outcome.[4]

With the opening up of "surplus" Indian lands to settlement beginning with the land run of 1889, Oklahoma came to be seen as a "promised land" for black southerners. By the last decade of the nineteenth century most black southerners found themselves locked into the debt-ridden life of a sharecropper, and many found their voting privileges and civil rights under attack from southern "Redeemers." Therefore many African Americans headed west to Oklahoma with the same pioneering spirit as their fellow white settlers—they sought to remove themselves to Oklahoma where they would be independent yeoman farmers. Emigrant aid companies were established with the express purpose of attracting black settlers to come to Oklahoma. Black newspapers and pamphlets were distributed throughout the southern states in an effort to attract migrants to the West.

Officials back in Washington had hoped that the freedmen of the Five Civilized Tribes and black migrants from the southern states would work as farm laborers for white or Native American landowners. Yet increasingly, African Americans began establishing their own farms and hence started working for themselves. In addition, by the close of the century, many African Americans began to move into the towns and to assume occupations normally reserved for whites. Due to the concentration of their population in certain electoral districts and their consistent support of the Republican Party, African Americans were able to garner a share of political power and patronage appointments. African Americans were sent to the territorial legislature, were appointed to territorial patronage jobs, served as deputy U.S. Marshals, and controlled the governments of more than twenty all-black towns.

4. Goble, *Progressive Oklahoma*, 138.

Had white politicians and reformers been ideologically consistent, they would have applauded the achievements of African Americans in Oklahoma as the very embodiment of the American Dream. Yet they did not. While white politicians and reformers hailed the pioneering spirit of white immigrants who became independent farmers and politically active citizens, and sought to inculcate these civic responsibilities in Native Americans, they found themselves uncomfortable when blacks came to challenge whites within the economic, political, and social realms.

Ironically, this study contends, white officials discouraged in African Americans the very ideals and values they so fervently sought to inculcate in Native Americans. While they clung steadfastly to their belief that contact between white and Native Americans would raise Native Americans to a level of sophistication close to that of Anglo-Americans, they held no such hope for African Americans. Instead, white officials worked to segregate African Americans from whites for fear that contact between the races would contaminate the white race rather than uplift the blacks. Hence while white officials were actively trying to entice Native Americans to attend white schools, adopt the Anglo-American justice system, establish themselves as independent yeoman farmers, and become American citizens with all the privileges and responsibilities thereof, they discouraged African Americans from pursuing the same goals. African Americans were segregated from both white and Native American children into separate and clearly inferior schools of their own. White officials did little to protect African Americans from the extra-legal vigilante lynch mobs which terrorized the black community in the territories. African Americans were expected to provide a cheap pool of farm labor upon which white and Native American landowners could draw; they were not expected to be landowners.

The difference in government policy towards African Americans and Native Americans resided in the contrast between the tripartite racial categorization that was made with respect to Native American mixed bloods and the one-drop rule that was applied to African Americans. Whites emphasized the white heritage of mixed bloods in a way that was never applied to mulattoes. Since whites were willing to recognize mixed bloods as partially white, this opened up the possibility of ultimate assimilation and dictated the course of federal Indian policy in the late nineteenth century. Native Americans, policy-makers realized, could ultimately be absorbed into white society through intermarriage and miscegenation. Therefore, the emphasis was placed upon preparing Indians for cultural absorption into Anglo-America. This was never an option for African Americans, as mulattoes were considered "niggers just like the rest of them." For African Americans, there was no escape from the indelible mark of their black skin.[5]

5. Crockett, *The Black Towns,* 100.

Whites, Native Americans, and African Americans were all willing to fight to promote their own interests because to all three racial groups, Oklahoma represented a promised land. The Indian Territory had been granted to Native Americans as their exclusive perpetual home, and they did all they could to try to force the government to live up to its obligations and promises. They sought to have white intruders removed from the territory, and they fought against attempts to incorporate the lands of the Indian nations into first a territory, and later into a state. But in return for Native Americans' losing sovereignty over their lands and the right of self-government, they were granted honorary membership in the dominant race in a society which increasingly only recognized whites and blacks. For when Jim Crow laws came to the new state, Native Americans were classified as "white." To African Americans, Oklahoma represented a place where they hoped to escape the oppression and debt of the southern states and start a new life where their freedom would have tangible meaning. For a short time, Oklahoma offered blacks the opportunity to vote, hold political office, send their children to schools, and most importantly, own their own land. But the virgin Indian lands also proved alluring to white settlers who were confronted with overcrowding and soil exhaustion in the East and therefore sought to conquer and settle this last American frontier. Clearly Oklahoma became a "contested territory." White settlers were willing to accept those Native Americans who were willing to adopt Anglo-American culture as their own. Those who were not were ostracized from white society. Whites fearful of a massive influx of black settlers seeking a place where their civil rights would be protected sought to discourage this potential immigration by passing strict segregation laws and disfranchising black voters. Thus, by the advent of statehood, whites had grabbed hold of the reins of power and overwhelmed the other groups with their sheer numbers. Control over the new state would no longer be contested—Oklahoma would be dominated by its overwhelming white majority.

BIBLIOGRAPHY

Printed Government Records and Documents

U.S. Department of the Interior. *Report of the Secretary of the Interior*. Washington, D.C.: Government Printing Office, 1865–1907.
U.S. Bureau of the Census. *Eleventh Census, 1890*. Washington, D.C.: Government Printing Office, 1890.
———. *Eleventh Census, 1890. The Five Civilized Tribes of Indian Territory*. Washington, D.C.: Government Printing Office, 1890.
———. *Indian Population of the United States—1910*. Washington, D.C.: Government Printing Office, 1910.
———. *Negro Population of the United States, 1790–1915*. Washington, D.C.: Government Printing Office, 1915.
———. *Thirteenth Census, 1910*. Washington, D.C.: Government Printing Office, 1910.
———. *Twelfth Census, 1900*. Washington, D.C.: Government Printing Office, 1900.

Microfilmed Government Records and Documents

National Archives of the United States: Washington, D.C.

Records of the Adjutant General's Office, 1780–1917
    Letters Received by the Office of the Adjutant General, RG 94, Microfilm Publication M619.
Records of the Bureau of Indian Affairs
    Correspondence of the Office of Indian Affairs (Central Office) and Related Records, Letters Received, RG 75, Microfilm Publication M234.
Records of the Bureau of Indian Affairs
    Records of the Superintendencies and Agencies of Indian Affairs, RG 75, Microfilm Publication M856.
Records of the Bureau of Refugees, Freedmen, and Abandoned Lands
    State of Arkansas, 1865–1869, RG 105, Microfilm Publication M979.

Records of the Department of the Interior
    Territorial Papers, Oklahoma Territory, 1889–1912, RG 48, Microfilm Publi-
    cation M828.
Records of the Secretary of the Interior
    Indian Division, Reports of the Inspection of the Field Jurisdictions of the Of-
    fice of Indian Affairs, RG 48, Microfilm Publication M1070.

Manuscript Collections and Documents

*Oklahoma Historical Society, Archives and Manuscripts Division,
Oklahoma City, Okla.*
    Athey, Thomas, Papers
    Barde, Fred, Papers
    Cherokee Nation, National Records
    Choctaw, Chickasaw 1875–1906 and Seminole 1845–1921 and Miscellaneous
        Papers 1874–1932
    Five Civilized Tribes Papers
    Grant Foreman Pioneer History Collection
    Oral History Project Collection, Pioneer Interviews
    Photo Collection
    Quapaw Agency, National Records
    Vertical Files Collection
    Womack, John, Papers

Western History Collection, University of Oklahoma, Norman, Okla.
    Boyd, David Ross, Papers
    Chapman, Berlin Basil, Papers
    Checote, Samuel, Papers
    Cherokee Nation Papers
    Chickasaw Nation Papers
    Choctaw Nation Papers
    Connelley, William E., Papers
    Creek Nation Papers
    Duke, Doris, Oral History Interviews
    Epton, Hicks Byers, Papers
    Ferguson, Walter Scott, Papers
    Gardner, Jefferson, Papers
    Garvin, I. L., Papers
    Harris, Johnson, Papers
    Historic Oklahoma Collection, Vertical Files—Afro-Americans, Colonization,
        Constitution, Racism
    Impson, Hiram, Papers
    Jarboe, W. C., Papers
    Johnston, Douglas H., Papers
    Jones, Wilson N., Papers
    Mayes, Samuel Houston, Papers

McCurtain, Edmond, Papers
McCurtain, Green, Papers
McCurtain, Jackson, Papers
Ogden, Florence, Papers
Parman, James Franklin, Papers
Pilburn, Anne Ross, Papers
Pitchlynn, Peter Perkins, Papers
Rister, Carl Coke, Papers
Robey, Roberta, Papers
Slover, James Anderson, Papers
Smith, Franklin Campbell, Autobiography
Tonkawa, Oklahoma, Public Library Collection
United States District Court Records, Western District of Oklahoma, Box 293, File Folders 2 and 4
Williams, John Robert, Papers

Archives and Manuscripts Division, Oklahoma State University, Stillwater, Oklahoma

Debo, Angie, Papers
Laws and Constitution of the Five Civilized Tribes
Cherokee M391 N9 Che C758
Chickasaw M391 L9 Chi C761
Choctaw M391 G9 Cho C758
Creek M391 N9 Cr C758
Seminole M391 N9 Se C758

Newspapers (Researched in the Newspaper Division, *Oklahoma Historical Society, Oklahoma City, Okla.*)

White and Indian Newspapers

Alva Review
Ardmore Appeal
Atoka Indian Citizen
Atoka Vindicator
Beaver Herald
Beaver Journal
Blackwell Times Record
Boston Daily Advertiser
Cache Clarion
Carnegie Herald
Cherokee Advocate
Cherokee Messenger
Cheyenne Transporter
Chickasha Daily Express
Chickasha Enterprise
Cleveland County Leader

Daily Ardmoreitte
Daily Oklahoman
Eagle Gazette
Edmond Sun
Edmond Sun-Democrat
El Reno News
Enid Weekly Eagle
Eufaula Indian Journal
Frederick Enterprise
Globe-Democrat
Guthrie Daily Leader
Hennessey Clipper
Kingfisher Free Press
Kingston Messenger
Krebs Eagle
Lawton Constitution
Lawton Weekly Enterprise
Lexington Leader
Lincoln Tribune
Mangum Star
Muskogee Daily Phoenix
Muskogee Indian Journal
Muskogee New-State Tribune
Norman Transcript
Oklahoma Capital
Oklahoma Eagle
Oklahoma Safeguard
Oklahoma State Capital
Oklahoma Weekly Times Journal
Perkins Journal
Purcell Register
Republican Bureau
Richmond Times Dispatch
Rochester Courier
Sayre Headlight
Shawnee Daily Herald
Stillwater Advance
Stillwater Gazette
Topeka Republic
Vinita Daily Chieftain
Wilburton News
Woodville Beacon
Woodward News

Black Newspapers

Boley Progress
Clearview Tribune

Indian Territory Sun
Langston City Herald
Langston Western Age
Muskogee Cimeter
Oklahoma Guide
Western World

Articles

Abbott, L. J. "The Race Question in the Forty-sixth State." *Independent* (July 25, 1907): 206–11.

Baird, W. David. "Are There 'Real' Indians in Oklahoma? Historical Perceptions of the Five Civilized Tribes." *Chronicles of Oklahoma* 67, no. 1 (1990): 4–18.

Balyeat, Frank A. "Segregation in the Public Schools of Oklahoma Territory." *Chronicles of Oklahoma* 39, no. 2 (1961): 180–92.

Berthrong, Donald J. "White Neighbors Come Among the Southern Cheyenne and Arapaho." *Kansas Quarterly* 3, no. 4 (1974): 105–15.

Bethel, Elizabeth. "The Freedmen's Bureau in Alabama." *Journal of Southern History* 14 (Feb. 1948): 50–92.

Bittle, William E., and Gilbert L. Geis. "Racial Self-Fulfillment and the Rise of an All-Negro Community in Oklahoma." *Phylon* 18, 3rd quarter (1956): 247–60.

Bloom, Leonard. "Role of the Indian in the Race Relations Complex of the South." *Social Forces* 19 (Dec. 1940): 268–73.

Brant, Charles S. "Indian-White Cultural Relations in Southwestern Oklahoma." *Chronicles of Oklahoma* 37, no. 4 (1959): 433–39.

Chapman, Berlin B. "Freedmen and the Oklahoma Lands." *Southwestern Social Science Quarterly* 29 (Sept. 1948): 150–59.

Christensen, Lawrence O. "J. Milton Turner: An Appraisal." *Missouri Historical Review* 70, no. 1 (1975): 1–19.

Clement, Rufus E. "The Church School as a Social Factor in Negro Life." *Journal of Negro History* 12, no. 1 (Jan. 1927): 5–12.

Cohen, William. "Black Immobility and Free Labor: The Freedmen's Bureau and the Relocation of Black Labor, 1865–68." *Civil War History* 28, no. 2 (June 1982): 221–34.

Crawford, Suzanne J., and Lynn R. Musslewhite. "Progressive Reform and Oklahoma Democrats: Kate Barnard versus Bill Murray." *Historian* 33 (spring 1991): 473–80.

Crockett, Norman L. "Witness to History: Booker T. Washington Visits Boley." *Chronicles of Oklahoma* 67, no. 4 (1989): 382–91.

Curry, J. L. M. "Industrial Education for Everybody." *Independent* 52 (Feb. 8, 1900): 357–58.

Duncan, Otis D. "The Fusion of White, Negro, and Indian Cultures at the Converging of the New South and the West." *Southwestern Social Science Quarterly* 14 (Mar. 1934): 357–69.

Fenner, Theodosia E. "Black Leadership in 1889." *Oklahoma's Historical Edition* 3 (1982).

Finney, Frank F., Sr. "Progress in the Civilization of the Osage, and their Government." *Chronicles of Oklahoma* 40, no. 1 (1962): 2–21.

Forbes, Jack D. "Mulattoes and People of Color in Anglo-North America: Implications for Black-Indian Relations." *Journal of Ethnic Studies* 17 (winter 1990): 17–53.

Frazier, E. Franklin. "The Negro in the Industrial South." *Nation* 125 (July 27, 1927): 359–60.

Gammon, Tim. "Black Freedmen and the Cherokee Nation." *Journal of American Studies* 11 (Dec. 1977): 357–64.

Hamilton, Kenneth M. "Townsite Speculation and the Origin of Boley, Oklahoma." *Chronicles of Oklahoma* 55, no. 2 (1977): 180–89.

Harris, Carl V. "Stability and Change in Discrimination against Black Public Schools: Birmingham, Alabama, 1871–1931." *Journal of Southern History* 51, no. 3 (Aug. 1985): 375–416.

Hill, Mozell C. "The All-Negro Communities of Oklahoma: The Natural History of a Social Movement." *Journal of Negro History* 31 (July 1946): 254–68.

———. "Basic Racial Attitudes toward Whites in the Oklahoma All-Negro Community." *American Journal of Sociology* 49 (May 1944): 519–23.

———. "A Comparative Analysis of the Social Organization of the All-Negro Society in Oklahoma." *Social Forces* 25 (Oct. 1946): 70–77.

———. "A Comparative Study of Race Attitudes in the All-Negro Community in Oklahoma." *Phylon* 7 (1946): 260–68.

Hill, Mozell C., and Thelma D. Ackiss. "Social Classes: A Frame of Reference for the Study of Negro Society." *Social Forces* 22, no. 1 (Oct., 1943): 92–98.

Hill, Mozell C., and Eugene S. Richards. "Demographic Trends of the Negro in Oklahoma." *Southwestern Journal* 2 (winter 1946): 47–63.

Holmes, William F. "Whitecapping: Agrarian Violence in Mississippi, 1902–1906." *Journal of Southern History* 25 (May 1969): 165–85.

Huggard, Christopher J. "Culture Mixing: Everyday Life on the Missions among the Choctaws." *Chronicles of Oklahoma* 70, no. 4 (1992): 432–47.

James, Parthena L. "Reconstruction in the Chickasaw Nation: The Freedman Problem." *Chronicles of Oklahoma* 45, no. 1 (1967): 44–57.

———. "The White Threat in the Chickasaw Nation." *Chronicles of Oklahoma* 46, no. 1 (1968): 73–85.

Jeltz, Wyatt F. "The Relations of Negroes and Choctaw and Chickasaw Indians." *Journal of Negro History* 33 (Jan. 1948): 24–37.

Johnson, Guy B. "Personality in a White-Indian-Negro Community." *American Sociological Review* 4 (Aug. 1939): 516–23.

Johnston, James H. "Documentary Evidence of the Relations of Negroes and Indians." *Journal of Negro History* 14 (Jan. 1929): 21–43.

Kremer, Gary R. "For Justice and a Fee: James Milton Turner and the Cherokee Freedmen." *Chronicles of Oklahoma* 58, no. 4 (1980): 376–88.

Krogman, Wilton M. "The Racial Composition of the Seminole Indians of Florida and Oklahoma." *Journal of Negro History* 19 (1934): 412–30.

Littlefield, Daniel F., Jr., and Lonnie E. Underhill. "Negro Marshals in the Indian Territory." *Journal of Negro History* 56, no. 2 (Apr. 1971): 77–87.

Makofsky, Abraham. "Experience of Native Americans at a Black College: Indian Students at Hampton Institute, 1878–1923." *Journal of Ethnic Studies* 17 (fall 1989): 31–46.

McPherson, James M. "White Liberals and Black Power in Negro Education, 1865–1915." *American Historical Review* 75 (June 1970): 1357–86.

Mellinger, Philip. "Discrimination and Statehood in Oklahoma." *Chronicles of Oklahoma* 49, no. 3 (1971): 340–77.

Perry, Thelma A. "The Education of Negroes in Oklahoma." *Journal of Negro Education* 16 (winter 1947): 397–404.

Porter, Kenneth. "Notes Supplementary to Relations between Negroes and Indians." *Journal of Negro History* 18, no. 3 (1933): 282–321.

———. "Relations between Negroes and Indians within the Present Limits of the United States." *Journal of Negro History* 17, no. 3 (1932): 287–367.

———. "The Seminole Negro-Indian Scouts, 1870–1881." *Southwestern Historical Quarterly* 55 (Jan. 1952): 358–77.

Rabinowitz, Howard N. "Half a Loaf: The Shift from White to Black Teachers in the Negro Schools of the Urban South, 1865–1890." *Journal of Southern History* 40, no. 4 (Nov. 1974): 565–94.

Richards, Eugene S. "Trends of Negro Life in Oklahoma as Reflected by Census Reports." *Journal of Negro History* 33, no. 1 (1948): 38–52.

Roberson, Jere W. "Edward P. McCabe and the Langston Experiment." *Chronicles of Oklahoma* 51, no. 3 (1973): 343–55.

Savage, W. Sherman. "The Role of Negro Soldiers in Protecting the Indian Territory from Intruders." *Journal of Negro History* 36 (Jan. 1951): 25–34.

Shepard, R. Bruce. "The Origins of the Oklahoma Black Migration to the Canadian Plains." *Canadian Journal of History* 23 (Apr. 1988): 1–23.

Strickland, Arvarh E. "Toward the Promised Land: The Exodus to Kansas and Afterward." *Missouri Historical Review* 69, no. 4 (July 1975): 376–412.

Taylor, Joseph H. "The Rise and Decline of a Utopian Community, Boley, Oklahoma." *Negro History Bulletin* (Mar. 1940): 90–93.

Tolson, Arthur L. "Black Towns of Oklahoma." *Black Scholar* 2, (Apr. 1970): 18–22.

Trennert, Robert A. "Educating Indian Girls at Nonreservation Boarding Schools, 1878–1920." *Western Historical Quarterly* 13, (July 1982): 271–90.

Warde, Mary Jane. "Fight for Survival: The Indian Response to the Boomer Movement." *Chronicles of Oklahoma* 67, no. 1 (1989): 30–49.

Washington, Booker T. "Boley, A Negro Town in the West." *Outlook* 88 (Jan. 4, 1908): 28–31.

Williams, Nudie E. "Black Men Who Wore the Star." *Chronicles of Oklahoma* 59, no. 1 (1981): 83–89.

———. "The Black Press in Oklahoma: The Formative Years 1889–1907." *Chronicles of Oklahoma* 61, no. 3 (1983): 308–18.

———. "They Fought for Votes: The White Politician and the Black Editor." *Chronicles of Oklahoma* 64, no. 1 (1986): 19–33.

———. "United States v. Bass Reeves: Black Lawman on Trial." *Chronicles of Oklahoma* 68, no. 2 (1990): 154–65.

Willson, Walt. "Freedmen in Indian Territory during Reconstruction." *Chronicles of Oklahoma* 49, no. 2 (1971): 230–44.

Womack, John. "Black Women Land Claimants the First Year in Oklahoma, 1889–1890." *Oklahoma Historical Society Papers* (June 1982).
———. "Statistics on Blacks in Oklahoma—The First Year." *Oklahoma Historical Society Papers* (June 1982).
Woodard, James E. "Vernon: An All Negro Town in Southeastern Oklahoma." *Negro History Bulletin* 27 (1963): 115–16.
Wright, Muriel H. "The Wedding of Oklahoma and Miss Indian Territory." *Chronicles of Oklahoma* 35, no. 3 (1957): 255–65.
Wrone, David R. "The Cherokee Act of Emancipation." *Journal of Ethnic Studies* 1, no. 3 (1973): 87–90.

Books

Anderson, James D. *The Education of Blacks in the South, 1860–1935*. Chapel Hill: University of North Carolina Press, 1988.
Andrist, Ralph K. *The Long Death: The Last Days of the Plains Indians*. New York: Macmillan, 1964.
Ayers, Edward L. *The Promise of the New South: Life after Reconstruction*. New York: Oxford University Press, 1992.
Bailey, M. Thomas. *Reconstruction in Indian Territory: A Story of Avarice, Discrimination, and Opportunism*. Port Washington: Kennikat Press, 1972.
Bailey, Ralph E. *The Story of Nelson A. Miles: Indian Fighter*. New York: William Morrow, 1965.
Baird, W. David. *A Creek Warrior for the Confederacy: The Autobiography of Chief G. W. Grayson*. Norman: University of Oklahoma Press, 1988.
Barney, Garold D. *Mormons, Indians, and the Ghost Dance Religion of 1890*. Latham: University Press of America, 1986.
Bentley, George R. *A History of the Freedmen's Bureau*. New York: Octagon Books, 1955.
Berlin, Ira. *Slaves without Masters: The Free Negro in the Antebellum South*. Oxford: Oxford University Press, 1974.
Billings, Dwight B. *Planters and the Making of a New South: Class Politics and Development in North Carolina*. Chapel Hill: University of North Carolina Press, 1980.
Billington, Ray A. *Westward Expansion*. New York: Macmillan, 1949.
Bittle, William E., and Gilbert Geis. *The Longest Way Home: Chief Alfred Sam's Back-to-Africa Movement*. Detroit: Wayne State University Press, 1964.
Bond, Horace M. *Education of the Negro in the American Social Order*. New York: Octagon Books, 1966.
Brundage, W. Fitzhugh. *Lynching in the New South: Georgia and Virginia, 1880–1930*. Urbana: University of Illinois Press, 1993.
Bullock, Henry A. *History of Negro Education in the South from 1619–Present*. Cambridge, Mass.: Harvard University Press, 1967.
Burton, Arthur T. *Black, Red and Deadly: Black and Indian Gunfighters of the Indian Territory, 1870–1907*. Austin: Eakin Press, 1991.
Butchert, Ronald E. *Northern Schools, Southern Blacks, and Reconstruction: Freedmen's Education, 1862–1875*. Westport: Greenwood Press, 1980.

Cash, W. J. *The Mind of the South*. New York: Alfred A. Knopf, 1941.

Clem, C. Douglas. *Oklahoma: Her People and Professions*. Kingfisher: Constitution Press, n.d.

Coleman, Michael C. *American Indian Children at School, 1850–1930*. Jackson: University of Mississippi Press, 1993.

Cooper, William J., Jr. *The Conservative Regime: South Carolina, 1877–1890*. Baltimore: John Hopkins Press, 1968.

Crawford, Isabel. *Joyful Journey: Highlights on the High Way*. Philadelphia: Judson Press, 1951.

Crockett, Norman L. *The Black Towns*. Lawrence: Regents Press of Kansas, 1979.

Cutler, James E. *Lynch-Law: An Investigation into the History of Lynching in the United States*. Montclair: Patterson Smith, 1969.

Debo, Angie. *And Still the Waters Run*. Princeton: Princeton University Press, 1940.

———. *The Road to Disappearance*. Norman: University of Oklahoma Press, 1941.

DeCanio, Stephen J. *Agriculture in the Postbellum South: The Economics of Production and Supply*. Cambridge, Mass.: Harvard University Press, 1974.

De Rosier, Arthur H., Jr. *The Removal of the Choctaw Indians*. Knoxville: University of Tennessee Press, 1970.

De Santis, Vincent P. *Republicans Face the Southern Question: The New Departure Years, 1877–1897*. Baltimore: John Hopkins Press, 1959.

Dillon, M. L. *The Abolitionists: The Growth of a Dissenting Minority*. DeKalb: Northern Illinois University Press, 1974.

Dinnerstein, Leonard, et al. *Natives and Strangers: Blacks, Indians, and Immigrants in America*. New York: Oxford University Press, 1990.

Dobyns, Henry F. *The Ghost Dance of 1889 among the Pai Indians of Northwestern Arizona*. Prescott: College Press, 1967.

Dunlay, Thomas. *Wolves for the Blue Soldiers: Indian Scouts and Auxiliaries with the United States Army, 1860–90*. Lincoln: University of Nebraska Press, 1982.

Dyer, Thomas G. *Theodore Roosevelt and the Idea of Race*. Baton Rouge: Louisiana State University Press, 1980.

Ellsworth, Scott. *Death in a Promised Land: The Tulsa Race Riot of 1921*. Baton Rouge: Louisiana State University Press, 1982.

Faulk, Odie B. *Oklahoma: Land of the Fair God*. Northridge: Windsor Publications, 1986.

Faust, Drew, ed. *The Ideology of Slavery: Proslavery Thought in the Antebellum South, 1830–1860*. Baton Rouge: Louisiana State University Press, 1981.

Federal Writers' Project. *Federal Writers Projects of the Works Progress Administration*. Vol. 6, *Ex-Slave Narratives, Oklahoma*. St. Clair Shores: Scholarly Press, 1976.

Fields, Barbara J. *Slavery and Freedom on the Middle Ground: Maryland during the Nineteenth Century*. New Haven: Yale University Press, 1985.

Filler, Harper. *The Crusade against Slavery, 1830–60*. New York: Harper, 1960.

Finkelman, Paul. *Lynching, Racial Violence, and Law*. New York: Garland, 1992.

Flynn, Charles L. *White Land, Black Labor: Caste and Class in Late 19th Century Georgia*. Baton Rouge: Louisiana State University Press, 1983.

Foner, Eric. *Nothing but Freedom: Emancipation and Its Legacy*. Baton Rouge: Louisiana State University Press, 1983.

———. *Reconstruction: America's Unfinished Revolution*. New York: Oxford University Press, 1988.

Forbes, Jack D. *Black Africans and Native Americans*. Oxford: Basil Blackwell, 1988.

Foreman, Grant. *The Five Civilized Tribes*. Norman: University of Oklahoma Press, 1934.

———. *Indian Removal: The Emigration of the Five Civilized Tribes*. Norman: University of Oklahoma Press, 1932.

Fowler, Arlen L. *The Black Infantry in the West, 1869–1891*. Westport: Greenwood Press, 1971.

Franklin, Jimmie Lewis. *Journey toward Hope: A History of Blacks in Oklahoma*. Norman: University of Oklahoma Press, 1982.

Franklin, Vincent P., and James D. Anderson, eds. *New Perspectives on Black Educational History*. Boston: G. K. Hall, 1978.

Fredrickson, George M. *The Black Image in the White Mind: The Debate on Afro-American Character and Destiny, 1817–1914*. New York: Harper and Row, 1971.

Fuchs, Estelle, and Robert J. Havighurst. *To Live on This Earth: American Indian Education*. Garden City: Doubleday, 1972.

Gaither, Gerald H. *Blacks and the Populist Revolt: Ballots and Bigotry in the New South*. Tuscaloosa: University of Alabama Press, 1977.

Gerteis, Louis. *From Contraband to Freedman: Federal Policy toward Southern Blacks, 1861–65*. Westport: Greenwood Press, 1973.

Gibson, Arrell M. *The History of Oklahoma*. Norman: University of Oklahoma Press, 1984.

———. *Oklahoma: A History of Five Centuries*. Norman: University of Oklahoma Press, 1981.

Gideon, D. C. *Indian Territory*. New York: Lewis, 1901.

Gillette, William. *Retreat from Reconstruction, 1869–79*. Baton Rouge: Louisiana State University Press, 1979.

Glasscock, Carl B. *Then Came Oil: The Story of the Last Frontier*. Westport: Hyperion Press, 1938.

Goble, Danney. *Progressive Oklahoma: The Making of a New Kind of State*. Norman: University of Oklahoma Press, 1980.

Grantham, Dewey W. *The Life and Death of the Solid South: A Political History*. Lexington: University of Kentucky Press, 1988.

———. *Southern Progressivism: The Reconciliation of Progress and Tradition*. Knoxville: University of Tennessee Press, 1983.

Green, James R. *Grass Roots Socialism: Radical Movements in the Southwest, 1895–1943*. Baton Rouge: Louisiana State University Press, 1978.

Green, Michael D. *The Politics of Indian Removal: Creek Government and Society in Crisis*. Lincoln: University of Nebraska Press, 1982.

Grinnell, George B. *Two Great Scouts and Their Pawnee Battalion*. Glendale: Arthur H. Clark, 1928.

Hagan, William T. *Indian Police and Judges: Experiments in Acculturation and Control.* New Haven: Yale University Press, 1966.

Hamilton, Kenneth M. *Black Towns and Profit: Promotion and Development in the Trans-Appalachian West, 1877–1915.* Urbana: University of Illinois Press, 1991.

Harlan, Louis R. *Booker T. Washington in Perspective: Essays of Louis R. Harlan.* Jackson: University of Mississippi Press, 1988.

———. *Separate and Unequal: Public School Campaigns and Racism in the Southern Seaboard States, 1901–1915.* Chapel Hill: University of North Carolina Press, 1958.

Harring, Sidney L. *Crow Dog's Case: American Indian Sovereignty, Tribal Law, and United States Law in the Nineteenth Century.* New York: Cambridge University Press, 1994.

Harris, Trudier. *Exorcising Blackness: Historical and Literary Lynching and Burning Rituals.* Bloomington: University of Indiana Press, 1984.

Higham, John. *Strangers in the Land: Patterns of American Nativism, 1860–1925.* New York: Atheneum, 1963.

Hoig, Stan. *The Oklahoma Land Rush of 1889.* Oklahoma City: Oklahoma Historical Society, 1984.

Holmes, Dwight O. *Evolution of the Negro College.* College Park: McGrath, 1969.

Holt, Thomas. *Black over White: Negro Political Leadership in South Carolina during Reconstruction.* Urbana: University of Illinois Press, 1977.

Horsman, Reginald. *Expansion and American Indian Policy, 1783–1812.* East Lansing: Michigan State University Press, 1967.

Howard, Oliver O. *My Life and Experiences among Our Hostile Indians.* New York: Da Capo Press, 1907.

Hoxie, Frederick E. *A Final Promise: The Campaign to Assimilate the Indians, 1880–1920.* Lincoln: University of Nebraska Press, 1984.

Jenkins, William S. *Pro-Slavery Thought in the Old South.* Chapel Hill: University of North Carolina Press, 1935.

Kappler, Charles J. *Indian Treaties, 1778–1883.* New York: Interland, 1972.

Kehoe, Alice B. *The Ghost Dance: Ethnohistory and Revitalization.* New York: Holt, Rinehart, and Winston, 1989.

Keller, Robert H. *American Protestantism and United States Indian Policy, 1869–1882.* Lincoln: University of Nebraska Press, 1983.

Knight, Thomas. *Sunset on Utopian Dreams: An Experiment of Black Separatism on the American Frontier.* Washington, D.C.: University Press of America, 1977.

Kousser, J. Morgan. *The Shaping of Southern Politics: Suffrage Restriction and the Establishment of the One-Party South, 1880–1910.* New Haven: Yale University Press, 1974.

Kusmer, Kenneth. *A Ghetto Takes Shape: Black Cleveland, 1870–1930.* Urbana: University of Illinois Press, 1976.

Leckie, William H. *The Buffalo Soldiers: A Narrative of the Negro Cavalry in the West.* Norman: University of Oklahoma Press, 1967.

———. *The Military Conquest of the Southern Plains Indians.* Norman: University of Oklahoma Press, 1963.

Leonard, William T. *Masquerade in Black*. Metuchen: Scarecrow Press, 1986.

Littlefield, Daniel F., Jr. *Africans and Creeks: From the Colonial Period to the Civil War*. Westport: Greenwood Press, 1979.

———. *Africans and Seminoles: From Removal to Emancipation*. Westport: Greenwood Press, 1977.

———. *The Cherokee Freedmen: From Emancipation to American Citizenship*. Westport: Greenwood Press, 1978.

———. *The Chickasaw Freedmen: A People without a Country*. Westport: Greenwood Press, 1980.

———. *Seminole Burning: A Story of Racial Vengeance*. Jackson: University of Mississippi Press, 1996.

Litwack, Leon. *Been in the Storm So Long: The Aftermath of Slavery*. New York: Vintage Books, 1979.

———. *North of Slavery: The Negro in the Free States, 1790–1860*. Chicago: University of Chicago Press, 1961.

Lomawaima, K. Tsianina. *They Called It Prairie Light: The Story of Chilocco Indian School*. Lincoln: University of Nebraska Press, 1994.

Lott, Eric. *Love and Theft: Blackface Minstrelsy and the American Working Class*. New York: Oxford University Press, 1993.

Mabee, Carleton. *Black Education in New York State: From Colonial to Modern Times*. Syracuse: Syracuse University Press, 1979.

Mandle, Jay R. *Not Slave, Not Free: The African American Economic Experience since the Civil War*. Durham: Duke University Press, 1992.

Mardock, Robert. *Reformers and the American Indian*. Columbia, Mo.: University of Missouri Press, 1971.

McBeth, Sally J. *Ethnic Identity and the Boarding School Experience of West-Central Oklahoma American Indians*. Washington, D.C.: University Press of America, 1983.

McLoughlin, William G. *After the Trail of Tears: The Cherokees' Struggle for Sovereignty, 1839–1880*. Chapel Hill: University of North Carolina Press, 1993.

McRill, Albert. *And Satan Came Also*. Oklahoma City: Britton, 1955.

Meier, August. *Negro Thought in America, 1880–1915: Racial Ideologies in the Age of Booker T. Washington*. Ann Arbor: University of Michigan Press, 1963.

Mihesuah, Devon A. *Cultivating the Rosebuds: The Education of Women at the Cherokee Female Seminary, 1851–1909*. Urbana: University of Illinois Press, 1993.

Miles, Nelson A. *Serving the Republic: Memoirs of the Civil and Military Life of Nelson A. Miles*. Freeport: Books for Library Press, 1911.

Mooney, James. *The Ghost Dance Religion and the Sioux Outbreak of 1890*. Chicago: University of Chicago Press, 1965.

Morgan, Anne H., and H. Wayne Morgan, eds. *Oklahoma: New Views of the Forty-sixth State*. Norman: University of Oklahoma Press, 1982.

Morgan, Anne H., and Rennard Strickland, eds. *Oklahoma Memories*. Norman: University of Oklahoma Press, 1981.

Morgan, H. Wayne, and Anne H. Morgan. *Oklahoma: A Bicentennial History*. New York: W. W. Norton, 1977.

Morris, John W., et al. *Historical Atlas of Oklahoma*. Norman: University of Oklahoma, 1976.

Nash, Gary B. *Red, White and Black: The Peoples of Early North America*. Englewood Cliffs: Prentice Hall, 1992.

Nathan, Hans. *Dan Emmett and the Rise of Early Negro Minstrelsy*. Norman: University of Oklahoma Press, 1962.

Newsom, D. Earl. *Kicking Bird and the Birth of Oklahoma: A Biography of Milton W. Reynolds*. Perkins, Okla.: Evans Publications, 1983.

Novak, Daniel A. *The Wheel of Servitude: Black Forced Labor after Slavery*. Lexington: University of Kentucky Press, 1978.

Nye, Wilbur S. *Carbine and Lance: The Story of Old Fort Sill*. Norman: University of Oklahoma Press, 1942.

———. *Plains Indian Raiders: The Final Phase of Warfare from the Arkansas to the Red River*. Norman: University of Oklahoma Press, 1968.

Oakes, James. *Slavery and Freedom: An Interpretation of the Old South*. New York: Alfred A. Knopf, 1990.

Oubre, Claude F. *Forty Acres and a Mule: The Freedmen's Bureau and Black Land Ownership*. Baton Rouge: Louisiana State University Press, 1978.

Perdue, Theda. *Nations Remembered: An Oral History of the Five Civilized Tribes, 1865–1907*. Westport: Greenwood Press, 1980.

———. *Slavery and the Evolution of Cherokee Society, 1540–1866*. Knoxville: University of Tennessee Press, 1979.

Perman, Michael. *The Road to Redemption: Southern Politics, 1869–79*. Chapel Hill: University of North Carolina Press, 1984.

Perry, Lewis, and Michael Fellman, eds. *Antislavery Reconsidered: New Perspectives on the Abolitionists*. Baton Rouge: Louisiana State University Press, 1979.

Powell, Lawrence N. *New Masters: Northern Planters during the Civil War and Reconstruction*. New Haven: Yale University Press, 1980.

Pratt, Richard H. *Battlefield and Classroom: Four Decades with the American Indian, 1867–1904*. New Haven: Yale University Press, 1964.

Prucha, Francis P. *American Indian Policy in Crisis: Christian Reformers and the Indian, 1865–1900*. Norman: University of Oklahoma Press, 1976.

———. *Documents of United States Indian Policy*. Lincoln: University of Nebraska Press, 1990.

———. *The Great Father: The United States Government and the American Indians*. Vols. 1 and 2, Lincoln: University of Nebraska Press, 1984.

———. *The Indians in American Society: From the Revolutionary War to Present*. Berkeley: University of California Press, 1985.

Rabinowitz, Howard N. *Race Relations in the Urban South, 1865–1890*. New York: Oxford University Press, 1978.

Ransom, Roger, and Richard Sutch. *One Kind of Freedom: The Economic Consequences of Emancipation*. New York: Cambridge University Press, 1977.

Rister, Carl C. *Land Hunger: David L. Payne and the Oklahoma Boomers*. New York: Arno Press, 1975.

———. *No Man's Land*. Norman: University of Oklahoma Press, 1948.

Roark, James R. *Masters without Slaves: Southern Planters in the Civil War and Reconstruction*. New York: W. W. Norton, 1977.

Rogin, Michael. *Fathers and Children: Andrew Jackson and the Destruction of American Indians*. New York: Alfred A. Knopf, 1975.

Rose, Willie L. *Rehearsal for Reconstruction: The Port Royal Experiment*. New York: Vintage Books, 1964.

Satz, Ronald N. *American Indian Policy in the Jacksonian Era*. Lincoln: University of Nebraska Press, 1975.

Savage, W. Sherman. *Blacks in the West*. Westport: Greenwood Press, 1976.

Scales, James R., and Danney Goble. *Oklahoma Politics: A History*. Norman: University of Oklahoma Press, 1982.

Shay, Frank. *Judge Lynch: His First Hundred Years*. Montclair: Patterson Smith, 1969.

Sheehan, Bernard. *Seeds of Extinction: Jeffersonian Philosophy and the American Indian*. Chapel Hill: University of North Carolina Press, 1973.

Sherer, Robert G. *Subordination or Liberation? The Development and Conflicting Theories of Black Education in Nineteenth Century Alabama*. Tuscaloosa: University of Alabama Press, 1977.

Shirley, Glenn. *Heck Thomas: Frontier Marshal*. Norman: University of Oklahoma Press, 1981.

————. *West of Hell's Fringe: Crime, Criminals, and the Federal Peace Officer in Oklahoma Territory, 1889–1907*. Norman: University of Oklahoma Press, 1978.

Sorin, Gerald. *Abolitionism: A New Perspective*. New York: Praeger Books, 1972.

Spivey, Donald. *Schooling for the New Slavery: Black Industrial Education, 1868–1915*. Westport: Greenwood Press, 1978.

Stein, Howard F., and Robert F. Hill, eds. *The Culture of Oklahoma*. Norman: University of Oklahoma Press, 1993.

Stewart, James. *Holy Warriors: The Abolitionists and American Slavery*. New York: Hill and Wang, 1976.

Strickland, Rennard. *The Indians in Oklahoma*. Norman: University of Oklahoma Press, 1980.

Takaki, Ronald T. *A Different Mirror: A History of Multicultural America*. Toronto: Little, Brown, 1993.

————. *Iron Cages: Race and Culture in Nineteenth Century America*. New York: Alfred A. Knopf, 1979.

Teall, Kay M. *Black History in Oklahoma*. Oklahoma City: Oklahoma City Public Schools, 1971.

Thompson, John. *Closing the Frontier: Radical Response in Oklahoma, 1889–1923*. Norman: University of Oklahoma Press, 1986.

Tise, Larry E. *Proslavery: A History of the Defense of Slavery in America, 1701–1840*. Athens: University of Georgia Press, 1987.

Toll, Robert C. *Blacking Up: The Minstrel Show in Nineteenth Century America*. New York: Oxford University Press, 1974.

Tolnay, Stewart E. *A Festival of Violence: An Analysis of the Lynching of African Americans in the American South*. Urbana: University of Illinois Press, 1995.

Tolson, Arthur L. *The Black Oklahomans: A History, 1541–1972*. New Orleans: Edwards Print, 1972.

Trelease, Allen W. *White Terror: The Ku Klux Klan Conspiracy and Southern Reconstruction*. New York: Harper and Row, 1971.

Trennert, Robert A., Jr. *The Phoenix Indian School: Forced Assimilation in Arizona, 1891–1935*. Norman: University of Oklahoma Press, 1988.

Utley, Robert. *Frontier Regulars: The United States Army and the Indian, 1866–1889*. New York: Macmillan, 1972.

———. *The Indian Frontier of the American West, 1846–1890*. Albuquerque: University of New Mexico Press, 1984.

———. *The Last Days of the Sioux Nation*. New Haven: Yale University Press, 1963.

Vaughn, William P. *Schools for All: The Blacks and Public Education in the South, 1865–1877*. Lexington: University of Kentucky Press, 1974.

Washburn, Wilcomb E. *Red Man's Land/White Man's Law: A Study of the Past and Present Status of the American Indian*. New York: Charles Scribner's Sons, 1971.

Washington, Nathaniel J. *Historical Development of the Negro in Oklahoma*. Tulsa: Dexter, 1948.

Watson, Harry L. *Liberty and Power: The Politics of Jacksonian America*. New York: Hill and Wang, 1990.

Wayne, Michael. *The Reshaping of Plantation Society: The Natchez District, 1860–1880*. Baton Rouge: Louisiana State University Press, 1983.

Weinberg, Meyer. *A Chance to Learn: The History of Race and Education in the United States*. Cambridge, Eng.: Cambridge University Press, 1977.

White, Howard A. *The Freedmen's Bureau in Louisiana*. Baton Rouge: Louisiana State University Press, 1978.

White, Richard. *The Roots of Dependency: Subsistence, Environment, and Social Change among the Choctaws, Pawnees, and Navajos*. Lincoln: University of Nebraska Press, 1983.

Williamson, Joel. *The Crucible of Race: Black-White Relations in the American South since Emancipation*. New York: Oxford University Press, 1984.

Wilson, Theodore B. *The Black Codes in the South*. University, Ala.: University of Alabama Press, 1965.

Woodward, C. Vann. *The Origins of the New South, 1877–1915*. Baton Rouge: Louisiana State University Press, 1951.

———. *The Strange Career of Jim Crow*. New York: Oxford University Press, 1974.

Wright, Gavin. *Old South, New South: Revolutions in the Southern Economy since the Civil War*. New York: Basic Books, 1986.

Wyatt-Brown, Bertram. *Honor and Violence in the Old South*. Oxford: Oxford University Press, 1986.

INDEX

Africa, 64

African American migration: and Choctaw freedmen, 12; and civil rights, 13, 31, 57, 63, 189, 210; and freedom from oppression, 33, 54, 64, 189*n*; and intermarriage, 35; and African American newspapers, 55, 56, 57, 58–59, 208; and McCabe, 55–58; and disfranchisement, 63, 203, 204, 210; and segregation, 85, 93, 189, 190; and education, 93; and Democratic Party, 179–80, 182, 190, 191, 196, 204; and "negro domination" threat, 179–80, 182, 200–1; and African American political participation, 184; and surplus lands, 208

African American newspapers: and African American stereotypes, 30–32; and intermarriage, 40; and African American migration, 55, 56, 57, 58–59, 208; and segregation, 87, 112–13, 188–89; and labor, 110, 111–12; and African American success, 114; and sandbar saloons, 148; and lynching, 160–62; and whitecappers, 165; and African American political participation, 185; and Republican Party, 186; and Jim Crow laws, 190, 197; and amendment to disfranchise African Americans, 201. *See also* specific newspapers

African American slaves: and Five Civilized Tribes, 2, 102, 103; and Indian removal, 4; and Indian Territory, 5; and Seminole tribe, 6, 9; and Reconstruction, 7; and minstrel shows, 29; emancipation of, 103–4, 114

African Americans: and racial inferiority slavery defense, 1; as inferior caste, 2; and Indian Territory, 12, 65; and Oklahoma Territory, 13, 30, 35, 55–59, 85, 88, 110, 180; stereotypes of, 15–17, 28–32, 34, 143; and labor, 16, 110–12, 116, 134, 165; and Anglo-American culture, 17, 29, 208; segregation of, 17, 29–30, 35, 41, 63, 64, 205, 209; and assimilation, 29, 59, 207–8; and state negroes, 31–32; opinions on segregation, 32–33, 112–13; and U.S. Army, 47–48, 133–36; and surplus lands, 54, 208; and land ownership, 55, 63, 109–10, 203, 210; and education, 56, 83–91, 93, 93*n*, 203, 210; lynchings of, 58, 154–63, 167, 209; political participation of, 63, 175–85, 191, 193, 194–96, 197–98, 200–2, 210; illiteracy of, 92, 93; and agriculture, 110; as entrepreneurs, 112–13; as jurors, 129; and U.S. judicial system, 129–30, 143, 145, 167; and alcohol consumption, 150; racial solidarity of, 163; and whitecappers, 164–66; and Native American judicial system, 167; and Republican Party, 175–87, 192, 195, 202–3, 208; and voting rights, 183–84, 187, 199–200, 201, 210; and Jim Crow laws, 194–95; and civil disobedience, 198. *See also* White American–African American relations

African Americans' civil rights: and African American migration, 13, 31, 57, 63, 189, 210; and education, 88–89; and Republican Party, 185, 191, 192, 195, 203; and

Indian Territory: creation of, 3; and effects of Civil War, 6; and Plains Indians, 7, 8; and race relations, 8, 13–14, 29–30, 163, 202, 203; and minstrel shows, 29; and all-black towns, 33; and education, 42, 46, 68–72, 85; as promised land, 46–47, 54, 65, 210; and boomers, 47; and Dawes Act, 52, 169; and land runs, 53, 54, 65, 208; and International Immigration Society, 64; and Oklahoma statehood, 66, 190; and segregation, 85; and white American laborers, 109; lawlessness of, 138–39, 145; temperance laws of, 147–49; lynchings in, 155, 156; statehood of, 170–71; factionalism in, 175
Indiana, 156, 195
Industrial education, 82, 93
Industrialization, 110
Intermarriage: and slave laws, 6; and Seminole tribe, 9, 36; and freedmen, 31, 35–36, 174–75; and citizenship, 35–36; and Native American–African American relations, 35, 40–41; and white American–Native American relations, 36–38, 155, 209; and one-drop rule, 40; and land allotments, 61; and statehood of Indian Territory, 171
International Immigration Society, 64
Iowa tribe, 54, 149

Jackson, Andrew, 1, 2–3, 4, 42, 180
Jails, 125, 128
Jefferson, Thomas, 1
Jim Crow laws: African American resistance to, 31, 198; and white settlers, 93; and African American deputy marshals, 138; and lynching, 161; and African American political participation, 187; and Democratic Party, 189, 190, 192, 193, 194, 197; and Native Americans as white, 210
Johnson, J. Coody, 63, 172
Johnston, Douglas H., 175
Jones, Mrs. Moses J., 31
Jones, Nelson M., 154
Jones, Robert M., 5–6
Jones, Wilson, 74
Judicial system. See Native American judicial system; U.S. judicial system

Kansas: white settlers from, 17–18; and surplus lands, 45; and boomers, 47, 48; all-black colonies of, 55, 57; and Indian land speculation, 62; and boarding schools, 78; and Indian raiding parties, 146; and white American–Native American relations, 152; and Republican Party, 177; and segregation, 190
Keetoowah society, 27–28
Kentucky, 33, 156
Kickapoo tribe, 54, 149
Kingston Messenger, 158–59
Kiowa tribe, 18, 45, 77, 97, 146
Knights of Pythias, 165
Krebs Eagle, 111
Ku Klux Kan, 164

Labor: and African Americans, 16, 110–12, 116, 134, 165; and manual labor schools, 68, 70–71, 72, 82; value of, 70, 94–95, 97–98, 100–1, 116; and freedmen, 82, 103–6, 115, 208; and white Americans, 106–9, 115; and mining, 110–11; and Indian police, 131; and U.S. Army, 134; and whitecappers, 165
Land. See Indian lands; Surplus lands
Langston, Oklahoma Territory, 33–34, 56, 88
Langston City Herald: and white American–African American relations, 32; and land ownership, 55; and Astor, 56; and African American immigration to Oklahoma Territory, 58–59; and labor, 110; and segregation, 112–13; and sandbar saloons, 148; and lynching, 160–61
Langston University, 56, 90
Langston Western Age, 161
Lawton, Oklahoma Territory, 185
Lawton Constitution, 185
Leckie, William, 135–36
Ledbetter, Bud, 198
Lexington, Oklahoma Territory, 165
Liberia, 64
Lighthorsemen: and Native American judicial system, 60, 130; and Seminole tribe, 122, 130; freedmen as, 151; and Native American–African American relations, 151
Lily-white movement: and segregation, 86; and disassociation with African Americans, 184–85, 203; and African American political participation, 185, 186; and African Americans' civil rights, 191; and white